TESI GREGORIANA

Serie Teologia

32

MARIA PASCUZZI CSJ

ETHICS, ECCLESIOLOGY AND CHURCH DISCIPLINE

A Rhetorical Analysis of 1 Corinthians 5

EDITRICE PONTIFICIA UNIVERSITÀ GREGORIANA

Roma 1997

Vidimus et approbamus ad normam Statutorum Universitatis

Romae, ex Pontificia Universitate Gregoriana
die 3 mensis maii anni 1997

R.P. Prof. James Swetnam, S.J.
R.P. Prof. Scott Brodeur, S.J.

ISBN 88-7652-767-2

GREGORIAN UNIVERSITY PRESS
Piazza della Pilotta, 35 – 00187 Rome, Italy

PREFACE

The present volume was originally presented and accepted as a doctoral dissertation at the Pontifical Gregorian University in May 1997. The dissertation is reproduced here in its entirety. While there are no substantial changes in content, I have introduced stylistic changes. Many of these were recommended by my mentor Rev. James Swetnam S.J. and defense examiner, Rev. Scott Brodeur S.J. I appreciate the concern to improve the quality and presentation of my thesis that their recommendations represent and I am most grateful to each of them for their enthusiastic endorsement of my work.

In addition to these changes, the form of the dissertation manuscript had to be revised in accordance with the publication requirements of *Tesi Gregoriana*. The revision work was carried out by Max Bonilla SSL who deserves a special word of thanks. Were it not for his precision and computer competence the publication of this book would have been significantly delayed. Thanks are also due to Rev. Roland Meynet S.J. the Director of *Tesi Gregoriana* and to Carlo Valentino, the technical director of the series.

In presenting this study of 1Cor 5 I am indebted to many but foremost to Rev. James Swetnam S.J. It was a pleasure to work under his careful guidance, draw on his wisdom and benefit from much sound advice always dispensed with clarity and kindness. As I go forward in my teaching and scholarly career it is my sincere hope that I may imitate and advance the scholarly excellence to which he is committed and engender the same enthusiasm for the study of Sacred Scripture that he has generated in so many.

Maria Pascuzzi CSJ

INTRODUCTION

1. The Problem

Paul's first letter to the Corinthians has provided a fertile field for biblical studies of some very controverted topics in contemporary Church life and teaching, in particular celibacy, sexuality, homosexuality, marriage and divorce, and the role of women in the church. Already in mid-first century A. D., Paul was engaged in discussions of these very same, and various other issues, with a small Christian community[1] born of his own missionary labors[2] in the active Roman port city, Corinth[3]. Paul's discussions of these issues are concentrated in 1Cor 6; 7; 11,2-15; 14,33-36 and these texts have been the focus of much scholarly attention. In notable contrast to the extensive interest in these texts to which the abundant literature[4] testifies, is the apparent dearth[5] of scholarly interest in

---

[1] Possibly numbering no more than 50 members (cf. J. MURPHY-O'CONNOR, *St. Paul's Corinth*, 156-58).

[2] Cf. Acts 18,1-11; 1Cor 3,6.10; 4,15.

[3] On Corinth cf. e.g. J. MURPHY-O'CONNOR, *St. Paul's Corinth*; W. WILLIS, «Corinthusne deletus est?», 233-241; R. OESTER, «Use, Misuse», 52-73; also D. ENGEL, *Roman Corinth*, who debunks views concerning the moral decadence of Corinth in Paul's era.

[4] A look at the *Elenchus of Biblica*, for example, will alert the reader to the profusion of relevant scholarly studies on these topics, hence there is no need to reproduce a list here.

[5] Besides commentary discussions, there are a few studies of 1Cor 5 in conjunction with broader topics, cf. e.g. G. FORKMANN, *Limits*; C.J. ROETZEL, *Judgement*; J.T. SOUTH, *Disciplinary Practices*. Beyond these, there is a respectable, but hardly extensive number of scholarly articles devoted to one or another aspect of this chapter. Except for some extended treatment by T. DEIDUN, *New Covenant Morality*, 28-30, 91, and L.W. COUNTRYMAN, *Dirt*, 197-202, studies devoted to NT or specifically Pauline ethics give marginal or no attention to 1Cor 5. This is notable in V. FURNISH, *Moral Teaching*. The author devotes more than sixty pages to sex, marriage, divorce and homosexuality, and only 14 lines to 1Cor 5 (cf. 69-70).

1 Cor 5, a short chapter dealing with a case of incest[6]. To date, as far as we know, no monograph has ever been devoted to this chapter. The meager interest is to some extent self-evident and understandable. Incest, while still a contemporary problem, is hard to detect and today's communities are hardly the close-knit social unit of fifty or so persons as was the case in Corinth where community pressure could be brought to bear on an offender in a palpable way. The disciplinary act, probably excommunication[7], prescribed in 1 Cor 5 and the language in which it is stated is so alien to modern thinking that the passage is rarely thought of as having contemporary relevance[8] Moreover, nowadays incest is more readily considered as socially deviant or criminal behavior rather than a religious issue. What concerns us here, however, is not the quantity of scholarship but some currents of interpretation issuing from this limited amount of literature. These currents converge to produce what we consider to be a problematic presentation of the situation of 1 Cor 5 and a misconstrual of Paul's aims here.

Apropos of this chapter, one reads in Fee[9], for example, that at stake in 5,1-13[10] is «the crisis of authority that was a large part of what lay behind 1:10-4:21». The author considers 1 Cor 5,1-13 something of a test of the community's obedience and asks, «will they [the arrogant] pay attention to him [Paul] on these matters when he is "with them in Spirit and the power of the Lord Jesus" or will they continue to follow their new prophets[...]?»[11]. He further states, «Paul uses this concrete example [i.e. the incest] to assert his authority [...]»[12]. In Havener one comes across the statement, «we have in this chapter a case of ecclesiastical discipline that is apparently carried out in a completely undemocratic, highly authoritarian manner by the Apostle Paul»[13]. Conzelmann maintains that «the community merely constitutes the forum» in which the judicial act

---

[6] Cf. F. HAUCK – S. SCHULZ, «pornè, pornos, porneia ktl», 579-595. The term *porneia* used by Paul at 5,1 has varied referents. In the context of 1 Cor 5 it connotes incest.

[7] To be discussed below in c. 5.

[8] One dissenter from this view, Pfitzner, argues for the relevance of this and other NT disciplinary texts for contemporary church life and believes that excommunication should still be carried out as an expression of the church's commitment to the gospel (cf. V.C. PFITZNER, «Purified Community», 48).

[9] G. FEE, *1 Corinthians*, 195.

[10] G. FEE considers the «crisis of authority» to be at stake in 6,1-11 and 12-20 as well (cf. 195).

[11] G. FEE, *1 Corinthians*, 195.

[12] G. FEE, *1 Corinthians*, 197.

[13] I. HAVENER, «A Curse», 334.

against the offender is carried out but «does not share in the action»[14]. Luedemann[15] considers the «enthusiasts» whom Paul addresses in 1Cor 5, to have been allied with Paul's opponents, thereby forming one united anti-Pauline front.

Other such comments will be cited during the course of this study. However, for the moment, this sampling of perceptions and interpretations suffices to show how they converge to produce a negative profile of both the community and Paul. With respect to the community the profile emerges of an incorrigible group of belligerents contesting Paul's authority every step of the way. Their tolerance and boasting of the reprobate who has married his step-mother is alleged to be an intentional challenge to Paul's apostolic authority. With respect to Paul, the portrait emerges of an authority figure, or worse, an autocrat, whose aim here in 1Cor 5 is to quell the challenge to his authority that this behavior allegedly comports. His decision is unilateral. His power is absolute. The community has no role beyond that of submitting to his authority and carrying out his orders. When Paul is seen in this light, the feminist claim that in 1Cor Paul promotes «compulsory authority based on the symbolization of ultimate patri-archal [sic] power»[16], does not seem so unreasonable.

Broadly speaking, one could say that these interpretations represent 1Cor 5 as reflecting a war of wills with Paul intent on insuring that *his* will prevail. What gives rise to such interpretations? It would appear that the text of 1Cor 5 is susceptible to interpretations which stress its alleged polemical character and which accord a negligible role to the community when a) the interpretation of 1Cor 5 is preconditioned by the overall perception that 1Cor as a whole reflects a continuing battle between Paul and the Corinthians over his apostolic authority; this perception is based on the reading of some sections of 1Cor as apologetic or defense rhetoric and also on the blurring of the distinction between the social situations of 1 and 2Cor, one of the results of failing to respect the literary integrity of 1Cor; and when b) little attention is paid to the rhetorical features of this chapter.

With regard to point a), in 1Cor 5,2 for example, Paul says that the Corinthians are «*pephysiômenoi*». But is this description a sufficient basis for assuming that the boasting was expressly intended to defy Paul's apostolic authority? Not necessarily, unless we are inclined to see this boasting as part of the alleged polemic between the community and Paul over his apostolic authority. In this same vein, consider that in 1Cor 5,

---

[14] H. CONZELMANN, *1 Korinther*, 97.

[15] G. LUEDEMANN, *Opposition*, 80.

[16] E. SCHÜSSLER FIORENZA, «Rhetorical Situation», 397.

after two opening verses, Paul solemnly articulates his own severe judgement. Does this necessarily mean that Paul was asserting his authority over a recalcitrant community or that he did not intend the community to make its own judgement? Again, not necessarily, unless we are inclined to read 1Cor 5 through the lens of polemic over Paul's authority.

Methodologically speaking it is of course admissible to bring to bear on the interpretation of one chapter or section of a letter information culled from the letter as a whole. But if Paul were not involved in a defense of his apostolic authority in 1Cor – a view that rests largely on the assumption that 1Cor 1-4 and 9 are apostolic apologies – would there be reason enough from the text of 1Cor 5 to interpret his response as an attempt to quell a threat to his authority? Would there be sufficient reason to claim that Paul acted in a highly undemocratic manner, suppressing any role that the community should have in this process? Would there be reason enough to consider the persons Paul addresses in 1Cor 5 as opponents, or to see 1Cor 5 as a situation of «Paul *versus* (my italics) the church»[17]? Granted a very serious issue is under discussion in 1Cor 5; but it is not at all certain that Paul's severity is caused by the boasting which he would have perceived as rebellion[18]. In fact, as we will argue, when the lens of polemic is removed and closer attention is paid to the text of 1Cor 5 it becomes clear that Paul's exigency and severity are due to theological concerns. With regard to point b), we note here that while many interpretations of 1Cor 5 are contingent on the alleged apologetic or defense rhetoric of 1Cor 1-4 and 9, little is said about the rhetoric of 1Cor 5[19]. In fact, it is striking that while considerations based on the alleged rhetoric in cc. 1-4 and 9 often tint the lens through which 1Cor 5 is viewed, when it comes to reading 1Cor 5, scholars rarely treat this chapter under the aspect of rhetoric! One example will suffice here to illustrate this point. Let us consider, 5,3-5, Paul's judgement pronouncement. On the one hand, these verses are studied with a view to explaining exactly what Paul intended by this sentence and what the community was concretely obliged to do. The underlying assumption in these studies is that, in making this

---

[17] Cf. G. Fee, *1 Corinthians*, 195.

[18] *Pace* A.Y. Collins, «The Function», 251, who claims that if boasting were not the issue Paul would have begun with a less drastic measure. Unfortunately this insinuates that Paul used the severe sentence to punish the community for its boasting instead of the sinner for his sin.

[19] There are two recent rhetorical studies of 1Cor: that of M. Mitchell, *Paul*, and B. Witherington, *Conflicts*. Both deal with 1Cor 5. Witherington spends more time exploring the background motives for the incestuous marriage and says disappointingly little about the rhetoric. A much more developed rhetorical study of the chapter is found in Mitchell which will be considered below in c. 5 § 3.

pronouncement, Paul did indeed intend something concrete and explicit which can be recovered with more research or the discovery of an appropriate parallel. But perhaps Paul did not intend to be quite so concrete and explicit as we modern readers might be inclined to assume. Yet, as we shall see, the explanation of this sentence is probably the subject of the greater part of the literature devoted to this chapter. On the other hand, these verses have been studied with a view to their form. It is claimed that vv. 3-5 constitute a prophetic judgement[20], a claim that could go a long way in accenting Paul's exclusive authority, reducing the role of the community to a vehicle for executing Paul's will and viewing Paul's judgement pronouncement as the central concern of the chapter. However, this claim may not stand up under examination, and even if it should, it does not exhaust the possibilities of what can be said about these verses, nor does it necessarily tell us their function in 1Cor 5.

For some twenty years now, thanks to the pioneering work of W. Wuellner[21], all those engaged in the study of Pauline texts have been sensitized to the fact that Paul's letters display a notable rhetorical sophistication[22] and can be approached within the realm of rhetoric understood as argumentation aimed at persuasion[23]. In essence this implies that we look at Paul's letters not simply in terms of literary genre[24] and with a view toward recovering the actual historical situation[25] but as carefully crafted

---

[20] Cf. E. KÄSEMANN, «Sentences», 66-81.

[21] Cf. below c. 1 n. 27, 28. Wuellner advocated not simply a revival of classical rhetoric but also an incorporation of the insights of the «new rhetoric» as advanced by C. PERELMAN – L. OLBRECHTS-TYTECA, *The New Rhetoric*, The latter was an attempt to move beyond modern philosophy's general disregard for rhetoric and establish rhetorical criticism as more than the study of literary rhetorical devices and style which the authors consider a serious limitation and distortion of rhetoric as understood and taught in antiquity. See further, C. PERELMAN, «Rhetoric and Philosophy», 15-25.

[22] On Paul's rhetorical skill in the use of digression in 1Cor cf. W. WUELLNER, «Greek Rhetoric», 177-188. Any lingering doubts about the importance of rhetoric in Paul and NT writers in general are set to rest in J.L. KINNEAVY, *Greek Rhetorical Origins*.

[23] Rhetoric, as set forth by ARISTOTLE, *Ars Rhetorica*, I.II, 2, was an act of persuasion and the science or art of rhetoric was concerned with the elaboration of argumentative strategies that would bring about the persuasion. (Unless otherwise noted, English translations of classical authors appearing in this study will be quoted or adapted from the LCL and referenced according to the book, chapter and line divisions found in the LCL).

[24] Cf. the discussion below c. 1.

[25] For example, in light of a recent rhetorical study of Rom 14-15, the common view that the references to the weak and strong are references to actual factions and reflect actual historical conditions in the Roman community should perhaps be jettisoned (cf. J.P. SAMPLEY, «The Weak», 40-52). Sampley's study stands as a reminder

arguments by which Paul endeavors to persuade his audience. If such is the case, then it is legitimate and perhaps necessary to examine 1Cor 5 as a carefully crafted argument in order to discover what was really at stake, what dynamics drove Paul's argument, what his aims were in this chapter and what the functions of each of the parts were. Failing to examine the rhetorical strategy that Paul employs in 1Cor 5 leads to misconstruing what is under discussion with the result that a polemic about authority, not ethics, is placed at the center of Paul's attention. In other words, because of this misunderstanding of the text, Paul's relationship with the community is placed at the center of his concern rather than the sanctified life of the community which he considers to be imperiled.

2. The Purpose of the Present Study

It is our contention that a rhetorical analysis of Paul's response in 1Cor 5 will reveal: a) that his aim in this chapter is to persuade the Corinthian community to change its own opinions, judgements and behavior and to take responsible action against the offender and b) that Paul's severe response to the immoral situation described in 1Cor 5 was motivated primarily by his Christological, ecclesiological and ethical concerns and not by a polemic about his apostolic authority. For Paul, Christianity is holy *koinônia*[26]. Here in 1Cor 5, Paul must deal with one of the problems that risks destroying Christianity at Corinth.

In the rhetorical analysis to follow, studied attention will be paid to the rhetorical strategy adopted by Paul in 1Cor 5 and in particular to the proofs the Apostle employs to persuade the community. In light of this analysis, it will, we believe, become evident that his response in this chapter is more correctly perceived as a carefully crafted argument aimed at persuasion rather than as a vehicle through which he attempts to reassert his apostolic authority.

The dissociation of the discussion of 1Cor 5 from the context of polemic opens the way for focusing on the Christological motivation of this chapter and for a much needed consideration of the ecclesiological and ethical suppositions that underpin Paul's argument. In the light of Paul's ideas about community, the moral reasoning set out in this chapter is fully understandable and the disciplinary sanction can be seen as positive, necessary and linked to theology rather than viewed as a situationally

---

that the text cannot always be taken as a description of the actual historical conditions in a community.

[26] Cf. e.g. 1Cor 1,9. On Paul's understanding of *koinônia* see G. PANIKULAM, *Koinônia*, esp. 55ff.

determined response to a desperate situation that reflects how far his authority has eroded.

The study will be developed in eight chapters. In Chapter 1, we must deal with the issue of the literary integrity of 1Cor. It is not our intention to undertake an exhaustive treatment of this question but to discuss two key problems of the partition approach to the text, viz., the equating of coherency with linearity and the study of a Pauline letter exclusively as *Briefgattung*. By examining advances in the understanding of ancient epistolography and compositional techniques, the relation of epistolography and rhetoric and the argumentative or rhetorical nature of a letter, it will become clear that partition hypotheses regarding 1Cor are not sustainable. In Chapter 2, we will begin by arguing the necessity of keeping the social situation of 1Cor and that of 2Cor, which is overtly polemical, distinct. Then we will examine the evidence ordinarily marshalled to support the claim that throughout 1Cor, Paul is involved in one long sustained effort to defend his apostolic authority. This will require determining whether 1Cor 1-4 and 9 constitute apostolic apologies since these are the two pillars, so to speak, which support the reading of the letter through the lens of polemic about apostolic authority. If these sections do not sustain this reading then there is no reason to read 1Cor 5 as one skirmish in a larger battle. Finally in this chapter we will consider some of the insights gleaned from social studies of early Christianity, particularly those of Meeks, that can also contribute to a more realistic understanding of the social setting of 1Cor. In Chapter 3, we will consider what ideology or false theology may have influenced the behavior under discussion in 1Cor 5. After considering some key theories, we will offer our own original reading on what factors may have influenced the Corinthians. If it is reasonable to consider that the Corinthians, as reflected in 1Cor 5, were operating out of Stoic conceptions and if the implications which we have drawn from this hypothesis are reasonable, then again the view that the Corinthians acted consciously to challenge Paul's authority is undermined. This will be followed by a brief Chapter 4 in which the literary and rhetorical limits of the text will be defined, the compositional arrangement of the text noted and the question raised as to whether this arrangement has hermeneutical significance. Chapter 5, the heart of the study, will be devoted to the rhetorical analysis of the passage. Here we focus attention on: how Paul unfolds his argument; the function of each of the parts of the argument; their relationship to each other; and the types of proofs used to persuade the Corinthians. It will become clear in the course of the analysis that the nerve center of Paul's argument is vv. 6-8. The material instruction to remove the offender derives from the criteria set out in these verses and attention will be focused on Paul's metaphoric language, both in terms of what it communicates and also leaves un-enunciated. After the analysis we will present an overview of our findings in schematic form and then attempt to answer questions raised at the beginning of the chapter about Paul's task in 1Cor 5, the role of the community and the rhetorical genre employed. This will be followed by a discussion of the criteria Paul uses in this argument and it will be argued that the Christological criteria in vv. 6-8 is what grounds Paul's argument and the command to remove the offender. Claims about the significance of the OT/Torah for Paul's response in 1Cor 5 will need to be considered. Finally we will note that while Paul effectively grounds his argument in this chapter on Christological criteria, account must be taken of the un-enunciated notions that inform this chapter which are best understood in light of Paul's ecclesiology. It is necessary, but not sufficient, to say that «new life» in Christ is the ground motive for Paul's argument here. What is «new life» in Christ and how does it inform the argument in 1Cor 5? These concerns lead into Chapter 6, where we will examine Paul's understanding of community to show how it informs his moral reasoning in 1Cor 5. By and large in studies of Paul's ethics, his ecclesiology is rarely expressly shown to have informed his ethical exhortation or material instructions. What we hope to show apropos of 1Cor 5 is that while the explicit Christological criterion grounds the argument, ecclesiological conceptions inform this discussion and contribute to the shape of the moral reasoning. In light of these conceptions we can gain insight into Paul's response in 1Cor 5 and have a better perspective from which to understand the disciplinary sanction which is remarkable for its severity. This severity is not conditioned by concern for scandal to the pagans; nor is it elicited by the community's boasting; nor is it a vehicle for re-asserting authority. Rather, the sanction is better understood as issuing from Paul's conception of the community as one and sinless. In Chapter 7, by way of conclusion, we will consider the question of the placement of the incest discussion *vis-à-vis* the ordering of the other practical issues under discussion in 1Cor. This will be followed wby a discussion in which we hope to highlight what appear to be some key flaws and lacunae in the Corinthian understanding of Christianity. Chapter 7 will be brought to a close by a summary statement of general conclusions issuing from the present study. In Chapter 8, we will present a theological reflection in which we will underscore and consider some of the implications of Paul's response to the situation described in 1Cor 5 *vis-à-vis* the church's ethical teaching, ecclesial discipline and Christian life and ethical choice today.

We now turn to the work of chapter 1 where we will take up the question of the literary integrity of 1Cor. Since the position adopted with regard to this question will affect the interpretation of the letter at every level, no study of any part of the letter can proceed without first addressing the question and stating a position.

CHAPTER I

The Question of the Literary Integrity of 1Cor

1. Beyond Partition Hypotheses: Methodological Considerations

The numerous partition hypotheses[1] advanced over the years could be viewed as an attestation to the seriousness with which many scholars have taken J. Weiss' comment that it is a «*methodologische Pflicht*»[2] to reject *a priori* the unity of 1Cor. Recently J. C. Hurd[3] has examined a number of partition hypotheses advanced since the publication of his book[4] and notes that with these new proposals there are now 15 text blocks whose assignment to a source stratum is at issue[5]. These hypotheses[6] are fraught with problems and it is not our purpose here to deal with each of the pivotal

---

[1] Cf. J.C. HURD, *Origin*, 45, table 4. Since the publication of Hurd's work other divisions and literary reconstructions of 1Cor have been proposed. Cf. e.g., E. FASCHER, *Erste Brief an die Korinther*, I, 42-43; R. PESCH, *Paulus ringt*; C. SENFT, *La première épître aux Corinthiens*, 17ff. W. SCHENK, «Der 1 Korintherbrief als Briefsammlung», 219-43; A. SUHL, *Paulus*, 208; G. SELLIN, «1 Kor 5-6 und der "Vorbrief"», 535-558.

[2] Cf. J. WEISS, *Der erste Korintherbrief*. For his partition proposal cf. XL-XLIII.

[3] Cf. J.C. HURD, «Good News», 38-62.

[4] Cited above n. 1.

[5] Cf. J.C. HURD, «Good News», 47.

[6] Not mentioned by Hurd in «Good News», but noteworthy, are two recent articles which propose interesting but problem-laden «middle» positions between integrity and non-integrity, cf. M. DE BOER, «The Composition», 229-245 and E. DE LA SERNA, «Los origines», 193-216; see also H. PROBST, *Paulus und der Brief*, who argues that 1Cor is a composite of four distinct, coherent letters written by Paul put together by a later redactor. Besides forcing epistolary structures on sections of the text, e.g. his treatment of 1Cor 5-7 (cf. 313-318), in order to make distinct letters, Probst multiplies the occasions to match the letters but does not demonstrate that there actually were four separate communications directed to Paul which elicited four separate letters.

points[7] on which partition theories hinge. They have been treated by various authors[8] who have demonstrated that much of what has been proffered as indisputable proof of compilation does not stand up to examination when other factors are considered[9]. Rather we wish to mention two theoretical problems attached to partition approaches and note the advances in understanding Paul's letters that are largely ignored by partition proponents and which call into question the whole partitioning enterprise. The first problem relates to the strict link partitioners see between «linearity» and coherency. The second is the problem of viewing a Pauline text exclusively as *Briefgattung*.

Apropos of the first problem, partitioners expect that a letter will have a beginning an end that encloses a body[10]. It is further expected that this

---

[7] They are essentially four: 1) that 1Cor 8,1-11,1 cannot be considered as deriving from the same letter given a) the apparent inconsistency between Paul's handling of the idol meat issue in 10,1-22 and 8,1-13; 10,23-11,1 and b) the alleged inappropriateness of c. 9 in the context of a discussion on idol meat; 2) the apparent incompatibility between Paul's information and views about schisms in 11,18 and his information and views on presumably the same subject in cc. 1-4. Apropos of this point, W. SCHMITHALS says that «the decisive observation for the fact that our canonical 1Cor contains pieces from various Pauline letters is to be made at 11,18[...]. If one compares this passage with Paul's statements in I, 1-4, it is simply inconceivable that both attitudes toward disputes could come from the same epistle» (*Gnosticism*, 90); 3) that 1Cor 6,12-20 clearly belongs to an earlier or previous letter and 4) the problem of the double occasion of 1Cor. This last point can be formulated most succinctly in the question: If Paul received two separate communications, one oral and one written, did each not occasion its own response?

[8] Most notably, J.C. HURD, *Origin*, esp. 70-81, 86-89, 126-141 and 142; H. MERKLEIN, «Die Einheitlichkeit», 153-183; D. LÜHRMANN, «Freundschaftsbrief», 298-314. More recently J.C. HURD, in «Good News», has again taken up the defense of the letter's integrity, this time zeroing in on the difficulties connected to the hypothesis of a redactor for 1Cor. After dealing with some specific problematic aspects of this hypothesis (cf. 47-52), Hurd moves to theoretical considerations about its contingent nature and states the view, «that an intelligent redactor has assembled 1 Corinthians from the surviving texts of two or three original letters which can themselves be reconstructed is not a hypothesis, but a pyramid of at least three hypotheses. At the bottom lies the hypothesis of the redactor» (52). On the problem of the redactor cf. further, J. MURPHY-O'CONNOR, *Paul. A Critical Life*, 254.

[9] An interesting argument against partitioning from a perspective other than form, literary or rhetorical, has been recently proposed by A. STEWART-SYKES, «Ancient Editors», 53-64. If the author is correct the editorial work needed to produce the compiled document that partitioners allege 1Cor to be would have been so arduous and impractical that some very compelling reason would have had to exist to justify such an undertaking. Given the lack of any indications that such an exigency existed, the author concludes that it is unlikely the task would have been undertaken and rejects the view that 1Cor is a compilation.

[10] On the form of the ancient letter, cf. J.L. WHITE, «Ancient Greek Letters», 85-106; M.L. STIREWALT, *Studies*; S.K. STOWERS, *Letter Writing*.

body should manifest a unity of thematic concept, i.e., an easily perceived ordering of more or less homogenous ideas, developed in a linear fashion[11] that purportedly signals text coherency. When these are the governing conceptions, and the expectations contingent upon them are not met, the critical task is reduced to highlighting proof of compilation and literary criticism rapidly devolves into source analysis[12]. However, in consideration of the following, it becomes immediately apparent that these governing conceptions are too rigid, as are the corresponding expectations: a) Though basic epistolary structures[13] existed, it is generally acknowledged that ancient writers were not reduced to a slavish following of form[14] but were flexible in their compositional activity, able to consider a range of aims or purposes[15] as required by the genre's occasional nature[16]. This same flexibility is evident in Pauline compositional activity and note has been taken[17] of the fact that Paul reflected on, unfolded and arranged his

---

[11] Apropos of linearity, Hurd remarks, «this linear view of the text must be what critics mean when they say they must deal with the literary problems» («Good News», 56). Precisely!

[12] The analytical fragmentation of the text that accompanies source analysis destroys the concentric patterns which must be considered when the question of coherency is raised. On the concentric pattern and method, cf. L. ALONSO SCHÖKEL, «Of Methods», 10.

[13] Cf. J.L. WHITE, «New Testament Epistolary Literature», 1730-1756.

[14] In «De Elocutione» the author maintained that a certain amount of freedom was necessary vis-à-vis the structure of a letter since it was not in the same vein as a tightly structured forensic speech for use in the courtroom, cf. DEMETRIUS, «De Elocutione», 229. To the point then is the recent comment that «Conventions have no binding force; their utility is a function of their flexibility whereby an appropriate, contextually shaped act of communication occurs» (M. DE BOER, «The Composition», 234).

[15] Cf. J.L. WHITE, «Ancient Greek Letters», 95; on the types of letters composed for various purposes see the 21 types mentioned in P.S. DEMETRIUS, «Typoi Epistolikoi». Cf. further, S.K. STOWERS, Letter Writing. The author lists 19 actions that people performed by means of letters (cf. 15) and stresses the flexibility that attended letter writing in antiquity (cf. 56).

[16] Cf. P.S. DEMETRIUS, «Typoi Epistolikoi». The author says, «Letters can be composed in a great number of styles, but are written in those which always fit the particular circumstances to which they are addressed» (line 1). Cf. further S.K. STOWERS, Letter Writing, 52-53. Apropos of the fact that 1Cor contains units treating distinct topics, J. MURPHY-O'CONNOR maintains that the topic alternation is caused largely by the fact that Paul was reacting to various pieces of information of various provenances (cf. Paul et l'art épistolaire, 124ff.). Murphy-O'Connor's highlighting of topic alternation by Cicero (cf. Ad QFr, III) points to the fact that in long letters an author's thoughts may appear disbursed. However, as he observes, this does not constitute evidence of distinct letters nor is the literary integrity of Cicero's composition questioned because of the variety of topics. Similarly, Paul's topic alternations do not necessarily imply a multiplicity of letters (cf. 124).

[17] Cf. J.-N. ALETTI, «La dispositio rhétorique», 394-396.

ideas in smaller literary units[18] a fact overlooked in the recent study of Probst[19]; b) It has long been recognized that the theological body of Paul's letters is characterized by dialogical and argumentative features that are influenced by oral traditions[20]. Moreover, it is well known and widely acknowledged[21] that Paul, especially in 1Cor, makes extensive use of a concentric[22], or ABA' literary pattern in which to arrange his thought[23]. By its nature, this pattern will not manifest the kind of linear flow that some literary critics expect as a sign of coherency. But this does not prove incoherence. Obviously if this surface literary pattern is ignored the coherency will be missed. As Talbert states, «recognition of this principle of organization in the Corinthian correspondence allows one to avoid the cliché that Paul's thought is disjointed when it does not seem to follow a linear line»[24]. Thus it is not unreasonable to say that when any partition argument is advanced that considers coherency only under the limited specter of linearity, that argument's value is proportionately limited.

Apropos of the second problem, the fact that partitioners persist in staying within the limits of *Briefgattung* when approaching 1Cor indicates a disregard both for the relation between epistolography and rhetoric[25] and

---

[18] Cf. e.g. Rom 1-4; 5-8; 9-11; 12-15 which are discreet units of thought.

[19] Cited above n. 6.

[20] Cf. J.L. WHITE, «Ancient Greek Letters», 99.

[21] Cf. E.B. ALLO, *Première épître aux Corinthiens*, LXI-III, 202, 319; K. BAILEY, «The Structure», Plate A, 156; A. BRUNOT, *Le génie litteraire*, 42-49; J.J. COLLINS, «Chiasmus, ABA' Pattern», 581; G. FEE, *1 Corinthians*, 16; N.W. LUND, *Chiasmus*, 145-196; J. MURPHY-O'CONNOR, *1 Cor*, 39 and passim; C. TALBERT, *Reading Corinthians*, xv.; J. WELCH, «Chiasmus in the New Testament», 211-249, esp. 215-217. Even Weiss recognized the significance of the ABA' schema. In reference to cc. 5-6, in particular 6,1-11, he writes, «in dem so häuftigen Schema aba ist b eine Einlage [...] aber doch irgendwie zur Beleuchtung des Hauptthemas dient» (cf. J. WEISS, *Der erste Korintherbrief*, 145). Unfortunately Weiss' penchant for partitioning did not allow him to capitalize on this insight.

[22] In «Good News», Hurd incorporates insights based on a recognition of the concentric schema, something not done in *Origin*. Apropos of 1Cor 8,1-10,1-22, Hurd maintains that when its concentric patterning is recognized then the «key argument of partition theories disappears because 1Cor 8,1 - 10,1-22 is the cornerstone of all partition theories» (61-62).

[23] This pattern will be discussed below in c. 4.

[24] C. TALBERT, *Reading Corinthians*, xv.

[25] The relationship between epistolography and rhetorical theory is concisely discussed in A. MALHERBE, ed., *Ancient Epistolary Theorists*, 2-6. In considering the «*Typoi Epistolikoi*» of PS. DEMETRIUS, Stowers has observed that of the 21 types, the accusing and apologetic types interface with forensic rhetoric, the advisory type of letter with deliberative rhetoric and most of the others with epideictic (cf. *Letter Writing*, 52).

for the insights offered by rhetorical criticism for understanding the dynamics of Paul's letters.

The overlap between letter and speech suggests two important dimensions for understanding the former. First, oratory was important in the Greco-Roman world and rhetoric occupied a central role in ancient education. Though primarily connected with oral delivery rhetoric had a profound affect on all genres of literature including letters[26].

Since his article on rhetoric in Romans[27], W. Wuellner has consistently[28] argued for the study of Paul's letters under the aspect of rhetoric, i.e., as arguments aimed at persuasion and not simply or exclusively as *Briefgattung*[29]. Wuellner's challenge came in the wake of a renewed interest in rhetoric and in particular a renewed understanding of rhetoric as argumentation[30]. In a different vein[31], H. D. Betz[32] began to explore the

---

[26] D.E. AUNE, *The New Testament*, 158. Though many would agree with Aune, it must be noted that the relationship between epistolary and rhetorical theory and with that the value of rhetoric for interpreting the Pauline epistles is a controverted issue. A window on the debate and the key issues involved is afforded in the following recent articles: S.E. PORTER, «Theoretical Justification», 100-122; J. REED, «Using Rhetorical Categories», 292-324; C. CLASSEN, «Paul's Epistles», 265-291. The debate over the application of rhetorical criticism is much too broad to be discussed in detail in this work. Certainly the distinction between rhetoric and epistolography needs to be kept in mind, and over-eager practitioners of rhetorical criticism may at times over-state their case. However, moving to the opposite extreme and denying the influence of rhetoric in Paul is hardly preferable. A moderate approach, respecting both the literary and the rhetorical dimensions of the text is advocated by J.-N. ALETTI, «La présence», 1-24; ID., «La *dispositio* rhétorique», 385-401.

[27] W. WUELLNER, «Paul's Rhetoric of Argumentation», 330-351. In the same year, in an unpublished paper entitled, «Methodological Considerations Concerning the Rhetorical Genre of 1 Cor,» Wuellner also proposed the use of rhetorical criticism based on Perelman's «New Rhetoric» as theory of argumentation.

[28] Among W. WUELLNER's other publications cf. e.g. «Greek Rhetoric and Pauline Argumentation», 177-188; «The Argumentative Structure of 1 Thessalonians As Paradoxical Encomium», 117-136.

[29] On the revival of interest in rhetoric, its application to the NT, the variety of approaches that are embraced by the term rhetorical criticism and an extended bibliography, cf. D.F. WATSON – A.J. HAUSER, *Rhetorical Criticism*, 101-125; or for a very precise summary, see A.C. WIRE, *Corinthian Women*, Appendix 1, 197-201.

[30] Cf. C. PERELMAN – L. OLBRECHTS-TYTECA, *The New Rhetoric*.

[31] On the relationship of the «classical rhetorical» and the «new» rhetorical approach to the text, cf. B. STANDAERT, «Lecture rhétorique», 190-191. Standaert sees no conflict between new and ancient rhetoric. He notes that the new rhetoric provides wider categories than those of ancient rhetoric which permit the study of biblical texts which have not undergone the influence that must be called Hellenistic. However, it can be argued that, in practice, there are significant differences to note, cf. D.L. STAMPS, «Rhetorical Criticism», 268-279; ID., «Rhetorical Criticism: Evaluations of Argumentation», 129-169.

[32] Betz's works are listed in D.F. WATSON – A.J. HAUSER, cited above n. 29.

application of the categories of classical rhetoric to Paul's letters. His commentary on Galatians, a first attempt to set a whole letter within the framework of Greek rhetorical categories, generated a greater interest in rhetorical criticism and with that, recognition of the need for a precise methodology. In response, G. Kennedy[33] developed a methodology based on the classical handbooks which is widely used in rhetorical studies of the NT. As with other methodologies, this also can be too rigidly applied[34]. However, when rhetorical analysis is not limited to an exercise in classifying[35] a letter according to the classical trigeneric schema[36], it provides an alternative tool for examining the text of a Pauline letter and allows us to ask the coherency question not simply in light of the literary flow but, in the context of argumentative strategies. Argumentative strategies may be

---

[33] G. KENNEDY, *New Testament Interpretation*, esp. 33-38. Kennedy's method is synthesized and critiqued in W. WUELLNER, «Where is Rhetorical Criticism?», 455-460. Apropos of Kennedy's understanding of the rhetorical situation, see the interesting comments of D.L. STAMPS, «Rethinking», 193-210. Stamps notes that following Kennedy's method, where the rhetoric of the text hinges on a correspondence of form and content with the historical or actual situation of the audience, can lead to a kind of «rhetorical form criticism» (198).

[34] A recent example of this tendency is found in M. MITCHELL, *Paul*. Having eschewed the «new rhetoric» as synchronic and given to skewed analysis, Mitchell takes the classical approach, argues that the genre of 1Cor is deliberative and insists that the genre of a text, by which she intends a whole composition, «cannot be begged in the analysis» (cf. 6-11). But is genre classification the point of rhetorical analysis? Second, even if rhetorical criticism were reducible to genre classification according to the categories of classical rhetoric (an assumption refuted by S.E. PORTER, «Theoretical Justification», 115ff.), here too Mitchell shows excessive rigidity, insisting that a literary composition is constituted by one and only one rhetorical genre (cf. 16-17). Yet even the masters of rhetoric admitted that the categories were somewhat artificial, cf. *Rhet. ad Her.*, III.IV, 7, and that genre overlap occurred, cf. QUINTILIAN, *Institutio*, III.VII, 1. Moreover, ancient epistolographic evidence reveals mixed types. In Ps. Libanius 92 one notes a mix of praise and blame and in Papyrus Bologna 5, Frag. XI, 6-27 congratulations and advice are interwoven. This evidence is collected in A. MALHERBE, ed., *Ancient Epistolary Theorists*.

[35] Even the best attempts will be unsatisfactory and this is due to the distinctness of the letter genre (cf. the remarks in S.K. STOWERS, *Letter Writing*, 52). In the same vein, it has been recently been commented that while models of Hellenistic rhetoric may help in the analysis of Paul's letters it must be born in mind that «Paul's letters not only accord with the pattern of ancient rhetorical convention; they radically differ from the pattern as well» (D.A. BLACK, «Discourse Structure», 21). Black proposes text linguistics as a more adequate method for approaching a Pauline text. His point is well made in reference to Hellenistic rhetorical categories. However, rhetorical analysis need not be limited to applying the schemas of classical rhetoric to Paul's letters as Wuellner's approach demonstrates.

[36] Cf. ARISTOTLE, *Ars Rhetorica*, I.III, 1-9.

composed of seemingly unrelated discreet parts[37] but this signals neither incoherence or compilation[38].

2. Conclusion to Chapter 1

In this chapter we have attempted to show why partition hypotheses should be rejected. Apart from the fact that the individual arguments upon which these hypotheses are founded have been substantially refuted, partition hypotheses are objectionable because their promotion comes at the cost of ignoring the insights of much solid scholarship that has taken account of both non-linear compositional patterns and the complex relationship that exists between rhetorical theory and epistolography. Although the conventions of rhetoric and epistolography are not identical, the techniques of oral communication do exercise influence on the writer and must be considered since the letter was a substitute for oral communication[39]. With regard then to 1Cor, the application of alternative rhetorical methods which look at both literary surface patterns and the dynamics of argumentation have made the recourse to partitioning unnecessary. There is no reason therefore to reject the literary integrity of 1Cor as the starting point for the study of the letter. With regard to 1Cor 5 in particular, despite the suddenness with which Paul appears to introduce this topic, we can proceed with the assumption that the chapter is in its original place. In fact, as we shall see below there are lexical links to note between c. 5 and what precedes and follows.

We are now ready to turn to the work of chapter 2 where we will look at the issue of the relationship that obtained between Paul and the Corinthian community, examine some of the chief evidence on which evaluations of this relationship are based and then give our own assessment of the situation.

---

[37] Cf. W.J. BRANDT, *The Rhetoric of Argumentation*, 49.
[38] Cf. J. MURPHY-O'CONNOR, *Paul et l'art épistolaire*, 124.
[39] J. MURPHY-O'CONNOR, *Paul et l'art épistolaire*, 100-101.

CHAPTER II

Social Relations Between Paul and the Corinthians

1. Keeping the Situations of 1 and 2 Corinthians Separate

While the relationship between Paul and the Philippians is commonly characterized as affectionate, and his relationship with the Thessalonians solicitous, the relationship between Paul and the Corinthians is commonly characterized as one of intense conflict in which the cardinal issue at stake is purported to be Paul's apostolic office and authority. This appears to be a correct characterization of the social situation reflected in 2Cor. In that letter, Paul is in open conflict with a newly arrived group of missionaries[1], the «superapostles»[2]. If the level of enmity in the social situation is measurable by the extent of the invective used[3], then clearly 2Cor, rife with invective, may be correctly considered as representing a critical situation of intense enmity[4]. These missionaries, judging by Paul's reactions, were

---

[1] With regard to the identity of these missionaries opponents, it has been suggested that they are Judaizers, identifiable with the opposition of 1Cor, «able to appeal to a real authority, indisputable in Christian eyes, namely the mother church» (H. SCHOEPS, *Paul*, 76); It has also been suggested that the opponents of Paul in 2Cor are Hellenistic Jewish Christian missionaries, distinct from the opposition of 1Cor (cf. D. GEORGI, *The Opponents*). Others hold that there is no reason to consider the adversaries referred to in 2Cor 10-13 as Judaizers since the Jewish authorities in Jerusalem and Jewish law seem to play no role in the debate (cf. e.g. E. LOHSE, «St Peter's Apostleship», 423).

[2] Cf. 2Cor 11,4. According to E. LOHSE, the term «super-apostle» should not be taken as a polemical allusion to Peter or James (cf. «St Peter's Apostleship», 423).

[3] Cf. P. MARSHALL, «Invective», 359-373.

[4] Examples of invective are given throughout Marshall's article, esp. 363-365. Important to note is that almost all the examples of Paul's use of invective which Marshall signals are located in 2Cor.

making allegations[5] intended to discredit him before the community. The strain on the relationship between Paul and the community, a result of the wedge driven into it by the rival missionaries, is apparent from the reading of 2 Cor. In his turn, Paul sought to relieve the strain by discrediting these false apostles[6] and entreating the community more than once to reconsider the merits of his apostleship[7].

What is true of the social situation in 2Cor is not likewise true of the situation reflected in 1Cor[8]. Fee remarked that «when turning to 2Cor from 1Cor one has the sense of entering a new world»[9]. Yet, notwithstanding this acknowledgement, he maintains that «this sense of newness turns out to be a surface reading of the letters» since «what holds them together are not the specific issues addressed in each but an overriding tension over Paul's apostleship [...]»[10]. In fact, Fee reads 1Cor as a kind of literary battlefield with Paul cast in a defensive role, dueling his way through successive attacks. Though acknowledging interior strife in the community, Fee insists that the greater division was between Paul and those in the community who were leading the church as a whole into anti-Paulinism[11]. Stated most succinctly, Fee's reading of 1Cor amounts to the following: 1Cor 9 is the «same kind of fierce defense»[12] of Paul's authority as found in cc. 1-4. The rest of the issues in 1Cor are understood as concrete challenges to that authority.

But is this characterization of the social situation of 1Cor as one of intense enmity sustainable? Granted there are problems in the community. Paul does admonish[13], shame[14] and even inject a bit of irony and

---

[5] For example, he was inconsistent (2Cor 1,17; 10,11); lived *kata sarka* (2Cor 10,3); lacked stature (2Cor 10,10); was deficient in oral communication (2Cor 10,10; 11,6) and that his refusal of Corinthian financial support attests that he is no legitimate apostle (2Cor 11,7).

[6] Besides decrying their boasting (2Cor 10,13ff.), Paul indirectly compares them to the deceiving serpent (2Cor 11,3), very bluntly calls them false apostles, deceitful workmen, apostolic impostors (2Cor 11,13) and then makes a direct comparison between them and Satan (2Cor 11,14).

[7] For example, that he is commended by the Lord (2Cor 10,18); has opted to support himself lest he be a burden to the community (11,9); has suffered greatly on account of his apostleship (11,16ff.); has had visions and revelations (12,1ff.), and has demonstrated through signs, wonders and mighty works the marks of a true apostle (12,12).

[8] Cf. the investigation of D. GEORGI, *The Opponents*.

[9] G. FEE, «"Another Gospel"», 111.

[10] G. FEE, «"Another Gospel"», 111.

[11] G. FEE, «"Another Gospel"», 6.

[12] G. FEE, «"Another Gospel"», 9.

[13] Cf. 1Cor 4,14.

[14] Cf. 1Cor 11,17ff.; 6,1-5.

sarcasm[15]. However, this in no way requires that 1Cor be read as a literary battlefield[16] and much less that we read the rhetoric as a window on to the actual social relationship that obtained between Paul and the community[17]. Since cc. 1-4 and c. 9 are the two main pillars on which the case for the defense reading of the whole letters rests, we must now examine these. The crucial question to be addressed is whether cc. 1-4 and c. 9 are apostolic apologies?

2. The Evidence

2.1 1Cor 1-4. An Apostolic Apology?

N. Dahl[18] developed an observation of F. C. Baur[19] and argued that cc. 1-4 are correctly considered an apostolic apology[20], in function of which Paul reasserts his authority as a preamble to addressing, in an authoritative way, the various disciplinary problems of the community which come to the fore beginning in c. 5. Dahl's thesis is not without subscribers[21] and

---

[15] Cf. 1Cor 4,8-10; 6,2.

[16] Probst rejects reading 1Cor under the aspect of polemic about authority and as apologetic. Drawing on information about the *Sitz im Leben* of the ancient letter *Gattung* he notes that: 1) «Alle argumentation geschieht durchaus im Rahmen freundliche Contenance und in der Stilform der beratenden *demegoria*»; 2) «Als Anlaß des antiken Briefes erscheint deshalb oft ein ursprünglicher Wunsch des Briefempfängers, einen Ratschlag des Autors zu erhalten, oder die eigene Absicht des Schreibers dem Empfänger einen guten Rat zuhommen su lassen»; 3) «Gegenseitige Akzeptanz und Achtung bilden die Grundlage des Briefes auch da, wo manch intensiver Konflikt durch die Kommunication beider Partner hindurchschimmert» (cf. H. PROBST, *Paulus und der Brief*, 101-102) Probst's observations are valid. However, his transference of these observations and their implications for 1Cor must be attended with caution since he assumes, but does not prove, that all the conditions pertaining to the occasion and composition of ancient letters are identical to the conditions that accompanied the writing of 1Cor.

[17] Cf. the discussion below, § 5.

[18] N.A. DAHL, «Paul and the Church», 313-335.

[19] Cf. F.C. BAUR, «Die Christuspartei», 61-206. While Dahl rejects Baur's claim that Paul's opponents were «Judaizers», he accepts and builds on Baur's thesis that cc. 1-4 are an apologetic unit intended as a justification for Paul's apostolic ministry and authority.

[20] Though he makes no claim that cc. 1-4 constitute an apostolic apology, W. SCHMITHALS remarks, in the same vein, that Paul had first to take care that his apostolic authority, denied by the Gnostics in function of Paul's «non-Pneumatic» status, was recognized in Corinth before he could re-establish order (cf. *Gnosticism*, 222).

[21] Cf. e.g. M. CHEVALLIER, «Construction», 109-129; J. WEIMA, *Neglected Endings*, 205; J.C. HURD, preface to the new edition of *Origin*, xx; E. SCHÜSSLER FIORENZA, «Rhetorical Situation» claims that the issue at stake in cc. 1-4 and restated throughout was Paul's *auctoritas* (cf. 394); but she goes beyond Dahl to claim that Paul is not re-establishing his authority but introducing unique authority claims as the sole founder and father of the community (cf. 397). Against such a claim stands the fact that Paul

was a significant attempt to explain the relationship of 1Cor 1-4 to the rest of the letter. Nonetheless it has problems[22]. One of these, which Dahl noted himself, is that chapters 1-4 are not written in the form of an apology[23]. This difficulty would appear to be overcome thanks to the rhetorical analyses provided by Bünker[24] and Pesch[25] which lend support to Dahl's thesis and provide the formal evidence needed to clinch his case. In fact, E. Schüssler Fiorenza finds corroboration for Dahl's position in the rhetorical analysis of Bünker who shows that 1Cor 1-4 has «the rhetorical structure of forensic or judicial discourse»[26]. Yet the rhetorical

---

includes in the superscription of 1Cor the name of a co-sender, Sosthenes, which could mean he was not at all intending to present himself as the exclusive authority in this situation. On this last point see D.L. STAMPS, «Rhetorical Criticism. Evaluations of Argumentation», 159.

[22] 1) Dahl says that Chloe's people could orally report both that there was strife in the community at Corinth and that there was some opposition to Paul (50). That Chloe's people reported *erides*, indicating the community lacked unity, is certain (1Cor 1,11). However, it is not clear that Chloe's people reported opposition to Paul or that the report of *erides* was tantamount to a report of opposition to Paul. 1Cor 1,12 is presumably Paul's restatement or perhaps reinterpretation (*legô de touto*), of the substance of this information. But v. 12 does not indicate opposition to Paul anymore than it indicates opposition to Peter or to Apollos or to Christ. Rather, it indicates that among community members quarrelling was going on which is somehow related to misunderstandings about ministerial figures; but it does not necessarily indicate that «the strife at Corinth was linked up with opposition to him [Paul]» (49), which Dahl further links with an alleged opposition to Stephanus (49-51) and the highly conjectural view that the quarrels were occasioned by Stephanus' recourse to Paul for his advice on the topics contained in the letter. 1Cor lacks any proof that within the community there were differences of opinion over the person to whom the community's questions should be addressed; 2) dwelling on the alleged «opposition» loses sight of the fact that Paul does not focus his energy here to refuting an opposition group, but is concerned to redirect the erring thinking of *all* concerning wisdom and ministers/ministry, even that of those who might be considered his own group of partisans. 3) The only concrete evidence Dahl sets out to prove that there was a center of opposition against Paul is the term *tines*, 4,18. This is very meager evidence. In fact we do not know if the arrogant *tines* formed a specific opposition group, nor whether as a group they were embedded within one of the so-called factions or whether the arrogant «some» were types.

[23] N. DAHL, «Paul and the Church», 61.

[24] M. BÜNKER, *Briefformular*, esp. 49-80. In schematic form Bünker's analysis is as follows: *Exordium* 1,10-17; *Propositio* 1,18; *Narratio* 1,18-2,16; *Probatio* 3,1-17; *Peroratio* I 3,18-23; *Refutatio* 4,1-13; *Peroratio* II 4,14-21.

[25] R. PESCH, *Paulus Ringt*, esp. 115-135 and 177-188. Pesch's analysis can be schematized as follows: *Exordium* 1,10-17; *Propositio* 1,18; *Narratio* 1,18-2,16; *Probatio* 3,1-17; *Peroratio* I 3,13-23; *Refutatio* 4,1-13; *Peroratio* II 4,14-16.

[26] E. SCHÜSSLER FIORENZA, «Rhetorical Situation», 392. However, she considers the fact that Bünker restricted his analysis to 1Cor 1-4 and 15, thereby failing to take account of the rhetorical genre of the whole letter, a weakness of the study. She concludes, with G. KENNEDY (cf. *New Testament Interpretation*, 87), that 1Cor is

analyses of both Bünker and Pesch purporting to demonstrate that cc. 1-4 are a unit of forensic or defense rhetoric are themselves problematic.

Beginning with broadest considerations it could be said that both analyses suffer from the same lamentable[27] tendency to impose on the text the ideal or complete form of the rhetorical *dispositio*. According to the classical handbooks a forensic speech had four[28] essential parts: *the exordium, narratio, probatio* and *peroratio*[29]. This four part schema represents the ideal arrangement of a forensic speech. However, we must not assume on the one hand that all the elements are always present and discernible in a Pauline text, nor should we subsequently force them on the text in view of assumptions about the rhetorical situation and the genre appropriate to it[30]. Nor must we assume on the other hand, that the absence of some elements indicates that Paul was not engaging in rhetorical argumentation. In fact the indispensable requirements for a rhetorical argument were two: the *prothesis* and the *pistis*[31]. When the *prothesis* or *propositio*[32] is isolated and the proofs studied then rhetorical analysis indeed becomes a useful tool that can allow us to center on and identify the import of Paul's argument[33].

---

largely deliberative with some judicial segments, as opposed to epideictic as W. WUELLNER suggests (cf. «Greek Rhetoric»).

[27] Cf. the critical remarks in J.-N. ALETTI, «La *dispositio* rhétorique», 385-387; ID., «La présence», 5-7.

[28] For the description of these four terms, referred to respectively as, *prooimion, diègèsis, pistis, epilogos*, and a discussion of their function cf. ARISTOTLE, *Ars Rhetorica*, III.XIV, 1 - XIX, 6

[29] QUINTILIAN, *Institutio*, III.IX, 1, considered the *probatio* divisible into two parts and thus named a fifth element, the *refutatio*. Among Latin authors, the classical forensic *dispositio* was seven-part: *exordium, narratio, explicatio, propositio, confirmatio, refutatio* and *peroratio*. This schema is discussed in T. LENCHAK, *A Rhetorical Critical Investigation*, 63-66.

[30] One of the risks in following the methodology outlined by G. KENNEDY in *New Testament Interpretation*, 33-37, is that having first established the rhetorical situation which Kennedy says «roughly corresponds to the *Sitz im Leben* of form criticism» (cf. 34) and having decided in advance to what exigency the writer addresses himself, the practitioner of rhetorical criticism may be overly pre-disposed to finding in the text the schema of that rhetorical genre proper to the pre-established rhetorical situation which should have been employed. The risk of forcing the text to configure to the appropriate rhetorical genre seems to inhere in this method. Cf. further the comments in J.-N. ALETTI, «La *dispositio* rhétorique», esp. 390-393.

[31] Cf. ARISTOTLE, *Ars Rhetorica*, III.XIII, 4.

[32] In the Latin authors the thesis is referred to as the *propositum*, cf. CICERO, *De Partitione*, XVIII, 61.

[33] Here we agree with J.-N. ALETTI, «La *dispositio* rhétorique» 390-391 and J. MURPHY-O'CONNOR, *Paul et l'art épistolaire*, 125-129, that rhetorical analysis which aims at understanding Paul's argument is more important than that which aims to apply to the text the whole schema as set forth in the handbooks. This is especially so

Moving to more specific considerations it can be argued that the rhetorical analyses of Bünker and Pesch are defective and do not make a convincing case that cc. 1-4 are a unit of defense or forensic rhetoric. Here we note three defects: 1) the incompatibility of the time frame of cc. 1-4 with that which is appropriate to the rhetorical genre established by Bünker and Pesch for these chapters; 2) the incorrect designation of 1,18-2,16 as *narratio* and 3) the failure to designate correctly the *propositio* or thesis of this unit of argumentation.

Regarding point 1, the defective nature of the analyses is evidenced rather immediately when we consider that the appropriate time frame of forensic speech is the past[34]. The time frame of cc. 1-4 is clearly the present. There is no judgement of things «past» but a consideration of the current state of affairs in the community with an eye to future comportment.

Regarding point 2, both Pesch[35] and Bünker[36] designate the *narratio* as 1,18-2,16. This is incorrect for the following reasons: a) as designated, this *narratio* is in violation of one of the chief rules regarding the *narratio*, held without exception by all the classical rhetoricians, viz., brevity[37]. The sections designated as *narratio* by both authors[38], actually turn out to be the longest segment of the argument; b) the *narratio* is, by definition, a disinterested recounting of past facts to prepare for the *probatio*[39]. What these authors have designated as *narratio* hardly fits the description[40]; c) according to both analyses the *narratio* is situated between the *propositio* and the proofs. Both Bünker and Pesch locate the *propositio* at 1,18, which is really to say that they consider the first verse of the section designated as *narratio* 1,18-2,16, to be the thesis. Both authors then say essentially the same thing regarding the unfolding of the narrative. Pesch says that Paul begins his *narratio* «mit einer These, (v. 18) deren Stichhaltigkeit er dann in drei Anläufen darlegt (1,19-25; 1,26-

---

in light of the fact that the order (*taxis*) of the speech could be altered as the rhetor saw fit depending on the circumstances (cf. *Rhet. ad Her.*, III.IX, 17).

[34] On the time frames appropriate to each of the three rhetorical genres, cf. ARISTOTLE, *Ars Rhetorica*, III.III, 4-6.

[35] R. PESCH, *Paulus Ringt*, 124-130.

[36] M. BÜNKER, *Briefformula*, 55-56.

[37] Cf. e.g. CICERO, *De Partitione*, IX, 31; QUINTILIAN, *Institutio*, IV.II, 104; *Ad Her.*, I, 9,14. See also «Narrationis virtutes et vitia» in H. LAUSBERG, *Handbuch*, I, 167-170.

[38] Cf. the schemas above n. 24; 25.

[39] Cf. CICERO, *De Partitione*, IX, 31-32; ARISTOTLE, *Ars Rhetorica*, III.XVI, 11; QUINTILIAN, *Institutio*, IV.II, 1.

[40] Also noted by P. LAMPE, «Theological Wisdom», 119. Cf. further, G. SELLIN, «Hauptprobleme», 2944.

31; 2,1-5) bevor er auf den Kernpunkt des Streites, der zwichen ihm und Gegnern in der korinthischen Gemeinde schwebt, eingeht (2,6-16)»[41]. Bünker says, «Der Aufbau des Abschnittes selbst [the narratio = 1,18-2,16] ist ganz klar. V. 18 stellt die These auf, die dann in einem dreifachen Beweisgang begründet wird: v. 19-25[...], v. 26-31[...]2,1-5[...]»[42]. But this order does not accord with the classical handbooks. After the *exordium*, the speaker will ordinarily state the facts, i.e., the *narratio*, then state the point he wishes to prove, i.e., the *propositio*, whereupon the proof/s of this point follow immediately[43]. In *breve*, the order is normally: *narratio, propositio, probatio*[44]. In the analyses of Pesch and Bünker, the *narratio* is designated as that which follows Paul's thesis or the point he wishes to prove. Moreover, both authors indicate that in what they designate as *narratio* Paul is effectively developing a threefold argument or proof of his thesis. But if in 1,18-2,5 Paul is already involved in setting out proofs then this section is a *probatio;* but it cannot be both *probatio* and *narratio* at the same time! While they are right that the section is already proof, they are wrong to consider it the *narratio*, which as already noted above is a disinterested recounting of past facts to prepare for the *probatio*. It is clear that there is no *narratio* here and one cannot be forced on the text for the sake of configuring the text to the ideal rhetorical schema. This brings us now to the third point mentioned above, the improper designation of the *propositio*.

According to the handbooks the *propositio* sets forth completely what the speaker intends to discuss or prove[45]. Moreover the *propositio* is characterized by brevity and is located immediately before the proofs or the argumentation proper[46]. Based on this information, the *propositio*[47], or point that Paul intends to argue in the first four chapters, appears to be contained in 1,17 and has two succinct parts: a) Paul is a preacher of the gospel not a baptizer (v. 17a), and b) human wisdom and the wisdom of

---

[41] R. PESCH, *Paulus Ringt*, 124.

[42] M. BÜNKER, *Briefformula*, 55.

[43] Cf. *Rhet. ad Her.*, II.X, 17; II.XVIII, 28; CICERO, *De Oratore*, II.XIX, 80. See also H. LAUSBERG, *Handbuch*, I, 148-149.

[44] Sometimes an *explicatio* is found between the *narratio* and *propositio*, cf. above, n. 29.

[45] Cf. ARISTOTLE, *Ars Rhetorica*, III.XII, 13; also *Rhet. ad Her.*, II.XX, 32.

[46] Cf. QUINTILIAN, *Institutio*, IV.IV, 2 - V, 28.

[47] Only by locating the *propositio*, which states the point to be argued and then reading the *probatio* (*pistis*) that follows immediately are we able to know, with precision, the point being argued by the author. This is more important than, and must necessarily precede, the establishing of the rhetorical genre of a unit. On the importance of determining the *propositio* of a rhetorical unit see J.-N. ALETTI, «La présence», 7.

the cross are incompatible (v. 17b). What follows the statement of the proposition is an unfolding of arguments[48] (*probatio*) relative to these two points[49]. In the setting out of the proofs, Paul argues the two points of the *propositio* in the reverse order in which they were first stated. He begins in 1,18 with an extended discussion of the wisdom of the cross (1,18-31) and of his decision not to preach with eloquent wisdom (2,1-16). These first arguments deal with the second half of the *propositio,* stated in 17b. After this, Paul discusses the work of true ministers of the gospel and the relationship that obtains among these ministers[50] (3,1-4,14), which relates to the first half of the *propositio*, stated in 17a. The two part *propositio* followed by arguments in support of each of its elements would appear to indicate that misapprehension regarding these two issues[51] is at the core of

---

[48] This is in accord with QUINTILIAN, *Institutio*, IV.IV, 2 - V, 28 on the order of *propositio* followed by *probatio*.

[49] Without using the rhetorical term *propositio*, Best correctly noted that v. 17b, «*ouk en sophia logou hina mè kenôthè ho stauros tou Christou*», which is the second half of the *propositio*, «forms the text for the following discussion» (cf. E. BEST, «The Power», 13).

[50] Paul's reference to the slogans, «I belong to Paul», «to Apollos» etc. may be taken as an indication that among community members there was some dispute revolving around perceptions and evaluations of ministers. Whether any dogmatic differences can be attached to the individual names, differences which would indicate a break up into theological factions, we cannot know with certitude. Based on the text information in cc. 1-4 Paul does not appear to be combatting any dogmatic tendencies which contradict his own. Paul seems to be condemning the fact of the disputes over ministers in so far as these disputes threaten the unity of the community.

[51] Relative to the issue of wisdom, Pogoloff makes an interesting case that the wisdom to which Paul refers should not be conceived in terms of content, as often argued, but rather in terms of rhetorical or cultural wisdom which the Corinthians would have understood as an important determinant of social status (cf. S. POGOLOFF, *Logos and Sophia*, 8-10). Pogoloff claims that the wisdom Paul rejects is not a counter-teaching or a counter-ideology; nor does he reject rhetoric *per se*. Rather, Paul rejects the cultural values and high social status that were attached to wise speech (121) especially in popular Stoic thought (115) which may have influenced the Corinthians. In the same vein as Pogoloff, cf. D. LITFIN, *Saint Paul's Theology of Proclamation*. In conjunction with Pogoloff's thesis, QUINTILIAN's characterization of a bad orator as one lacking «eloquence» and «power» ought to be signalled, cf. *Institutio*, VIII Pr. 17. Interestingly, Paul disclaims as personal characteristics both eloquence and power, intentionally, it seems, disowning good orator status, cf. 1,17. He preached «*ouk en sophia logou*», usually rendered «not in eloquent wisdom», lest the cross of Christ be emptied of *its* power. This rejection of eloquence and focus on the power of the cross as opposed to his own, could lend support to the claim that Paul sought to distance himself from the profile of the good orator with its concomitant high social status. However, on a primary level, Paul may have intended to distance himself from the seductive rhetoric that only obfuscates, and is moreover inadequate to express, the stark reality of the cross which is God's power forcing upon Christians

the disunity in Corinth[52]. Paul's aim in speaking to these two issues is to correct misunderstandings in order to achieve his main purpose, the conciliation of the community, since it is the unity of the community that is at stake. Paul addresses himself to the misunderstanding over ministers and wisdom that puts the unity in jeopardy and guides the community in a correct line of thinking[53]. It would appear beyond question then that the argument Paul unfolds in these chapters is not aimed at defending his apostolic status and authority.

In sum, once the formal evidence advanced to demonstrate that cc. 1-4 are a unit of forensic rhetoric is shown to be inadequate, the evidence advanced by Dahl to support his reading of cc. 1-4 as an apostolic apology is neither sufficient nor incontrovertible proof. Content, tenor and one piece of lexical evidence, *tines*, and what its use by Paul allegedly implies about his awareness of the existence of a center of opposition to him, do not compel the adoption of Dahl's reading of the unit as an apology for Paul's apostolic authority. It seems more likely, considering Paul's *propositio* and proofs, that this first argumentative unit of text in 1Cor is devoted to the correction of misapprehensions that threaten the unity of the community[54]. Despite various hypotheses[55] advanced to show on what grounds Paul's authority was being contested, text evidence is insufficient to support the claim that Paul is engaged in the defense of his apostolic authority in 1Cor 1-4. On the contrary, it would appear that the fact of his apostolic authority constitutes the basis for Paul's conciliating activity and call for unity.

---

a whole new order to which they must submit. This last point has been forcefully expounded in R. HAMMERTON-KELLY, *Sacred Violence*, 84.

[52] An interesting discussion on Paul's rhetorical skill in «covertly» relating these two discussions to the problem of disunity in Corinth is offered in P. LAMPE, «Theological Wisdom», esp. 117-127.

[53] Cf. E. BEST, «The Power», 14.

[54] Kuck has correctly observed both that the heart of the issue here is ecclesiology, since what is threatened by the Corinthian zeal for Wisdom is the unity of the Body of Christ, and that 1Cor 1-4 is not «theological polemics or self-defense» (cf. D. KUCK, *Judgment*, 234-235).

[55] For example, it has been suggested that Paul's apostolic status and authority were contested in light of theological reasons, cf. C.K. BARRETT, «Christianity at Corinth», 269-287; ID., «Cephas in Corinth», 1-12; or sociological or political reasons, cf. e.g. G. THEISSEN, *Social Setting*; P. MARSHALL, *Enmity in Corinth*; L.L. WELBORN, «Discord», 85-111.

2.2 1Cor 9. An Apostolic Apology?

Though a number of scholars consider 1Cor 9 an apology[56], there is sufficient reason to doubt that this chapter is an apology in which Paul is allegedly refuting specific charges[57] of real opponents[58]. Recent studies[59] make it clear that construing the passage as an apology, reflecting actual conditions in which Paul found himself under attack, can only be done at the expense of viewing c. 9 apart from its context[60] and its rhetorical or paraenetic function in that context. According to Malherbe, by using the phrase, «*hè emè apologia tois emè anakrinousin estin autè*», «Paul is not indicating that there were people who were bringing specific charges against him which required a self-defense»[61]. Rather he has in view «the anticipated reaction of his readers to his warning in 8.9 that their *exousia* not become a *proskomma* to the weak»[62]. Moreover, even if the text could justifiably be treated apart from the context, still it is not clear that its form can be considered that of an apology. As both Willis[63] and

---

[56] Among others, cf. e.g., R. HOCK, *Social Context*, 59-62; D. DUNGAN, *The Sayings*, 4ff.; G. LUEDEMANN, *Opposition*, 65ff; R. PESCH, *Paulus Ringt*, 224-229.

[57] On what the charge/s were which could have actually been brought against Paul and the historical plausibility of the suggestions, cf. M. MITCHELL, *Paul*, 245-246. She notes that «all attempts to analyze 1Cor 9 as a true defense against actual charges have failed» (244).

[58] It has been suggested that the «same opponents are certainly in mind» in 1Cor 9 and 2Cor 11,1ff. (cf. W. SCHMITHALS, *Gnosticism*, 115). However, there is absolutely no evidence of outside intruders who are behind the issues addressed in 1Cor; nor is there evidence to support Schmithal's identification of these alleged intruders as Palestinian Jews. Moreover, such suggestions betray disregard for the distinctiveness of the situation of 1Cor.

[59] Cf. M. MITCHELL, *Paul*, esp. 130 and 243ff.; W. WILLIS, «An Apostolic Apologia?», 33-48; Stowers considers both 1Cor 9 and 1-4 paraenetic (cf. *Letter Writing*, 96).

[60] It has often been thought that 1Cor 9 is a digression, in the sense of a departure from the discussion about the right, *hè exousia* (8,9), to eat idol meat. As such, c. 9 was thought to have been located here by a redactor. However, various scholars have called attention to Paul's use of the rhetorical technique *digressio* (cf. e.g. W. WUELLNER, «Greek Rhetoric», 177-188; B. STANDAERT, «1Co 13», 128; ID., «Lecture rhétorique», 190-91). Understood as a *digressio*, in the technical rhetorical sense of the term, it is now clear that 1Cor 9 is an integral part of Paul's discussion on idol meat which begins in 1Cor 8,1 and extends to 11,1. On the rhetorical technique, *digressio*, cf. QUINTILIAN, *Institutio*, IV.III, 12-14).

[61] A. MALHERBE, «Determinism», 240. Apropos of Malherbe's point see further G. LYONS, *Pauline Autobiography*, esp. 95-105. This author discusses the methodological questionability of reading every Pauline denial as evidence of real accusations against him.

[62] Cf. A. MALHERBE, «Determinism», 240.

[63] W. WILLIS, «An Apostolic Apologia?», 34.

Mitchell[64] have pointed out, the presence of the forensic terms *apologia* and *anakrinein* does not *ipso facto* signify that what follows is a genuine apology. Recourse to the tone of the section to sustain this view is also tenuous since defensive tone and self-justification do not necessarily signal an apology[65].

A closer look at this argumentative unit reveals that Paul is problematizing his apostolic freedom and stressing his renunciation of this freedom as a model for the community. With regard to the specific right to eat idol meat (1Cor 8,1ff.), the community must consider not only its freedom to exercise this right, but also the possibility of freely renouncing that right when its exercise negatively impacts some members of the community with weak consciences (8,9).

Willis correctly argues that vv. 4-14 are not a defense of Paul's rights but a strong establishment of them[66]. In fact the questions posed with the negative *ou/ouk,* 9,1.2.4.5.12, all expect a positive answer. Yes, Paul is free, is an apostle and he does have all the rights to which the questions refer. Paul establishes these rights by a reference to apostolic practice in vv. 4-6, by simple examples based on the soldier, the vine planter and the shepherd in v. 7 and finally by a reference to the law, vv. 8-10. With these points firmly established Paul can now illustrate how he has freely given up these rights and thus present himself as an exemplar of renunciation of rights which is itself an exercise of freedom. Why does Paul do this? He says himself in 12b., *hina mè tina enkopèn dômen to evangeliô tou Christou.*

Paul is clearly speaking to the exercise of freedom[67] in this chapter. Unfortunately attention often turns immediately to the terms «apostle» and «apology» and the significance of the leading question, «am I not free?», is mostly overlooked. Yet this lead question really betrays another underlying question which Mitchell has aptly formulated: «if I am free, then why do I have to curtail my freedom from doing things which I am admittedly free to do?»[68]. The answer to this question is what Paul's so-called «defense» is actually all about: how true freedom can be expressed in renunciation of rights without being construed as mere weakness. For

---

[64] M. MITCHELL, *Paul*, 243.

[65] S.K. STOWERS, *Letter Writing*, 96.

[66] W. WILLIS, «An Apostolic Apologia?», 33-34.

[67] On the similarities between Paul's argument here and popular philosophical debates on the sage's independence especially as it related to determinism and free will, cf. A. MALHERBE, «Determinism», esp. 242-55.

[68] M. MITCHELL, *Paul*, 247

the cognitively empowered[69] (strong) whom Paul addresses beginning in 8,1, for whom freedom and the exercise of power went hand in hand, the idea of renunciation of the exercise of power could only appear to be weakness and slavery[70]. Indeed Paul picks up on this in 9,19 and says that he made himself a slave. But this slavish freedom is true freedom manifested in adaptability to the needs of others who are saved (9,22), by the exercise of freedom rather than destroyed (8,11)[71]. Paul wants to see the same kind of adaptability on the part of the Corinthian strong when it comes to the issue of eating idol meat and the problems this creates for the weak.

The results of the recent rhetorical analysis of c. 9 by Mitchell[72] corroborate the conclusions emerging from Willis' analysis. Both studies have convincingly shown that in form and in function c. 9 should be understood as paraenetic[73] and not as apologetic. In fact, given its placement between c. 8 and c. 10, where Paul is urging the renunciation of the right to eat idol meat, the paraenetic function of c. 9 is evident. But it cannot be paraenetic and apologetic in function at the same time[74]. For if Paul were defending himself against actual accusations then we would have to assume that at least some in the community were being adversely affected by his course of action. Perhaps they were even offended or angered by his refusal of financial support. Following through logically on this, one would have to admit that Paul's renunciation of support would have effected in the community the exact result which he wants them to avoid, viz., giving offense by counseling them to a course of action that must at times include renunciation of rights. Paul's example of renunciation of rights for the sake of avoiding giving offense would fail if

---

[69] It is widely held that in 1Cor 8,1 Paul is citing a Corinthian slogan, «*pantes gnôsin echomen*», which he then modifies in v. 7, «*all' ouk en pasin hè gnôsis*». The «strong» were those who were cognitively empowered and conversely we might understand the «weak» to refer to those without this cognitive power. Given this, we are inclined to agree that the terms weakness and strength are references primarily to cognitive status (cf. A. MALHERBE, «Determinism», 233) and not to social standing (cf. G. THEISSEN, *The Social Setting*, 121-143), though they may also refer to social status on a secondary level.

[70] The interesting possibility that Stoic conceptions of power/freedom and weakness/slavery are at the heart of Corinthian views in c. 8 and that Paul seeks to overturn these conceptions in c. 9, is expounded in A. MALHERBE, «Determinism», 231-255.

[71] Cf. A. MALHERBE, «Determinism», 252.

[72] Cited above, Introduction n. 19.

[73] M. MITCHELL refers to c. 9 by the rhetorical term, «exemplary argument» (cf. *Paul*, 250).

[74] «Paul plays with the idea of apology in 1Cor 9:3-12 but the larger context of the chapter and the letter itself are hortatory» (S.K. STOWERS, *Letter Writing*, 173).

indeed he had offended, irritated or scandalized members of the community. Surely, one of these would have had to have been the case if Paul were defending himself. But he is not. As Mitchell says, «1Cor 9 is no defense speech by Paul. Instead Paul calls it defense to justify rhetorically his use of himself as the example of imitation, a rhetorical stance paralleled in antiquity [...]»[75]. In fact, as shown, it makes no sense in its present context as an apostolic apology. What logic would Paul's closing command in 11,1 have? How should the Corinthians imitate him? By choosing a course of action that would stir adverse reaction and require defense? Of course not! Moreover, that Paul so resolutely offers himself as a model of imitation makes sense only if he were not currently under attack.

3. Medial Summary

What should be apparent from the foregoing discussions of 1Cor 1-4 and 9 is that these units do not provide evidence that can be used to sustain the reading of 1Cor as a largely defensive letter in which Paul must stave off attacks by opponents against his apostleship. In consequence, one can reasonably say that there is no compelling reason to construe Paul's relationship with the community as one of enmity or to assume that the Corinthian behavior under discussion in this letter betrays a posture of hostility. Besides the fact that the rhetoric does not support such claims, this flawed reading of the text and the social situation also indicates a disregard for a number of very important factors which point away from such a reading. The following factors, for example, should be noted: 1) The Corinthians were the ones who had recourse to Paul, initiating the communication with him both orally and in writing. The fact that Paul was approached by the community can reasonably be taken to insinuate that he was held in regard and was to a large extent considered the spokesperson of its values. 2) Twice in the letter, at 4,16 and 11,1, Paul offers himself as a model to be imitated. How does one explain these two facts if his relationship with the community was not sound?[76] Indeed

---

[75] M. MITCHELL, Paul, 246. Cf. further B. FIORE, The Function, esp. 26-44, 181-184.

[76] The reply that Paul was here only addressing a limited number within the community who challenged his authority does not work. It is clear from the text that Paul addresses the whole community from the beginning of the letter to the end. Throughout there is consistent use of the 2nd person pl. except for a few cases of 2nd pers. sing. as found in 4,7; 7,21,27; 8,10; 14,16-17; 15,36-37. In the last case, the 2nd sing. clearly refers to an imaginary interlocutor. In the other cases, the alternation in

these appeals to imitate him would be quite fatuous if he were currently under attack! 3) Not only does 1Cor lack the harsh invective of 2Cor[77] but in this letter Paul refers to the Corinthians as his beloved children[78] and to himself as their father[79], responsible for introducing them to new life and responsible also for their behavior[80]. It is precisely in light of this relationship that Paul can urge them to be his imitators (cf. 1Cor 4,16). Again, what sense would any of this make were Paul's relationship with the community not solid? 4) If Paul were actually dealing with adversaries would he risk playing into their hands by referring to himself as weak and disreputable (cf. 4,10)? 5) Finally, if Paul's relationship with the community were one of animosity, how does one explain the concluding greeting, «my love be with you all in Christ Jesus» (1Cor 16,24), especially since Paul concludes no other letter with this greeting! Apropos of this last point it has been recently argued by J. Weima[81] in his study on the form, content and significance of Paul's letter closings that the conclusion of 1Cor with its unique stress on love is, contrary to what we have just suggested, an indicator of the strained relationship between Paul and the Corinthian church. He claims that «a careful reading of the letter's epistolary conventions, as well as its content reveals the fact of a growing conflict between Paul and the Corinthians»[82]. He asserts that Paul's main aims in the letter were: a) to reassert his authority in a situation where it had seriously eroded and b) to convince his readers to change their behavior and errant theology[83]. Weima uncritically accepts the claims of Dahl and particularly Fee and appears to configure his conclusions about the letter ending of 1Cor to support their reading of the letter as apologetic, defensive and reflective of extreme conflict between Paul and the community: in sum, as a continuous attempt by Paul to reassert his authority. Even though he insists that a careful reading of the letter's epistolary conventions sets the conflict in relief and that acknowledging the conflict is crucial to understanding the epistolary conclusion, his assertions rely heavily on the disputable positions of others[84], except where he marshals evidence from his own analysis of the superscription

---

number is a question of moving the issue from a general plain to a particular application and in no way indicates a change of group addressed.

[77] Cf. above, n. 4.
[78] Cf. 1Cor 4,14.
[79] Cf. 1Cor 4,15.
[80] Cf. J.H. SCHÜLTZ, *Paul and the Anatomy*, 209.
[81] J. WEIMA, *Neglected Endings*, esp. 201-207.
[82] J. WEIMA, *Neglected Endings*, 203.
[83] J. WEIMA, *Neglected Endings*, 204.
[84] J. WEIMA, *Neglected Endings*, 205.

and thanksgiving section of 1Cor. The results of this analysis, he maintains, corroborate the view that the situation was one of conflict between the Apostle and the community. Apropos of the thanksgiving section, which Weima sees as «foreshadowing the tension»[85], he observes that the notable omission of certain elements in the thanksgiving of 1Cor[86] already signals a seriously strained relationship between Paul and the Corinthians. However, as always, arguments based on omissions have the potential to prove everything or prove nothing. For example, he observes that, in the thanksgiving, Paul fails to mention any cause for thanking God which originates in the Corinthian church itself. Rather, Paul's reason for thanks is exclusively rooted in God. While this observation is correct, does it in fact prove anything about Paul's relationship with the Corinthians, let alone that it is evidence of a strained relationship? Weima's use of Galatians as a comparative basis for establishing the situation of 1Cor is also questionable. He points up similarities between Galatians, a letter reflecting a situation of tension between Paul and the community, and 1Cor in order to show that 1Cor, like Galatians, must also be taken as reflecting great tension between Paul and the community. Yet he fails to mention a major difference between Gal and 1Cor which could seriously undermine his case, viz., that despite whatever omissions are notable in the thanksgiving section of 1Cor, the fact is that it *does* have a thanksgiving section, whereas Galatians does not. This is a significant difference which cannot be selectively overlooked. In sum, Weima's observations about the concluding section of 1Cor, and specifically the love salutation, need to be taken with caution. His pre-conditioned starting point for reading 1Cor prejudices his conclusions. Weima has not argued convincingly that the love salutation is in fact a gauge of conflict rather than a genuine token of affection.

In light of the preceding considerations, it makes it all the more difficult in our opinion to sustain the view that in 1Cor a relationship of animosity obtained between Paul and the community. Perhaps it would be better to adopt Wuellner's position that «whenever Paul refers to himself and his apostolic office in 1Cor, rather than seeing in it evidences of "apology" we should be seeing in it evidences of epideictic which is related to education»[87].

---

[85] J. Weima, *Neglected Endings*, 205.

[86] J. Weima, *Neglected Endings*, 204.

[87] W. Wuellner, «Methodological Considerations», 5. Wuellner's understanding of epideictic is based on an amplified understanding of this genre as set forth in C. Perelman – L. Olbrechts-Tyteca, *The New Rhetoric*, esp. 52-54.

4. Distinguishing the Rhetorical and the Historical Situation

In the preceding pages we have attempted to show that it appears incorrect to consider cc. 1-4 and c. 9 as apologies. Leaving aside that evaluation for the moment, here we wish to move to another level of consideration and take up the question of the relationship between rhetoric and the establishing of the actual historical situation. Can one argue through the rhetoric to the historical situation? It appears that a misreading of the situation of 1Cor as one of opposition and intense conflict results not only from the misconstrual of the rhetorical genre but also from the assumption that once the arrangement can be determined and with that, the genre, one can and should proceed to an identification of the actual historical situation. This seems to be the operating assumption in the reading of 1Cor in those cases where scholars argue through the rhetoric to the an actual historical situation of conflict. Apropos of 1Cor 1-4, and 9, we have seen that the establishment of defense rhetoric or apostolic apology allowed scholars to argue to a real situation of opposition for 1Cor. Identities were then assigned to the «opponents»[88] of Paul and motives supplied for why he is being opposed[89]. Practiced this way, and aimed at uncovering the real historical situation, there is little distinction between the notion of situation in rhetorical criticism and that of historical criticism. In fact, except for the introduction of rhetorical terminology and the highlighting of the rhetorical arrangement, the rhetorical situation is bypassed and the text is read as a mirror which reflects the real situation. But is a Pauline text ever only a mirror of an actual historical situation? Is there then no distinction between a rhetorical situation and the historical situation? If so, what bearing has this on the interpretation of 1Cor?

In a recent article, D. Stamps[90] provides a number of important insights to help in dealing with these questions. First, he sets out to define the difference between the rhetorical and the historical situation. Relying on Wuellner's[91] formulation of the difference between the rhetorical and

---

[88] For example, it has been suggested that the opposition was composed of the high status, highly educated members of the community,(cf. M. Bünker, *Briefformular*, 17, 51-52). This conclusion is in line with the views of G. Theissen regarding the source of trouble in Corinth (cf. *The Social Setting*, essays 2 and 3). The sociological approach to the text as advocated by Theissen is shared by W. Meeks, *The First Urban Christians* and has had a generally positive reception. However, it is not without critics, cf. R.L. Rorhbaugh, «The City», 68.

[89] Cf. N. Dahl, «Paul and the Church», esp. 48-52.

[90] D.L. Stamps, «Rethinking», 193-210.

[91] D.L. Stamps recognizes that Kennedy's reformulation (cf. *New Testament Interpretation*, 34-35), of Bitzer's definition of rhetorical situation (cf. L. Bitzer, «The Rhetorical Situation», 1-14), is the prevailing conception among NT scholars.

historical situation, Stamps maintains that the historical situation is not defined by the correspondence between extrinsic factors and text strategy but by the correspondence between text form and its ability to persuade[92]. In other words, the rhetorical situation is a text phenomenon, something inscribed in the text. Second, apropos of our question of whether the text is simply a mirror of the historical situation, a comment of Stamps is helpful in clarifying the relationship between the text and the actual situation. He writes,

> While it may be granted that any text, and an ancient NT epistle in particular, stems from certain historical and social contingencies which contribute to the rhetorical situation of a text, it is also true that a text presents a selected, limited and crafted entextualization of the situation. The entextualized situation is not the historical situation which generates the text and/or which the text responds to or addresses, rather, at this level, it is that situation embedded in the text and created by the text which contributes to the rhetorical effect of the text[93].

Third, he points out that it is the textual presentation of the inscribed situation which is crucial for understanding the argument of the letter since the rhetoric of the letter operates from the situation as it is constructed and presented in the letter[94]. Otherwise stated, the argument of the letter is a response to the situation presented in the text. How one isolates the rhetorical situation embedded in the literary presentation and what significance this has for interpretation occupies Stamps in the remainder of his article[95]. Stamps concludes by noting that in the material

---

However, Stamps maintains that Kennedy insufficiently distinguishes between the rhetorical and historical situation (cf. D.L. STAMPS, «Rethinking», 194-198).

[92] Cf. D.L. STAMPS, «Rethinking», 196.

[93] D.L. STAMPS, «Rethinking», 199.

[94] D.L. STAMPS, «Rethinking», 210.

[95] Stamps' full treatment of 1Cor is soon to appear in a monograph. In the present article (cf. 200ff.), he presents streamlined comments about the rhetorical situation inscribed in the text of 1Cor. His insights are certainly worth consideration. Apropos of the material in 1Cor 7,1ff., Stamps points out that: a) Paul's presence is not involved and b) despite the situation specificity, the responses take on a very general tone. In fact, though the questions are presumed to be introduced through the Corinthian letter, Paul makes no specific application of the situation to Corinthian life, nor does he revert to a discussion of church practice in Corinth as a basis for dealing with the issues. Instead his responses are general and could apply to any church. In fact, some responses are drawn from the general church praxis which seems to mitigate the situation specificity of his response. Why so? Stamps explains that on a rhetorical level the lack of specificity has a double effect: 1) the occasional reminder that what Paul is saying apropos of Corinthian cases is what is also taught elsewhere, in effect, places the discussion above the particular level. As Stamp states, «Implicitly, the audience is told there is a general catholic stand which provides uniformity and expects conformity»; 2) the lack of particularity creates a distance between the author and the

beginning in 7,1 Paul sets up a rhetorical situation in which he purposefully distances himself from the local controversy in order to persuade. If he is correct, then even with regard to Paul's responses to the so-called written inquiries from Corinth, the view that Paul was engaged in a battle with the opposition[96] should be abandoned.

What these insights suggest is that a) a Pauline text, as rhetoric, is not simply a step by step mirroring of the historical situation; b) to deduce a situation from the rhetoric and present it as the actual historical situation misses the point of the rhetorical situation and c) to speak of «entextualizing the situation» is to speak of the conscious and autonomous activity of the author. This is not to say that the entextualized situation as presented by the author is totally dissociated from the audience, but rather to emphasize that the author's presentation is not limited to being a direct correspondence with the actual historical situation. That being the case, one needs both to proceed with caution when making affirmations about the actual historical situation and to keep the distinction between the historical and rhetorical situation clearly in view.

5. Reassessing the Situation

Finally, let us return to the level of actual historical situation. Even apart from rhetorical considerations we might ask, do the standard views on the situation of 1Cor overstate the hostility between Paul and the Corinthian community, especially when it comes to the characterization of the Corinthians? Let us consider for a moment the depiction of the Corinthians. The standard view of the Corinthians is that they are arrogant, contentious and head-strong[97]. Moreover, the community is often referred to as opponents[98], a term often used uncritically[99] and without

---

Corinthian situation by subsuming it under the rubric of common doctrine. By remaining above the level of local controversy, Paul is attempting to persuade by conviction. Thus he is not engaging in a battle with the opposition. Building on Stamps' insights, it might be added that the posture of distancing Paul adopts, coupled with the general tenor of his responses and the reminders about solidarity with the other churches (e.g. 1,2; 11,2; 11,16; 16,1-3), probably indicates that beyond the actual Corinthian audience Paul also has in mind a much wider audience for whom he also intends these responses to be relevant.

[96] D.L. STAMPS, «Rethinking», 209-10.

[97] Cf. J. MURPHY-O'CONNOR, 1 Cor, ix.

[98] This term in the full sense should be restricted to 2Cor as noted by W. SCHRAGE, 1 Korinther, 39.

[99] Cf. M. McDONALD, «Women», 161-181. The author consistently calls the persons with whom Paul dialogues in 1Cor 7, his «opponents». The fact that some in the community may behave in ways that Paul finds inappropriate does not make them his opponents.

discriminating in application among some, all, insiders and outsiders. What one comes away with based on these evaluations is tantamount to an accusation of regressive behavior on the part of the Corinthians. This is certainly one way to look at the situation, especially when one is pre-disposed to an inverse tendency to absolutize Paul's theology and stress his authority[100]. However, if the insights of studies on the social situation that obtained in the early Christian communities in general are integrated into the picture of Corinth, perhaps there is further reason to re-consider views on the Corinthian situation and especially characterizations of the Corinthians.

There is a tendency in conceptualizing early Christian converts to assume that a) they existed in a social and cultural vacuum – living empty vessels, so to speak, into which the message of Christianity was poured; or b) they were formed in a particular social and cultural context but with the conversion to Christianity they somehow spontaneously and defini-tively cut the cord between themselves and the formative environment in which their lives had, more or less, already taken shape. Contained in such notions, clearly in need of revision[101], is the idea that the passage to Christianity entailed both immediate re-socialization and moral transfor-mation. That these conceptions do not conform to the reality is repeatedly asserted by W. Meeks[102] who maintains that the presumed re-socialization that took place in the conversion to Christianity, described as a dying and rising with Christ, a second birth, an adoption into a new family etc., was not in reality, despite the radicality of the metaphors, ever so radical and complete[103]. Hence, as he points out, it is essential to keep in mind that «the Christians whose moral formation we are trying to understand lived in the world of the early Roman Empire, and that world also lived in them: in their thinking, in their language, in their relationships»[104].

Applying this information to the situation at Corinth, one could say that the people addressed by Paul were attempting to live Christianity and develop their understanding of its implications interactively, actually the

---

[100] The penchant for negatively casting the Corinthians may be the necessary correlate to positive affirmations of Paul and his authority. Cf. the comments in A.C. WIRE, *Corinthian Women*, 9-11.

[101] See the comments in H. KOESTER, «Epilogue», 473.

[102] W. MEEKS, *Moral World* and ID., *The Origins*. For similar views cf. E. FERGUSON, *Backgrounds*, 135.

[103] Cf. W. MEEKS, *Moral World*, 13. The same was no doubt true for converts to Judaism. Even though PHILO's language would lead us to believe that the conversion was radical (cf. *De Virtutibus*, 102-04; *De Specialibus*, IV, 178), and that moral trans-formation was immediate (cf. *De Virtutibus*, 180-82), elsewhere he concedes how difficult it is to educate and change a disbeliever (cf. *De Praemiis*, 49).

[104] W. MEEKS, *Moral World*, 13.

only way possible unless they opted out of their social context, which Paul advises against (1Cor 5,10)[105]. By «interactively» what is intended is that their faith and moral formation were taking shape in the interplay between their formative world, itself a pluralistic construct of diverse and even opposing values, and this whole new world of Christianity. The Corinthian community member then, is more realistically characterized as a Christian in the process of emerging from this interaction, as someone who might be called, borrowing a term from modern social analysis, a tentative character type[106]. Understanding the Corinthian as an emerging Christian, involved in a dynamic process of growth and integration, allows the situation of 1Cor to be viewed, all the problems notwithstanding, as essentially one of a continuing advance toward a fuller comprehension of the goals of Christianity and not necessarily as a negative situation of regression. As Ortkemper remarks, «Wir müssen uns hüten, aus diesen Informationem ein Negativbild der Gemeinde zu zeichen. Im Grunde hatte sie sich sehr gut entwickelt, war sie sehr lebendig. 1 Kor I,4-8 ist sicher nicht nur liebenswürdige Höflichkeit des Apostels!»[107]. In fact, 1Cor 1,4-8, taken at face value, is a powerful testimony to the spiritually rich existence that characterized this community.

Viewing the Corinthians under the aspect of regression, for which all the text references to arrogance etc. are mustered as proof, may derive from the tendency to envision a static situation wherein all the problems that did emerge or ever could emerge in the interaction between Christianity and the receptor cultures into which it was introduced were already confronted and settled. But they were not. In fact, 1Cor is a testimony to the dynamic process through which both Christianity and Christian people were emerging. When the situation is understood this way, one could say that Paul and the Corinthians were not fighting each other, but were arguing over the ramifications deriving from this interactive process especially when they resulted in ways of engaging Christianity or in certain types of behavior that Paul deemed incompatible with the goals of Christian life. If what has just been suggested is reasonable, we can entertain the following: 1) Paul is better perceived as a pastor engaged in a continued effort to instruct and guide the Corinthians in the on-going process of becoming Christian, which means becoming a holy community and

---

[105] That Paul also had sectarian and separatist expectation need not be denied, cf. J. BARCLAY, «Thessalonica and Corinth», 56.

[106] Cf. R. BELLAH, *Habits*, 39.

[107] F.J. ORTKEMPER, *1 Korintherbrief*, 11.

sharing in the *ethos* that characterizes the whole church[108]; 2) it would seem better to consider the Corinthians as healthy co-protagonists in a developing story rather than as Paul's enemies, which appears to be an unfair and unfounded characterization. If these ideas can be reasonably entertained, then the exegesis of 1Cor ought to be carried out apart from the thesis that has dominated studies of this letter, viz., that Paul is addressing opponents.

6. Conclusion to Chapter 2

In regard to the social relationship between Paul and the Corinthians we offer the following conclusions: 1) the social situations of 1 and 2Cor are distinct and the tendency to attribute aspects of the situation of 2Cor to that of 1Cor should be avoided; 2) from the text evidence, especially 1Cor 1-4 and 9, it cannot be shown that Paul was engaging in defense rhetoric or apostolic apologia and with that, doubt arises as to the accuracy of generalized descriptions of the situation between Paul and the Corinthians as one of hostility revolving around the contestation of the apostle's authority; 3) the issues and behavior in 1Cor might be better and more realistically understood when viewed within the broader context of the dynamic emergence of Christianity and Christians within concentric circles of social and cultural influence; 4) too much accent on the conflict over authority runs the risk of seeing authority and not moral behavior as the center of the debate between Paul and the Corinthians. This is not to say that in the debate over behavior the issue of Paul's authority to speak to these issues did not come into play. On the contrary, it did! Not however, as something contested[109], but rather as an important basis out of which he could and should speak to the problems of the community.

If what we have set forth and argued in this chapter and the conclusions issuing from it are reasonable, then we have some grounds to suggest that interpretations of 1Cor as a situation of intense conflict over authority which tend to lay stress on Corinthian contentiousness and to find reason

---

[108] 1Cor contains many reminders that the community at Corinth is part of the church everywhere. This is stated directly in 1,2. Moreover, Paul reminds the Corinthians of what is practiced in all the churches (cf. 11,15; 14,33) and advises that what they do should give no offense to «the church of God» (10,32).

[109] *Pace* G. FEE, *1 Corinthians*, 9 and passim. The authority issue seems even to impact the resolution of the *crux interpretum* in 1Cor 5,3-5 (cf. e.g. I. HAVENER, «A Curse», 334-344), even though it must be resolved on grammatical grounds, as will be discussed below c. 5 § 8.1.

in this alleged contentiousness to justify Paul's alleged spiritual absolutism, should be set aside.

It will be the work of the next chapter to examine Corinthian behavior and attitude as discussed in 1Cor 5, to look at what has been proposed as motives for this behavior and to try to determine whether the behavior and attitudes arose from misunderstanding, and if so, to try to identify what it was they misunderstood and why, or whether the behavior and attitude really betray a hostile rejection of Paul, his teaching and his authority.

CHAPTER III

The Historical-Religious Background of 1Cor 5

1. Motives for the Behavior Under Discussion in 1Cor 5

1.1 *Information from the Text*

Before beginning our study of motives we need to review briefly what was under discussion in 1Cor 5. Paul states the issue immediately in v. 1. There is a concrete case of *porneia* in the community. To this is added the specification «*hôste gynaika tina tou patros echein*», which makes it clear that the *porneia* is a case of incest[1] The fact of this relationship had been communicated orally[2] to Paul, judging by *akouetai* in 5,1. Beyond this we

---

[1] The *gynaika tou patros* was someone distinct from one's mother as evidenced by the double injunction in Lev. 18.7,8; one refers to *mètèr sou*, the other to *gynaikos patros sou*. The term, father's wife, was understood to refer to one's step-mother (cf. Str-B, 343ff.). *Echein* with *gynaika* or *andra* is used technically to indicate having sexual intercourse, though marriage is not necessarily implied, cf. H. HANSE, «*echô ktl*», 287, n. 5. In some instances *gynaika echein* does indicate marriage, cf. e.g. 1Cor 7.2,12; Lk 20.28,33. In Mk 6.18 *echein* is interchangeable with *gameô*, at 6.17. The scholarly consensus about 1Cor 5,1-13 is that the son and step-mother were married. Countryman takes *echein* to connote possession, arguing that Paul treats this case of incest as a property, not purity, issue (cf. L.W. COUNTRYMAN, *Dirt*, 197-202). However, if this were so, one should expect Paul to treat the issue from the point of view of the individual who was the victim of this offense. Instead, Paul treats the matter as an affront to the entire church.

[2] J. MURPHY-O'CONNOR confidently asserts that the informants of 1Cor 5 are identifiable as «those of Chloe» (cf. *Paul. A Critical Life*, 278-279). He further asserts that Paul asked these people who were travelling to Corinth from Ephesus «to assess» the situation in the community. Of the areas pointed out by Paul for assessment, «sexual morality was certainly one» (cf. 279). Given the lack of information, these assertions are highly speculative. Moreover, it is curious that Murphy-O'Connor can assert both that Paul entrusted these persons with the task of assessment and also that Paul would have considered their report as «no more than gossip» (cf. 279). With

learn that the community is *pephysiômenoi* (v. 2a), obviously the wrong response to the fact that a community member[3] is living in an incestuous marriage since Paul immediately injects what he considers the appropriate response, *epenthèsate* (v. 2b).

The curiosity of readers is justifiably piqued as to the motives for both the individual's and community's behavior discussed in c. 5. Though the mention of «in house» bickering in cc. 1-4 curbs any illusions about the model status of this community, the reader is hardly prepared for the contents of c. 5. How could Christians, and relatively recent converts at that, engage in such outrageous behavior? Unfortunately Paul says little in the remaining verses of c. 5 to satisfy such curiosity. There is no reference in the text to what motivated the offender or where he got the idea that he could live in this type of relationship with impunity. Nor do these thirteen verses disclose anything about the community's motives for boasting of this relationship[4]. The only reasonably certain thing we can adduce from the text information is that the community did not consider the incestuous relationship a bad thing and possibly even considered it something good. This is deductible from v. 6a where Paul expressly states, to the contrary, that their *kauchèma*[5] i.e., the incestuous relationship, the object of their boast, is *ou kalon*.

The lack of information leads to hypothesizing about what ideological or false theological factors[6] influenced the behavior of the community.

---

regard to the identity of the informants, perhaps the most that can be said is that they may have been those of Chloe, cf. J.C. HURD, *Origin*, 77-78.

[3] All of Paul's references in this chapter are masculine sing., cf. e.g. v. 2c *ho praxas*; v. 3 *ton katergasamenon*; v. 5 *ton toiouton*; v. 13 *ton ponèron*. It is the male who is singled out for criticism and disciplinary measures. Many, e.g. G. FEE, *1 Corinthians*, 201; C.K. BARRETT, *1 Corinthians*, 121; H. CONZELMANN, *1 Korinther*, 96, assume the woman was not a believer and was left unimplicated on that account. Though this is not certain it is likely given Paul's statement in v. 12a that he is not responsible for judging outsiders. Nonetheless, it cannot be excluded that the sentence extended to the step-mother even though she is not named. If in 1Cor 5,5 Paul intended the *karet* penalty, such a penalty could extend to the person's whole line, wife and descendants, cf. J. MILGROM, *Numbers*, 405-408.

[4] W. SCHMITHALS suggested that the absence of a discussion of motives was due to Paul's unfamiliarity with gnostic ideas (cf. *Gnosticism*, 237).

[5] Based on Pauline usage, cf. Rom 4,2; 1Cor 9,15.16; 2Cor 1,14; 9,3; Gal 6,4; Phil 1,26; 2,16, the neuter *to kauchema* refers to the object of, or grounds for boasting, which here equals the incestuous relationship. Notwithstanding this evidence, it has been recently argued, though unconvincingly, that the Corinthians were boasting «despite» the immorality, cf. A. CLARKE, *Secular and Christian Leadership*, 76-77.

[6] Sociological factors, with which we will not concern ourselves, are also adduced to explain the situation of 1Cor 5. Cf. e.g. G. HARRIS, «The Beginnings», 1-21; J.K. CHOW, *Patronage*, esp. 130-134, considers greed to have been the motive for the marriage and the high social status of the step-son as a deterrent to the community's

Since a background for 1Cor 5 is usually not conceived apart from comprehensive attempts to account for the influences and motivations underlying all the issues and behavior addressed throughout 1Cor, it is necessary to route our discussion of 1Cor 5 through these. Some, or perhaps one of these, may give us insight into the behavior discussed in c. 5. Here we will treat the main comprehensive hypotheses. In order to keep the focus on 1Cor 5, only what is necessary to understand the main contours of each hypothesis will be stated. The question of whether and how the individual hypotheses account for the specific behavior in 1Cor 5 will then be considered. The hypothesis of realized eschatology linked to pneumatic enthusiasm, to which many adhere, will justifiably claim more attention. For the sake of conciseness we divide the hypotheses into two broad categories. After these have been reviewed and evaluated we will offer our own hypothesis concerning the background against which 1Cor 5 might reasonably be read.

2. **Various Hypotheses (Category A)**

Hypotheses which look to ideas introduced into the community apart from Paul which would have influenced its thinking and behavior, creating the situation addressed in 1Cor.

In this category we locate the hypotheses of Baur[7], Schmithals[8], Pearson[9] and Horsley[10]. Before looking at these we mention one problem common to the hypotheses of Baur and Schmithals, viz., each relies on the alleged mediation of counter missionaries or persons extraneous to the community who would have introduced the community to the false theology that allegedly influenced its behavior. This is unlikely since there is no mention anywhere in the text of 1Cor of interlopers responsible for introducing counter preaching or another gospel as was the case

---

taking action against him. A. CLARKE, *Secular and Christian Leadership*, 73-88, obviously unaware of Chow's work, came up with the same novel but unconvincing hypothesis concerning 1Cor 5. It has been recently suggested that the behavior in question in 5,1-6,20 may not be due to a new theological program at all. It may simply reflect what is ordinary, socially acceptable, Greco-Roman behavior, which the Corinthians continued to practice after conversion, cf. J. BECKER, *Paul*, 199-200. But why then would the Corinthians boast over the incestuous marriage if it were such typical behavior? Why not boast over law-suits and frequenting brothels as well? The boasting does not square with Becker's suggestion.

[7] Cited above, c. 2 n. 19.

[8] W. SCHMITHALS, *Gnosticism*.

[9] Cited below n. 41.

[10] Works cited below, n. 42.

elsewhere[11]. In fact, the case for neither hypothesis can be made without retro-reading[12] the information about opponents mentioned in 2Cor 11 onto the situation of 1Cor in order to justify the claim that the problems Paul addresses in 1Cor were the result of outside influences on the community[13]. In addition to this difficulty each of these hypotheses has its own share of unique problems.

2.1 *A Judaizing Faction: Baur*

Baur's study of the Corinthian community and its *schismata* lead to his assertion that the situation in Corinth represented a bilateral[14] struggle between Paul and a Jewish opposition[15]. Though Baur's thesis had a great impact on subsequent studies[16], dissenting voices were never lacking[17]. At present, the majority of scholars[18] would be likely to agree with Schmithals that «there is probably no assertion in theological-critical

---

[11] Cf. Gal 1,6 or 2Cor 11,4.

[12] A problematic approach since the situations are distinct as we noted in chapter 2; Cf. also W. SCHRAGE, *1 Korinther*, 39.

[13] Baur retro-reads 2Cor 10-13 on to the situation of 1Cor and considers the interlopers to be Judaizers with whom the so-called «Christ party» of 1Cor 1,11 is aligned. Schmithals, on the other hand says, «This much is sure, that the opposition to Paul in Corinth did not develop out of Paulinism, does not represent a continuation or extension of the Pauline community, but has been brought into it from without by those whose religious history followed a course independent of Paul [...]» (cf. *Gnosticism*, 123). In light of 2Cor 11,22, Schmithals argues that Paul's opponents were alien teachers of Palestinian Jewish origin who introduced gnostic ideas resulting in innovations in cultus and doctrine which constituted the point of the debate between Paul and these opponents in both Corinthian epistles.

[14] This accords with Baur's portrayal of earliest Christianity based on his study of Paul's ministry. Baur sets Paul's ministry in the context of an adversarial dialectic and reduces the picture of early Christianity to a split between Paul's religion of *Geist und Freiheit* and Judaism (cf. F.C. BAUR, *Paulus*, II, 253). However, it is now widely recognized that earliest Christianity was a complex and diversified phenomenon, cf. e.g. J.D.G. DUNN, *Unity*. On the assumed conflict between Peter and Paul and their respective approaches to Christianity see the recent discussions in P. PERKINS, *Peter*; E. LOHSE, «St. Peter's Apostleship», 419-435. Lohse rejects the bilateral view, undermining Baur's use of Gal 2.11-21 to argue for the conflict (431-32). With regard to 1Cor, Baur applied the same dialectical lens and reduced the so-called parties to two: Paul/Apollos representing Gentile Christianity and Cephas/Christ representing a Judaizing front.

[15] J. Munck rejects this two-party division as totally arbitrary and argues against the existence of parties altogether (cf. J.MUNCK, «The Church», 135-167).

[16] It is still upheld by C.K. BARRETT, «Cephas in Corinth», 1-12 and was recently re-proposed, with modifications (cf. below n. 22).

[17] Cf. E. E. ELLIS, «Paul», 80-115.

[18] See the survey of scholarly opinions in N. DAHL, «Paul and the Church», 313-315.

research that has been defended with greater certainty and wider distribution and at the same time with less evidence than the assertion that in the Corinthian epistles Paul is dealing with Judaizers»[19]. The exegetical basis in 1Cor to support the claim that Paul is polemicizing about issues that have a specifically Jewish character with a Judaizing faction is lacking. In fact, certain statements in the text of 1Cor manifestly contravene Baur's claims or are at least difficult to reconcile with them, as many scholars have already noted[20]. In this regard, one has only to consider Paul's emphasis on keeping the commandments of God (1Cor 7,19), and the non-polemical reference to circumcision in this passage. Moreover, neither the argument for the eating of idol meat (1Cor 8,1ff.), nor the sexual immorality discussed in 5,1-13 and 6,12-20 can be reasonably associated with Judaizers who were totally dependent on the Mosaic law, as Baur insists[21]. Notwithstanding the multiple problems which render Baur's hypothesis improbable, M. Goulder[22] has recently re-proposed it with modifications[23]. This attempt also runs aground[24] and not surprisingly, especially with regard to sexual immorality and the issue of idol meat. These issues cannot be reconciled with the agenda of Jewish nomists[25].

2.2 *Gnosticism: Schmithals*

Schmithals' study[26] emerged as a *tour de force* in setting the Corinthian correspondence within the framework of a developed system of gnosticism[27]. His thesis, most succinctly stated is this: There existed a

---

[19] W. SCHMITHALS, *Gnosticism*, 118.

[20] Cf. e.g. W. SCHRAGE, *1 Korinther*, 47.

[21] Cf. F.C. BAUR, «Die Christuspartei», 78.

[22] Cf. M.D. GOULDER, «*Sophia*», 516-534.

[23] Goulder modifies Baur's understanding of *sophia* as Greek Wisdom. He argues that, as used by Paul's alleged Judaizing opponents, *sophia* was really interchangeable with Torah (520). From this he argues that Paul's opponents, though using Greek terminology, were effectively promoting a life lived according to the Law. The controversy turned not on the opponents' advocacy of the law *per se*, but in their going beyond the law by advancing their own allegedly spirit-inspired *halakha*. In sum, Paul would be opposed to the *dibrè hokmah* of his opponents which he considered mere human extrapolations (522). The rest of Goulder's article is an attempt to show how dispute over the law underlies all of 1Cor.

[24] See the critique in C. TUCKETT, «Jewish Christian Wisdom», 201-220.

[25] To resolve this problem Goulder (cf. 534), follows T.W. MANSON, «St. Paul in Ephesus» 101-120. In both we find a pyramid of questionable assumptions on which the solution to this problem is based.

[26] Cf. W. SCHMITHALS, *Gnosticism*.

[27] Gnosticism was also proposed as a factor to be reckoned with in 1Cor by U. Wilckens, but his study was delimited to 1Cor 1-2 and focused on a *Sophia*-Christ

pre-Christian system of Jewish Christ Gnosticism[28], introduced to the Corinthians by outsiders[29], which mediated their approach to Christianity, conditioning the thought and behavior under discussion in 1 and 2Cor. It was to this gnostically conditioned engaging of Christianity with its correlative patterns of behavior that Paul responded. This heretical system was anchored in a dualistic Christology[30] and a dualistic anthropology[31]. The dualistic anthropology leads to both the denigration of the body and an over-emphasis on the pneumatic and further, to a doctrine of freedom that accommodated both the ascetic and libertine tendencies at Corinth[32].

Besides the lack of evidence in 1Cor for any extraneous mediators of gnostic ideas in the community, Schmithals' thesis has some other

---

Redeemer Myth that allegedly influenced Corinthian belief and practice, cf. U. WILCKENS, *Weisheit*. But see the critical comments in M. HENGEL, *Judaism and Hellenism*, I, 154 and II, n. 300 and also in R. SCROGGS, « ΣΟΦΟΣ and ΠΝΕΥΜΑΤΙΚΟΣ», 33.

[28] Cf. W. SCHMITHALS, *Gnosticism*, 25-86. He holds that Gnosticism was an independent pagan religion, temporally antecedent to Christianity, which was objectified in three major mythological motifs. His focus is on the «primal man myth» which finds unique expression in Gnosticism as Christ gnosticism owing to the centrality of a Messiah figure. Keeping with his claims that this Christ system is pre-Christian, and aware of the centrality of the Messiah figure, Schmithals avers that the pre-Christian Christ Gnosticism necessarily has to do with Jewish Gnosticism (36). He reconstructs this gnostic system by inferences from information contained in *The Great Apophasis*, a post-Christian Simonian gnostic writing referred to by Hippolytus (*Refutatio* Bk VI 9-18). Anticipating objections Schmithals says, «we are not asking about the age of the *Apophasis* as a literary document, but about the age of the system portrayed in it [...]» (40). Later in reference to the lack of literary evidence for Jewish Gnosticism he claims that the essential nature of the gnosticism obviated the need for revelational literature (79).

[29] W. SCHMITHALS, *Gnosticism*, 115-6. However as noted, he relies on 2Cor 11,22 and assumes that they are the same opponents Paul has in mind in Epistle B. By Epistle B, Schmithals designates almost all of what is intended by canonical 1Cor, except for 1Cor 6,12-20; 9,24-10,22; 11,2-34, c. 15 and 16,13-24 (cf. 100).

[30] W. SCHMITHALS, *Gnosticism*, 125-55. His discussion can be summarized as follows: In the dualistic Christology, Jesus *kata sarka* is rejected. This same rejection is evident at 1Cor 12,3. In consequence, the cross is emptied of its significance as reflected in 1Cor 1,17, and its wisdom is replaced by a new *sophia*. Paul is faulted by the community for failing to have preached this new wisdom and defends himself against this charge at 1Cor 2,6-3,3. This new wisdom is nothing less than an aspect of Gnosticism which the vaunting Corinthians, rejecting Paul's preaching as inferior, claimed to possess. *Gnosis*, a global term under which Paul subsumes all of the individual errant features of the Corinthian theology, is explicitly used in discussions at 1Cor 8-10 and 1Cor 12-14.

[31] W. SCHMITHALS, *Gnosticism*, see the author's discussion, 155-237.

[32] W. SCHMITHALS, *Gnosticism*, 232-36.

drawbacks. The majority view[33] that gnosticism should be accorded no essential role in NT hermeneutics undermines Schmithals' hypothesis *ab ovo*. Moreover, accepting Schmithals' thesis requires accepting his two points of departure: 1) that the situation of both 1 and 2Cor are for all practical purposes identical[34] and 2) the rejection of the literary integrity of 1Cor[35]. Neither of these starting points is acceptable, as we have already argued in the first two chapters of this study.

Apropos of 1Cor 5, Schmithals applies his thesis to the behavior in question but without pressing the issue[36]. The claim that the case of incest «happened under the appeal of Gnostic libertinism»[37] is posited on the basis of Schmithals' allegation of a bifurcated gnostic sexual ethic deriving from dualistic anthropology. However as R. McL. Wilson points out, when the information from the Nag Hammadi texts is carefully considered and the heresiological evidence is more critically appraised, it becomes apparent that in gnostic ethics the expressed tendency was toward asceticism, especially in the sexual sphere, and that groups or individuals drawing libertine conclusions from gnostic doctrine were quite the exception[38]. This evidence casts doubt on Schmithals' hypothesis of a bifurcated gnostic sexual ethic as influential in the Corinthian community of Paul's day. Indeed, if any continuity were to be posited between allegedly gnostic sexual tendencies at Corinth and later full blown gnostic sexual ideas and praxis as attested in the literature, the continuity could only be safely suggested with regard to the tendency to asceticism[39] This being

---

[33] On the *status quaestionis*, cf. E. YAUMACHI, «Pre-Christian Gnosticism», 26-33. In *breve*, the issue comes down to a) whether one holds to a restricted view of Gnosticism as a post-Christian heretical development as confirmed by extant literary documents, in which case gnosticism is held to have NO decisive role in NT hermeneutics; or b) whether one understands gnosticism more broadly as a pre-Christian phenomenon, part of the spirit of late antiquity, the influence of which cannot be discounted for lack of literary evidence. I am inclined to the majority opinion. Though it may be true that lack of documentation does not prove non-existence as adherents to position b) claim, it is also true, as R. McL. Wilson has pointed out, that even if ideas can be traced back before texts, this is no guarantee that in the pre-literary phase they were gnostic ideas (cf. McL. WILSON, «How Gnostic?», 68).

[34] Cf. W. SCHMITHALS, *Gnosticism*, 101-115.

[35] W. SCHMITHALS, *Gnosticism*, 87-96.

[36] «Obviously it cannot be proved that this happened under the appeal to Gnostic *eleutheria*, but in view of the total situation at Corinth this is certainly the most likely assumption» (W. SCHMITHALS, *Gnosticism*, 237).

[37] W. SCHMITHALS, *Gnosticism*, 237.

[38] Cf. R. McL WILSON, «Ethics», 440-449.

[39] This tendency is notable in 1Cor 7. But even in regard to sexual asceticism factors other than gnosticism may have influenced the Corinthian position. For other

the case, it is highly doubtful[40] that the immorality in 1Cor 5 was influenced by or reflects gnostic libertine ideas on sex.

2.3 Hellenistic Diaspora Jewish Wisdom Speculation: Pearson and Horsley

The hypothesis of Hellenistic Diaspora Jewish Wisdom Speculation as the background against which to read 1Cor is strongly advocated by Pearson[41] and Horsley[42]. In essence Pearson argues that: 1) key terms in 1Cor, alleged to be gnostic technical terms, are in fact not gnostic[43], and 2) passages in 1Cor containing these terms are more appropriately understood against the background of Hellenistic Judaism. According to Pearson, this thought world, manifest in its particular terminological contrasts, exegetical traditions and wisdom speculation, clearly informs the positions and best accounts for the errant theological ideas against which Paul polemicizes[44]. Pearson claims that his thesis also has the advantage of according well with the historical conditions[45]. In

---

views cf. e.g., B. PRETE, *Matrimonio*, 81-87; D. BALCH, «Backgrounds» 351-364; O.L. YARBROUGH, *Not Like the Gentiles*, 117-122; W. DEMING, *Paul on marriage*, 39.

[40] Likewise for the hypothesis of W. LÜTGERT, *Freiheitspredigt*. Lütgert never attempted to identify or reconstruct a whole gnostic system but he did claim that Paul was dealing with gnosticizing pneumatic types (cf. 43), who under the influence of gnostic ideas, perverted Paul's teaching (cf. 102-135). They had a dualistic spiritualism (cf. 115-117), and this allegedly accounts for both ascetic and libertine tendencies. Under the influence of gnostic ideas, the Corinthians turned Paul's freedom teaching into licentiousness. This explains the sexual licentiousness discussed in 1Cor 5 and 6,12-20. However, the merit of Lütgert's work was that, unlike Baur before him and Schmithals after, he did not rely on positing an opposition group from outside but argued that the problems in 1Cor were due to the gnosticizing hyper-Paulinists who distorted Paul's preaching. However, for much of his information he relies on 2Cor.

[41] B.A. PEARSON, *The Pneumatikos-Psychikos Terminology*.

[42] In three studies: R.A. HORSLEY, «How Can Some?», 203-231; «Gnosis», 32-51 and «Spiritual Marriage», 30-54.

[43] E.g. *pneumatikos, psychikos, teleios, nèpios* and *gnosis*. According to Pearson, 8, when these terms are found in gnostic texts they are employed with gnostic intent. But it does not follow that terms found in gnostic texts must be gnostic technical terms. Ergo, in 1Cor, we do not necessarily have gnostic technical terms.

[44] Pearson claims that: a) the *teleoi/nèpioi* contrast as intended in Diaspora Judaism is the key to understanding the discussion in 1Cor 2 (27-30); b) the *pneuma/psychè, pneumatikos/psychikos* contrast as intended in Diaspora Judaism linked with particular Diaspora Judaism exegesis of Gen 2,7 and 1,7 informs the community position in 1Cor 15 which is based on the doctrine of «a-somatic immortality» (15-23); c) Philo's understanding of prophetic ecstasy is the best backdrop against which to consider 1Cor 12-14 (44-50).

[45] Pearson refers to the existence of a Hellenistic Jewish Synagogue in Corinth and the presence of Apollos. Pearson takes Acts 18,24-28 at face value and claims that

conclusion, he argues against the possibility of defining the Corinthians as Gnostics[46] and offers his own definition of Gnosticism and theory of its origins[47].

In the same vein, R. A. Horsley argues in three studies[48] that the background of the Corinthian opposition theology is located in the concept world of Hellenistic Diaspora Judaism. In each article he notes the key Corinthian terms or ideas present in texts under study, viz., 1Cor 1-4, 8-10 and 7. Then, looking to the literature of Hellenistic Judaism, in particular Philo and *Wis of Sol*, where vocabulary and ideas parallel to that found in the Corinthian texts are used, Horsley identifies the complex of ideas expressed by this language or these motifs[49] in the religious tradition of Hellenistic Judaism. Finally he proposes, on analogy, that these same complexes of ideas from Hellenistic Judaism can and should be understood as underlying the positions and behavior discussed in the Corinthian texts he has studied. These ideas of Hellenistic Judaism came to Corinth through Apollos[50]. In a particular way, the community became obsessed with *sophia*[51] as he preached it[52].

Apollos' exegetical ability is «of great moment for our understanding of the doctrines of the Corinthian opponents» and further, that «Apollos' role in Corinth is a factor of great importance for the development there of a Christianity influenced by the traditions of Diaspora Judaism» (17-18). In strong support of this view is N. HYLDAHL, «The Corinthian "Parties"», 21-23, though this author sees no connection between Apollos and a «party» Older views on the role of Apollos are discussed in J.C. HURD, *Origin*, 96-107.

[46] Cf. B.A. PEARSON, *Pneumatikos-Psychikos Terminology*, cc. 6 & 7.

[47] Pearson concludes that Gnosticism was essentially a radically new and different religion, with a new hermeneutic and therefore cannot simply be equated with «the spirit of late antiquity» (84). This new religion was born out of a revolt against Judaism, arising on Jewish soil out of a profound disillusionment with its God and its hermeneutic (85).

[48] Cited above n. 42

[49] For example, in «How Can Some?», Horsley examines key Corinthian terms used in 1Cor 1-4, all of which appear extensively in the literature of Diaspora Judaism. In this tradition, especially as represented by Philo, Horsley observes that these terms are part of a «set combination of language and motifs that express the self-consciousness of Hellenistic Jews who had attained the highest spiritual status» (212). Ergo, used by the Corinthians, these terms express their own comparable self-understanding as *sophia*-possessing, high spiritual status persons.

[50] Cf. R.A. HORSLEY, «How Can Some?», 229-230. Murphy-O'Connor also considers Apollos «the obvious channel by which Philo's philosophical framework entered the community» (cf. J. MURPHY-O'CONNOR, *Paul. A Critical Life*, 282). However, there is little evidence available in Acts based on which Apollos' theology can be reconstructed and reasonably identified as Philonic. Thus, «conclusions

How do the ideas of Hellenistic Judaism inform the behavior discussed in 1Cor 5? The studies of Pearson and Horsley, taken together, point up the influence of ideas allegedly taken over from Hellenistic Judaism on almost all of the issues of 1Cor, with the notable exception of cc. 5 & 6[53]. In fact the thesis cannot be applied to the cases of immorality any more than Baur's could. Fee rejects such a background for cc. 8-10 as well. He remarks with regard to the discussion on the right to eat idol meat that «one can scarcely imagine the context in which a Diaspora Jew would so argue – even Philo would be horrified here»[54] This remark, *mutatis mutandis*, applies equally well to the case of incest.

That the thesis cannot be applied to 1Cor 5, does not on that account exclude it as a possible explanation for the background to other issues in 1Cor. However, problems and unresolved questions do eclipse its merits[55] and point up its improbability. We note three: 1) The language in the texts under discussion is Paul's[56]. Whether it was also the Corinthian's and what this could signify about their actual self-perception we do not know with certitude[57]. 2) That the addressees of 1Cor were converts from the

---

regarding his [Apollos'] theology (via Philo) are precarious» (H. CONZELMANN, *1 Korinther*, 33, n. 22).

[51] Horsley claims that *sophia*-obsession is also at the basis of Corinthian sexual renunciation, cf. «Spiritual Marriage», 30-54, a claim rejected recently by W. DEMING (cf. *Paul on Marriage*, 12-16). In «Gnosis», Horsley studies the term *gnosis* as used in Diaspora Jewish texts. He concludes that *gnosis*, like *sophia*, was part of a pattern of religious self-understanding. In Diaspora Judaism, the possession of both *sophia* and *gnosis* testified to an enlightened spiritual status. The spiritually elite adopted an enlightened ethical stance, considering themselves beyond the risk of moral corruptibility. Horsley finds these same ideas, expressed in the same language, in 1Cor 8-10.

[52] N. HYLDAHL refers to the problem in Corinth as «Apollos' *sofia*-movement» («The Corinthian Parties», 26).

[53] Pearson disregards these chapters. In «How Can Some?» Horsley notes a parallel to 1Cor 6,12 in Diaspora Jewish literature but does not develop the point (cf. 225).

[54] G. FEE, *1 Corinthians*, 14.

[55] 1) It looks to a literarily attested pattern of religious thought that could have influenced the Corinthians. 2) It does not rely on persons extraneous to the community to account for Corinthian ideas and behavior.

[56] Both authors try to deal with the difficulty this poses. Pearson (31) says Paul takes over and reinterprets Corinthian terminology. Horsley does not insist that the terminology belongs to the Corinthians. But he takes Paul's use of these terms as a linguistic mirroring of the Corinthian self-perception as spiritually elite (cf. «How Can Some?», 212). Curiously though, in his argument against realized eschatology (cf. «Spiritual Marriage», 44), Horsley takes «already» (1Cor 4,8), as expressing Paul's view and not that of the Corinthians!

[57] The difficulties of constructing a thesis on vocabulary assumed to be the opponents' are noted in J. BARCLAY, «Mirror Reading», 81. See further G. LYONS, cited above c. 2, n. 61.

synagogue is an assumption based on the existence of a diaspora synagogue in Corinth. However, the explicitly gentile features of this letter[58], especially the remark in 12,2, point to the contrary, making this particular assumption unlikely and the hypothesis of Hellenistic Diaspora Jewish ideas even more unlikely. 3) Identifying Apollos as the conduit of the ideas of Hellenistic Diaspora Judaism raises still unanswered questions[59]. Apollos' presence in Corinth and his stature as a skilled preacher can hardly be denied. But there is no evidence from 1Cor that Paul is speaking to a community which had been mislead by teaching subsequent to his own, let alone through that of Apollos[60].

2.4 Summary and Evaluation of Category A

Of the three hypotheses examined in this category none can possibly account for the behavior and attitudes under discussion in 1Cor 5. Moreover, as hypotheses intended to account for the whole background to the discussions and problems of 1Cor, those of Baur and Schmithals are constructed on assumptions that must be rejected. In the case of the hypothesis of Hellenistic Diaspora Jewish ideas, none of the starting assumptions need be immediately rejected, but the unanswered questions they generate and evidence to the contrary make them very doubtful. Overall, we consider the hypotheses discussed in this category as highly improbable.

3. Various Hypotheses (Category B)

Hypotheses which consider Paul's own preaching to have been responsible, in some way, for Corinthian ideas and behavior that resulted in the problems and issues addressed in 1Cor.

---

[58] Noted by G. FEE, *1 Corinthians*, 4. According to J. Murphy-O'Connor, the problems treated in the letter attest to the fact that «the predominant group in the Corinthian church was made up of Gentiles [...]», cf. *Paul. A Critical Life*, 273; cf. further A.C. WIRE, *Corinthian Women*, 64.

[59] If Apollos were the disseminator of problematic ideas in Corinth two questions emerge: Why would Paul have «strongly urged him to visit» (cf. 16,12) the Corinthians again? Why does Paul so stress (cf. 3,1ff.) the integrated nature of his and Apollos' ministries? That the stress on the unity highlights the rift is not a plausible response, *pace* R.A. HORSLEY, «Wisdom», 231. A very recent attempt to demonstrate that Apollos with his Encratite theology was the source of the difficulties in Corinth and constituted Paul's main rival has been advanced by P.F. BEATRICE, «Apollos», 1232-1275. This article offers novel insights on the person of Apollos, his theology and role in Corinth. However, we are not convinced by the author's argument that 1Cor 3,1ff., and 16,12 insinuate hostility between Paul and Apollos.

[60] Cf. J. BARCLAY, «Thessalonica and Corinth», 66.

3.1 *Early Paulinism: Hurd*

In *The Origin of 1 Corinthians*, J. C. Hurd attempted to reconstruct both
the content of Paul's earlier preaching at Corinth and the «Previous
Letter» mentioned in 1Cor 5,9, in which Paul, as Hurd claims, abandons
the radical stance of his earlier preaching[61]. According to Hurd, Paul's
«about-face» in the «Previous Letter» was not well received in Corinth
and precipitated the situation of confusion and anger that in turn occasioned canonical 1Cor in which Paul allegedly hedges between his earlier
position and that represented in the «Previous Letter» in order to placate
the community. This thesis keeps the discussion of causes for the positions and problems in Corinth in an intramural context. Hurd considers
Paul's four-stage[62] relationship with the Corinthians as representing a
self-contained dialogue characterized by statement, counter-statement and
compromise[63]. Moreover, Hurd locates the source of difficulty not in the
Corinthians who go beyond or radicalize[64] what Paul has said[65], but rather
in Paul who recants in compliance with the Apostolic Decree[66]. This
thesis depends entirely on the proposed reconstruction of events[67] allegedly leading to Paul's «about face».

---

[61] See the discussion, *Origin*, 213-96. The contents of the «Previous Letter» are
irretrievable. Hurd attempts a hypothetical reconstruction of its contents (cf. c. 6).
However, he admits that such reconstruction becomes more precarious the further one
ventures from canonical 1Cor (cf. 213). The question, whether a part of the «Previous
Letter» is present at 2Cor 6,14-7,1 is debated (cf. V. FURNISH, *II Corinthians*, 375-
383). Hurd responds in the affirmative (cf. *Origin*, 235-237).

[62] Stage 1 = Paul's initial preaching; Stage 2 = the Previous Letter; Stage 3 = the
Corinthian reply letter; Stage 4 = canonical 1Cor.

[63] Cf. J.C. HURD, *Origin*, 273

[64] This is key to the Realized Eschatology/Pneumatic Enthusiasm hypothesis to be
discussed next.

[65] Hurd appears to contradict this later on (cf. 276-278), when he considers the
problems of 1Cor 5 and 7 as stemming from an over-enthusiastic application of Paul's
ideas on spiritual marriage. To be consistent, Hurd would have to say that, *vis-à-vis*
spiritual marriage, the Corinthians were simply doing what Paul advised, but in
canonical 1Cor, Paul was backing down on his earlier endorsement of spiritual
marriages.

[66] Cf. J.C. HURD, *Origin*, 261.

[67] To summarize: 1) Hurd first proposes a hypothetical reconstruction of the
contents of the Previous Letter (213-39); 2) Then he reconstructs the situation which
prompted Paul to write this letter; 3) In light of parallels between the alleged contents
of the Previous Letter and the Apostolic Decree (259), Hurd postulates that the
Previous Letter was written as a result of this decree, a decree formulated and
promulgated subsequent to Paul's initial preaching at Corinth (cf. 261); 4) In order to
bring his preaching and Corinthian praxis into conformity with the decree's contents,

Hurd's discussion of c. 5 is scant. He situates the problem of 1Cor 5 within the context of what he alleges was part of the content of Paul's original preaching in Corinth. Hurd reconstructs the content of the preaching that he assumes has relevance for 1Cor 5 from information in 1Cor 7. In *breve*[68], Hurd alleges that in addition to Paul's preaching that it was best for a man not to touch a woman, he probably also inaugurated[69] the institution of «spiritual marriage» during his original visit to Corinth, an institution about which Paul, in canonical 1Cor, expresses modified views. Based on this, Hurd suggests that the parties to the incestuous relationship may have considered themselves joined in a «spiritual marriage». This appears to be quite an improbable explanation for the behavior in 1Cor 5. First of all, Hurd concludes that 7,36-38 refer to an institution, i.e., spiritual marriage. However nothing in these verses points distinctly to such an idea[70] and referring to vv. 36-38 in terms of «spiritual marriage» is anachronistic[71]. Moreover, even given the remotest possibility that Paul did intend «spiritual marriage», or something like it, in 7,36-38, that the offender and his step-mother considered themselves to be living in a spiritual marriage is unlikely[72]. The fact is, theirs was a sexual relationship as the text language makes clear[73]. Moreover, even a superficial reading of 1Cor 5 makes it clear that Paul is in no way treating this case as a lack of continence in spiritual marriage but rather a case of gross and vulgar immorality. Whatever other merits[74] Hurd's thesis may have, his suggestion for what informed the behavior in 1Cor 5 is not at all compelling.

3.2 *Realized Eschatology: Thiselton*

A. C. Thiselton is neither the first nor only scholar to advocate reading 1Cor against the background of realized eschatology. However, against the protest[75] that such a background is usually assumed[76] but never ade-

---

Paul wrote the Previous Letter; 5) Their negative reaction to this letter occasioned a response, viz., canonical 1Cor.

[68] See Hurd's full discussion, 274-278.

[69] Hurd's claim that Paul inaugurated such an institution is considered «highly questionable» by W. SCHRAGE, *1 Korinther*, 49 and most scholars. One recent exception is J. BASSLER, «*Skeuos*», esp. 53-66.

[70] Cf. W. DEMING, *Paul on Marriage*, 42.

[71] W. DEMING, *Paul on Marriage*, see the author's discussion, 40-47.

[72] Harris also considers it unlikely that the couple considered themselves joined in a spiritual marriage (cf. G. HARRIS, «The Beginnings», 4).

[73] Cf. above n. 1

[74] Noted in C.K. BARRETT, *1 Corinthians*, 6-8 and G. FEE, *1 Corinthians*, 13. However, both authors advise against full adherence to the thesis.

[75] Cf. E.E. ELLIS, «Christ Crucified», 69-74.

quately demonstrated as the appropriate background of 1Cor, Thiselton took up the task of establishing the case and so we begin by focusing on his study[77]. Based on the cumulative evidence of 1Cor, Thiselton concludes that the problem of realized eschatology is evident in all of the issues considered in 1Cor, provides a key to unlocking the whole situation and also confirms the literary integrity of the letter[78].

Crucial to Thiselton's case is to explain the basis for the Corinthian self-understanding as people already involved in full end-time living. Here Thiselton has recourse to an intramural context to account for the provenance of Corinthian concepts and suggests that in all probability, rather than misunderstanding Paul, the Corinthians felt they were legitimately developing his own line of thinking[79], albeit in a most radical way. By combining and radicalizing Paul's freedom and new creation preaching the Corinthians reasoned to the conviction that they were already fully participating in end-time living[80]. The essence of eschatological living is enunciated in the phrase at 1Cor 6,12 and 10,23 «panta moi exestin» which Thiselton considers the heart of the matter from 5,1-11,1[81]. Freedom, the hallmark of eschatological living, is to be understood as both a consequence and testimony to the reality of eschatological status. It is under the aspect of testimony to the reality of this newness of eschatologi-

---

[76] Cf. e.g. H. VON SODEN, «Sakrament», I, 1-40; E. KÄSEMANN, *Essays*, 171; F.F. BRUCE, 20-21; J.M. ROBINSON, «Kerygma», 30; J. MUNCK, *Paul*, 165; C.J. ROETZEL, *Judgement*, 109-112 and more recently cf. e.g. N. WATSON, *First Epistle to the Corinthians*, xxv-ii; M. MCDONALD, «Women», 161-181; C. TUCKETT, «Jewish Christian Wisdom» 201-220; P.H. TOWNER, «Gnosis» 95-124; Gundry Volf refers to the Corinthians' «highly realized eschatology and their sense of living according to new norms in the power of the eschatological gift of the Spirit as those already resurrected to new life» (cf. J. GUNDRY VOLF, «Male and Female», 119); Yarbrough operates out of what he considers the *communis opinio*, i.e., that there were some in Corinth who claimed that they had already experienced the resurrection (cf. O.L. YARBROUGH, *Not Like the Gentiles*, 117).

[77] A.C. THISELTON, «Realized Eschatology», 510-526.

[78] Though Thiselton's purpose was not primarily to confirm the literary integrity of 1Cor, still this aim, announced at the end of the article (cf. 525-526), significantly conditioned his study as evidenced in the forced reading of cc. 1-4 which he then admits does not accord well with the text information where the problem in view is the «over» not undervaluing of ministers (cf. 513). While realized eschatology may be heuristically useful if one is attempting to put all the issues in 1Cor under the same banner, it may be unnecessary. On this last point cf. W. BAIRD, «"One Against the Other"» 116-136. Moreover, it is not essential to the argument for literary integrity to show that only one issue is addressed throughout 1Cor (cf. above c. 1 n. 16).

[79] Cf. A.C. THISELTON, «Realized Eschatology», 512. This harkens back to Lütgert's position, above n. 40, *sans* the gnostic factor.

[80] A.C. THISELTON, «Realized Eschatology», 516.

[81] A.C. THISELTON, «Realized Eschatology», 515.

cal life characterized by freedom, that Thiselton considers the behavior referred to in 1Cor 5[82]. In other words, Thiselton claims that the couple, whose relationship Paul considers incestuous, entered into this union as a testimony to or expression of the spiritual liberation characteristic of «New Age» living[83]. Before we consider the implications of such a view and make some general observations about the hypothesis, a comment is called for on the idea that the Corinthians radicalized Paul's freedom teaching.

Thiselton accents the word freedom (*eleutheria*) as the semantic link between Paul's preaching and the Corinthian slogan. The fact that freedom was taught by Paul and touted by the Corinthians is not however proof that the notion of freedom that guided the Corinthians in their behavior was a radicalized form of Paul's. Freedom was a widely cherished principle not only in the Christian community at Corinth but in Greco-Roman society at large[84]. *Eleutheria* was a common *topos* of the philosophers[85] who considered freedom «a noble and precious thing»[86]. The slogan «*panta moi exestin*», expressive of the prerogative of the Cynic[87] or the Stoic[88], was linked to a whole perspective on freedom quite distinct from Paul's[89]. It appears beyond question that this well known philosophical slogan[90] had meaning for Paul's contemporaries apart from whatever meaning it had in his Christian preaching. Hence one must proceed with caution when asserting that the Corinthian Christians' brand of freedom can be explained as a radicalization of Paul's freedom teaching. Corinthian adults who converted to Christianity no doubt brought with them, *inter alia*, their own well-entrenched ideas on freedom. Moreover, as we stated in c. 2, in line with the insights of Meeks, it would be rash and naive to imagine that these ideas were discarded or ever

---

[82] A.C. THISELTON, «Realized Eschatology», 516.

[83] Also thought to be the case by others. Cf. e.g. C. SENFT, *La première épître de Saint Paul*, 73; J. MURPHY-O'CONNOR, *1 Cor*, 40; ID., «1 Cor V,3-5», 240.

[84] Vollenweider notes that new conceptualizations of world order, freedom and the role of the individual in this order needed to be forged in the aftermath of the fall of the Greek *polis*. Freedom talk was rampant and philosophical discourse, particularly that of the Stoics, decisively contributed to an understanding of *eleutheria* from the perspective of the individual (cf. S. VOLLENWEIDER, *Freiheit*, 23). The accent was placed on inner individual freedom to live according to nature which became «a salvation doctrine in a hard world» (B. GERHARDSEN, «*Eleutheria*», 5).

[85] Stoics, in particular, contributed to the revival of freedom talk, cf. EPICTETUS, *Discourses*, I.XII, 8ff; III.XXII, 38ff; IV.I, 1ff.

[86] EPICTETUS, *Discourses*, I.XII, 12.

[87] Cf. DIOGENES LAERTIUS, *Lives*, VI, 104.

[88] DIOGENES LAERTIUS, *Lives*, VII, 125.

[89] Cf. R. BANKS, *Paul's Idea*, 20-25.

[90] Cf. A. MALHERBE, «Determinism», 235.

totally re-imbued with exclusively Christian connotations. Thus to say that the community's notion of freedom represented a radicalization of Paul's notion of freedom appears to be too simplistic an explanation of a situation whose dynamics were apparently more complex.

We return now to the implications of this hypothesis for 1Cor 5 and our observations about the hypothesis as a whole. Apropos of the latter, we begin with a question that the hypothesis invites: Why in Corinth alone among the diverse venues where Paul preached, did his message, apparently constant[91], lend itself for such radical development and commensurately radical behavior? What was so peculiar to the Corinthian community that impelled it to radicalize Paul's preaching to such an extent? Thiselton does not say. Fee[92] asserts that it was the consciousness of being «*pneumatikoi*» that awakened the community to the conviction that it was involved in full eschatological living since the outpouring of the Spirit signalled the eschaton[93]. But to this answer one could still query: Were the Corinthians the only community so endowed with the Spirit and «spirit enthusiasm» that only they believed themselves caught up in full end-time living? Surely other communities had been richly endowed and every Christian had received the Spirit[94]! Either one must accept that Corinth reflects a truly unique happening in earliest Christianity, a possibility not to be discounted for lack of testimony to similar situations in other communities, or one must look to an additional factor/s within the Corinthian community.

Returning to a more particular level, the text evidence to support the claim for realized eschatology is slim and Ellis has convincingly argued

---

[91] The evidence from the authentic letters seems to indicate that Paul's basic message remained constant. In fact in 1Cor 4,17 Paul says of his «ways» that he teaches them «everywhere in every church». Paul's «ways» may mean his ethical ways or his doctrine. More likely it means both since Paul's doctrinal and ethical teaching were apparently inseparable, cf. 1Thess 2,10-11; 4,1-2. According to A. Seeberg, «ways» refers to Christian *halakha* which was based on an early Jewish catechism (cf. A. SEEBERG, *Der Katechismus*; P. Carrington speaks of a «neo-levitical» catechism related to the Jerusalem decree and therefore to the Levitical law of holiness (cf. P. CARRINGTON, *Early Christian Church*, I, 118-119 and P. CARRINGTON, *The Primitive Christian Catechism*).

[92] G. FEE, *1 Corinthians*, 12, coins the term «spiritualized eschatology» to accommodate his belief that it was their pneumatic status that brought them to consider themselves as living in the eschaton.

[93] Thiselton had already rejected such a view, considering Spirit enthusiasm as issuing from realized eschatology and not as responsible for it. Regardless of which comes first, most scholars who consider realized eschatology as the background to 1Cor see it as yoked to spirit enthusiasm.

[94] Cf. e.g. Rom 5,5; 8,9; 15,14; Gal 3,2.5; 4,6; Eph 1,3.13.

that 1Cor 15[95] cannot be equated with 2Tim 2,18 (those who claim «the resurrection is past already») and therefore cannot be taken as support for the interpretation of 1Cor 4,8[96] along the lines of realized eschatology. Thiselton circumvents this lack of hard proof by qualifying the notion of realized eschatology. While other advocates of this view still speak of Corinthians as believing themselves already resurrected to new life[97], Thiselton had suggested that realized eschatology is not really about whether the Corinthians believed that the resurrection had fully and finally taken place but about how much weight they placed on the experience of transformation in the present, so much so, that future life and the resurrection were all but forgotten[98]. Unless one accepts this qualified notion of realized eschatology, this hypothesis would be senseless since the main event of the eschaton is the victory over death made concrete in the resurrection of believers[99]! Nevertheless, despite the qualification, the

---

[95] According to E.E. ELLIS, 1Cor 15 reflects Platonic dualism (cf. «Christ Crucified», 69-74). He considers the error contained in the false wisdom at Corinth to be «not in affirming the reality of a present participation in Christ's resurrection life and power but rather in misconceiving the way in which that reality is presently to be manifested», 73. Cf. further the comments of K. BERGER, «Die impliziten Gegner», 387-388.

[96] The key term in 4,8 is ἐδὲ. In the hypothesis of realized eschatology, ἐδὲ is held to have eschatological significance and is taken as evidence that the Corinthians saw themselves as «already» enjoying full end-time living. In the Pauline corpus, the word ἐδὲ is employed 7 other times at Rom 1,10; 4,19; 13,11; 1Cor 5,3; 6,7; Phil 3,12; 4,10. At Rom 13,11 and Phil 3,12 it has apocalyptic significance. In the other 5 occurrences ἐδὲ is either part of an idiomatic expression or stands absolutely with no more than a temporal connotation. Hence, apart from 1Cor 15, which Ellis has shown is no evidence that the Corinthians believed the resurrection had «already» taken place, there is no reason based on Pauline usage elsewhere to take this term with eschatological significance either from Paul's or the Corinthians' point of view. If the Corinthians did see themselves as «already» sated etc. still this does not necessarily mean that eschatological parameters marked this view. The Corinthian perspective may have been simply non-eschatological (cf. J. BARCLAY, «Thessalonica and Corinth»). K. Berger states, «Der *locus classicus* dieser Hypothese (1 Kor 4,8) ist ironische Invektive des Paulus gegen das Sich-Aufblähen im Parteienstreit. Mit der Eschatologie der Korinther hat das nichts zu tun [...]» (K. BERGER, «Die impliziten Gegner», 387).

[97] Cf. above n. 76. For many advocates of the realized eschatology hypothesis, the A), denial of the resurrection, is taken as B), a claim that the Corinthians believed the resurrection had already taken place. But if A is true, it does not follow that B is necessarily true. It may have been that the Corinthians simply did not think the resurrection was necessary, cf. E. SCHWEIZER, *The Church*, 27-29. For a schematic presentation of what scholars have assessed to be the position of the 'deniers', the substance of their denial and what, by implication, they were thus affirming, cf. M. DE BOER, *The Defeat of Death*, 96-97.

[98] Cf. A.C. THISELTON, «Realized Eschatology», 523.

[99] Cf. 1Thess 4,13ff; Rom 6,5; Phil 3,10-11.20-21.

situation of Corinth still remains couched in the context of the struggle between present and future eschatological existence with Paul tipping the scales with reminders of the latter to offset the weight the community puts on the former. But is this really the problem? Or could it be a matter of not enough transformed living? After all, the Corinthians are transformed in Baptism[100] and have been brought from death to new life[101]; they «belong to another, to Him who has been raised from the dead»[102]. They are a new creation[103] and have been set free for freedom[104]. This is the reality! The problem seems rather to be that these are people who do not live extensively enough the true implications of present transformed existence but a pseudo-Christian life of their own making pumped up by false wisdom (1,18ff.), characterized by indiscreet judgement (esp. cc. 5-6,11) and special insights geared more to personal pursuits (8,1-3) and self-aggrandizement (14,4a) than community upbuilding (8,2; 14,4b) and *koinônia* (1,9). It would appear from the text that Paul is not faulting the community for pre-empting eschatological privileged living or over-emphasizing its reality in the present but rather for living in a way that has nothing whatsoever to do with Christian eschatological living, which, both in the present and the future, is truly transformed living[105] to which their behavior does not configure.

Let us focus now on 1Cor 5. The advocates of the hypothesis of realized eschatology share the assumption that Paul's freedom/new creation teaching, radicalized in some way, was the catalyst for the licentious behavior. The incest and the community attitude toward it, is just one instance. As noted at the beginning of this chapter, Paul does not discuss the motives of the man who contracted this marriage or the community members who boast in it. However, if their criteria were theological extrapolations from Paul's own teaching, radicalized in the service of incest, which, despite Thiselton's disclaimer, is tantamount to saying that they misunderstood Paul's teaching, a curiosity emerges: why would Paul fail to mention the theological principle/s being evoked, albeit in a radicalized way, and attempt to correct or modify them as he does elsewhere? In 1Cor 8,4-6, for example, the principles that obviously relate to the issue under discussion are mentioned. Paul affirms that these are sound principles but he adds social factors that must be brought to bear on the discus-

---

[100] Cf. Rom 6,3-5; Gal 3,27; 2Cor 5,17.
[101] Cf. Rom 6,13.
[102] Rom 7,4; cf. also Gal 3,29.
[103] Cf. 2Cor 5,17.
[104] Cf. Gal 5,1.
[105] Cf. D. DOUGHTY, «The Presence», 63.

sion of exercising the right to eat idol meat. Hence, the clarification of sound theological principles is preliminary to the discussion. In the case of 6,12a.c principles are stated which Paul modifies in 12b.d before the discussion can proceed. Similarly, we see a statement of principle and modification in 7,1.2. Now if the Corinthians were invoking a radicalized brand of Paul's own theological teaching to justify or tout incest, would Paul have omitted to correct this radicalization which for all practical purposes amounted to an abuse of his teaching? Would he not have wanted to clarify the principles? Moreover, it is difficult to concede that Paul's freedom-from-the-law teaching was being radicalized by the Corinthians to mean freedom from all moral constraint[106]. This type of suggestion insinuates a split between Paul's doctrinal and ethical teaching as if in his original preaching at Corinth, for 18 months, Paul preached a freedom-from-the-law doctrine unaccompanied by any moral exhortation concerning sexual comportment. In fact, Countryman makes the sweeping statement that «in writing 1 Corinthians Paul could not simply remind the congregation of what he had already told them, but had to begin at the beginning to instruct them about sexual ethics»[107]. But Paul's doctrinal preaching seems to have been consistently accompanied by moral exhortation[108]. Had the Corinthians never before heard his injunctions against *porneia*? How then can we understand the behavior in 1Cor 5 as a radicalizing of Paul's freedom teaching to the point of practicing that which he also taught must be avoided? This would indeed point to open defiance. Or is it that they did not think this particular type of relationship fell under the category of immoral sexual relations? This would apparently need to be the case if the community could even consider the incest something in which to boast unless it were somehow totally out of touch with reality[109] or unless it were operating out of another set of principles thought somehow, albeit incorrectly, to coincide with Christianity.

---

[106] *Pace* L.W. COUNTRYMAN, *Dirt*, 196. A similar but nuanced view is found in G. HARRIS, «The Beginnings», 11.

[107] This statement (cf. 97), is based on Countryman's view that in 7,10-11, Paul is citing a tradition which he claims not to have previously handed on to the community. It has been held, to the the contrary, that Paul was «reminding» (cf. E.E. ELLIS, «Traditions», 488). But even had Paul not previously handed on *one* Jesus tradition about divorce, it is a long jump from this to Countryman's generalization.

[108] Cf. above n. 91; also W. SCHRAGE, *Die konkreten Einzelgebote*, 34.

[109] Thiselton suggests this, pointing to 5,1-13 as the clearest indication of the disjuncture with reality that realized eschatological living entailed. But, if end-time living was so unreal, so transmundane, how then to explain Corinthian recourse to law courts for *kritèrion elastikôn* (cf. 6,1ff.), trivial quotidian matters that should have hardly made a difference to persons living exalted existences? No answer is found in Thiselton.

One extended attempt to understand the motives for the specific issue of 1Cor 5 and to put the matter in a more real and positive light has been made by D. Daube[110] and requires consideration. Rather than a case of radicalizing the freedom-from-law teaching, Daube argues that 1Cor 5 is about the exercising of a privilege that accompanied the «new creation» status accorded by baptism, on analogy with Jewish proselyte baptism practices and privileges[111] which, according to Daube, Paul incorporated *in toto* into his own Baptism catechesis[112]. This privilege consisted in the dissolution of all pre-conversion relationships[113] thereby allowing, in principle, for marriages between persons who, before baptism, were related. Seen in this light, the «offender» of 1Cor 5 was simply exercising a post-baptism, «new creation» privilege. To marry his step-mother was no longer incest/*porneia*, but a valid and licit relationship, a sign of new living, indeed something over which the community should have boasted! In light of this, Daube suggests that far from openly condoning a gross case of immorality, the Corinthians «in this case seriously claimed that what was being done was their privilege as new creations»[114]. Now this begins to make sense of what seemed otherwise to be some very strange behavior! But then why does Paul react so severely? This is a question to which we should expect an answer. But we do not get one. Instead Daube shifts gears, re-contextualizing the issue of 1Cor 5 within the sphere of other concerns and issues in the letter, thereby mitigating the gravity of the issue and Paul's response. In light of a Rabbinic proviso[115] Daube suggests that Paul, though operating within this Rabbinic scheme, went beyond the proviso's concern for the individual proselyte to a concern over the incestuous marriage *vis-à-vis* what is «better» and «upbuilding» for the community[116]. By setting this issue in the context of what is

---

[110] D. DAUBE, «Pauline Contributions», 224.

[111] Cf. Str-B, 343-362, esp. 353-354.

[112] Cf. D. DAUBE, «Pauline Contributions», 224. But, it has been claimed to the contrary that «Paul betrays no knowledge of such a doctrine or of its applicability to a situation like this» (F.F. BRUCE, 54).

[113] The Rabbis held that a gentile has no father and a gentile become proselyte is like a newborn child (cf. P.J. TOMSON, *Paul*, 100). Therefore a proselyte with his new status would not transgress the stipulations of Lev 18, except if he married maternal kin. In other words, he could marry with impunity any paternally related female (cf. Str-B, 353).

[114] Cf. D. DAUBE, «Pauline Contributions», 224.

[115] That is, in cases where marriages, though now theoretically possible, are forbidden by pagan law, they cannot be contracted, for fear that the proselyte be scandalized and believe himself to have «come from a weightier sanctity into a lighter one» (D. DAUBE, «Pauline Contributions», 224).

[116] D. DAUBE, «Pauline Contributions», 226.

«better» and «upbuilding» for the community Daube accents the continuity of 1Cor 5 with the rest of 1Cor[117]. He adds that as elsewhere in the epistle, here too, «what Paul is anxious to stop is the making of a fetish of some, in itself, praiseworthy notion, and especially one peculiar to Christians»[118]. This appears hardly to be the case and here we must begin to register some serious reservations about Daube's hypothesis. First, even if one should assume that Paul took over the rabbinic scheme *in toto*, Daube's thesis also relies on the questionable assumption that converts largely from paganism, as the text evidence seems to indicate[119], knew the ins and outs of Jewish proselyte baptism and were operating in the context of proselyte privileges and provisos[120]. Second, the continuity Daube alleges between 1Cor 5 and passages discussing matters to be weighed in terms of the beneficial or the upbuilding is simply not supported by the text. The key terms he cites, *sympherô* and *oikodomeô* are not found in 1Cor 5 nor is there any indication that here Paul is deliberating or discerning with the community in terms of what is better[121], beneficial[122] or upbuilding[123] for it. Paul treats this as a gross sin, «not some in itself praiseworthy notion». There is not a shred of evidence or even a hint in 1Cor 5 that he possibly thought the latter. Nor is this a case of something which may be beneficial to the individual, but whose practice must be tempered by «love», «consideration» or «caring» as Daube suggests[124]. This type of marriage is not a right on a par with, for example, the right to speak in tongues (cf. 1Cor 14). Paul's severe response in the case of the former and moderate response in the case of the latter makes this clear. In fact, the one calling himself a brother who marries incestuously is classified by Paul with rank sinners (cf. 5,11). Third, according to Tomson[125], Strack-Billerbeck, on which Daube relies, inaccurately presents the rabbinic position with regard to a proselyte marrying his step-

---

[117] Daube remarks, «Once the nature of this case [incest] is grasped the Epistle gains hugely in thematic unity» («Pauline Contributions», 227). However, this is a forcing of the text of 1Cor 5 which is not admissible, even in the interests of affirming the letter's unity.

[118] D. DAUBE, «Pauline Contributions», 227.

[119] Cf. above, p. 56.

[120] Daube insinuates that Jewish proselyte Baptism was a well-established phenomenon, temporally antecedent to Christian Baptism, with a well-defined system of privileges and provisos. But see the discussion in S. MCKNIGHT, *A Light*, esp. 82-85.

[121] Cf. 1Cor 7,38 where e.g *kalôs* is juxtaposed with *kreisson.*

[122] Cf. 6,12b; 10,23; 12,7.

[123] Cf. 1Cor 8,1; 10,23; 14,4 (bis).17; and *oikodomè*, 14,3.5.12.26.

[124] Cf. D. DAUBE, «Pauline Contributions», 227.

[125] Cf. P.J. TOMSON, *Paul*, 101.

mother as lenient. Tomson asserts, to the contrary, that the rabbis unanimously prohibited such marriages[126]. To be sure Paul's response in 1Cor 5 is severe and shows total opposition to the incest and the community's response to it. The problem with Daube's reading is that it effectively ignores the severity of Paul's response in 1Cor 5 and incorrectly links 1Cor 5 to the other issues under deliberation in the letter. These problems may be due to an inaccurate starting point with regard to the Rabbinic position or to an over-eagerness to show how 1Cor 5 is in continuity with the rest of the letter, or both. Whatever the case, the text of 1Cor does not support Daube's hypothesis as presented[127].

3.3 Summary and Evaluation of Category B

The hypotheses of Early Paulinism and Realized Eschatology examined in this category have the advantage of offering the possibility of locating the factors that influenced Corinthian behavior and positions within the confines of developments in the community relative to Paul's own teaching. This at least accords better with the text information which makes no mention of outsiders, or a different gospel to combat. However, like the hypotheses evaluated in category A, these latter tend also to over-homogenize the Corinthian position, so that whether the conflict is traced to intramural or extramural factors, still the whole community is presented as ideologically monolithic[128]. In any event, of the two, Hurd's shows itself the less probable, based as it is on reconstructions of events, exchanges between Paul and the community, speculation about what Paul originally preached and, not least of all, a chronology[129] that has not compelled wide adherence[130]. In particular as it related to 1Cor 5, Hurd's speculation that Paul introduced and endorsed the institution of spiritual marriages, even if it could be proved, does not seem to have much prob-

---

[126] P.J. TOMSON, *Paul*, 100-101. An earlier study by W.G. BRAUDE, *Jewish Proselyting*, showed the *halakhic* tradition less uniform than is claimed by Tomson.

[127] Further critical comments are found in A. CLARKE, *Secular and Christian Leadership*, 75.

[128] On the inadequacy of the one-front, one-ideology reading of 1Cor, cf. W. BAIRD, «"One Against the Other"», 116-136. Cf. further K. BERGER, «Die impliziten Gegner», 383-384.

[129] In the preface to the second edition of *Origin*, Hurd quite humbly admits and takes responsibility for what he considers some of the «more fanciful aspects of this study, particularly my theory concerning the Apostolic decree», xiv.

[130] Besides Hurd and R. JEWETT, *A Chronology*, who follows J. KNOX, *Chapters*, the majority of contemporary chronologists set the date of the Apostolic Conference at 48 or 49 A.D., i.e., before Paul's second missionary journey. Interestingly, Hurd elsewhere places the «previous letter» before the apostolic conference essentially jettisoning the sequence established in *Origin* (cf. J.C. HURD, «The Sequence», 198).

ability as the motive for the incestuous marriage and the community's boasting in it. That leaves the hypothesis of realized eschatology with an advantage over Hurd's and all others reviewed so far. Besides looking to internal developments, the hypothesis of realized eschatology does not require the reconstructive machinations of Hurd. Eliminating the hypothesis of Daube, done so with good reason as we believe to have shown, eliminates a viewing angle on to the situation which had the merit of injecting some rationality into the incest case and the accompanying boasting. Thus we are left with a view of community so out of touch with reality, so caught up in pneumatically charged «New Age» living, that one of its members could claim, in function of a radicalized notion of Christian freedom, that marrying incestuously was testimony to this eschatological life[131]. The community not only tolerated this but made it the grounds of their boasting! The text of 1Cor 5, indeed the whole situation of 1 Corinthians, perhaps cannot be pressed for explanations that would appear more rational. That being the case, the hypothesis of realized eschatology/pneumatic enthusiasm may have the most to recommend it, at least for the present.

Before proceeding it might be good to pause, step back from what we have seen and take a moment to consider what the components of a reasonable and satisfactory explanation of the background of 1Cor 5 might be. In the first place, such an explanation would have to avoid recourse to persons and ideas extraneous to the community. In the second place, unless one is content to settle for the picture of irrationality resulting from realized eschatological/pneumatic living, the explanation would need to account for the community's assessment of the incest as something good. In the third place, since it is difficult to concede the direct link between Paul's theology and preaching and a grossly immoral sin such as incest, no matter how much allegedly legitimate development or radicalization was engaged in, a more satisfactory hypothesis would have to show that other ideas influenced the behavior and comportment in 1Cor 5, ideas which may have intersected with, but did not necessarily flow from Paul's thought as a direct radicalized outgrowth. This would require showing that something intrinsic to the community could have been mixed with Paul's preaching, resulting in ideas that motivated behavior which Paul may have considered incongruous with the claims of Christianity but which the Corinthians may have considered coherent and congruous with these same

---

131 J. MURPHY-O'CONNOR, «1 Cor V,3-5», 241, makes the suggestion that the incestuous man actually did this «in the name of the Lord Jesus» and settles part of the *crux interpretum* of vv. 3-5 so that it supports this view. See the discussion below c. 5 §8.1

claims. In light of what we have just noted it may be worth considering whether Stoic ideas may have been instrumental in contributing to the behavior under discussion in 1Cor 5.

4. Testing a Stoic Hypothesis

From the outset, let it be stated that our intention is not to show that Stoic ideas permeated all of 1Cor and provide the background to the all the discussions in the letter[132]. Diversity and pluralism were the hallmarks of Corinth[133] and there is no reason to doubt that the Christian community was dynamic and heterogeneous. Therefore, to argue for a single front or single ideology at work in the Corinthian situation is, as now admitted, unduly restrictive[134]. Rather, a case will be made that some Corinthian Christian converts, formed in a mega-culture where Stoic ideas[135] were *koinè*[136], could have contained within themselves the possibility of fusing Christian preaching with some of the pervasive ideas or categories of Stoicism which may have produced the kind of behavior we come across in 1Cor 5. This might be especially true if among the Corinthian converts endowed with the Spirit of wisdom and baptized into the freedom wrought through Christ's redemptive act, some of them somehow infused their Christianity with ideas and behavior that were appropriate to the ideal Stoic whose hallmarks were wisdom and freedom.

4.1 *Some Key Concepts of Stoicism*[137]

First we must consider the Stoic philosophy of nature, *physis*. Succinctly stated, by *physis* Stoics meant the power or principle[138] which uni-

---

[132] Stoic ideas and influence have been detected at various places in 1Cor. See the studies of e.g. W. DEMING, *Paul on marriage*; ID., «The Unity»; S. POGOLOFF, *Logos and Sophia*; A. MALHERBE, «Determinism»; D. BALCH, «1Cor 7:32-35 and Stoic Debates», 429-439; T. PAIGE, «Stoicism», 180-193; R.M. GRANT, «Hellenistic Elements», 60-66.

[133] «Korinth war mit seiner sehr gemischten und fluktuierenden Bevölkerung und seiner heterogenen Kultur ein Ort zahlreicher Kulte und Tempel, sozusagen ein Modellfall des antiken Synkretismus» (W. SCHRAGE, *1 Korinther*, 27).

[134] Cf. above n. 128.

[135] Though Stoicism and Cynicism were distinct philosophical schools it is well known that by the Roman period Stoicism had incorporated many of the ideas of Cynicism. This has been recently illustrated with regard to the Stoic-Cynic debate on marriage in W. DEMING, *Paul on Marriage*, 50-107.

[136] By the Roman period Stoic ideas, language and especially their ethics were dominant, cf. H. KOESTER, *Introduction*, I, 153; also G. VERBEKE, «Le stoïcisme», esp. 35-39; F.W. WALBANK, *The Hellenistic World*, 180ff.

[137] Full treatments of Stoicism can be found in F.H. SANDBACH, *The Stoics*; M. COLISH, *The Stoic Tradition*, I.

fies or gives coherence to the universe, penetrates all things and brings all things into being[139]. This universal rational principle was variously termed the soul or mind of the world, or god or nature[140]. The fact that Stoics use the terms god and nature interchangeably points to major differences[141] between their understanding of god and the Christian understanding of God and His will for humans[142].

Second, the Stoics integrated their physics with ethics[143] and considered the goal or norm of all virtue to be a life lived in accord with this universal principle. In other words, the *summum bonum* for the Stoic was to live in accord with nature[144]. This was one's moral purpose or *telos* and to pursue it was an individual right. As the Stoic would say:

> Control over the moral purpose is my true business, and in it neither shall a tyrant hinder me against my will or a single individual, nor the stronger man nor the weaker; for this has been given by god to each man as something that cannot be hindered[145].

The absolute autonomy with which Stoics acted in ethical matters did not pose a conflict of interests between the individual and the group as one might be inclined to presume. On the contrary, the Stoic considered himself to be exercising a divine right. Thus as Colish observes, «it is inconceivable for the Stoics that there could be any conflict between the good of the individual, the good of the group and the good of the universe for the same *logos* permeates and rules them all»[146]. In other words, as long as an individual exercised his freedom[147] to pursue a life according to nature, his individual actions were perceived as in no way capable of producing ultimately negative ramifications for others.

---

[138] Conceived as fire, cf. DIOGENES LAERTIUS, *Lives*, VII, 156.

[139] DIOGENES LAERTIUS, *Lives*, VII, 148-9.

[140] DIOGENES LAERTIUS, *Lives*, VII, 136. According to Diogenes Laertius, Zeno maintained that this universal structuring principle was identical with Zeus, cf. *Lives* VII, 88; cf. also CICERO, *De Natura*, II. esp. cc. IX, X, XI.

[141] See comments in e.g. R.H. NASH, *Christianity*, 68; A. SCHWEITZE, *Paul*, 96; M. HENGEL, *Judaism and Hellenism*, I, 148-149. In EPICTETUS, *Discourses* I.XIV, 1ff. or II.VII, 10ff., god is portrayed in a more personal way. However, as Vollenweider observes, this personalization of the character of God «ist nur eine Akzentierung der pantheistischen Grundstruktur der stoischen Religion» (S. VOLLENWEIDER, *Freiheit*, 27); the Christian God is «personnel et transcendent» while the Stoic god is «impersonnel et immanent» (A. JAGU, «La morale d'Epictète», 2194).

[142] Cf. J. RIST, *Human Value*, 10, 147ff.

[143] Cf. M. COLISH, *Stoic Tradition*, I, 36.

[144] Cf. DIOGENES LAERTIUS, *Lives*, VII, 87; EPICTETUS, *Discourses*, I. XXVI, 1ff.

[145] EPICTETUS, *Discourses*, IV.V, 34.

[146] Cf. M. COLISH, *Stoic Tradition*, I, 36.

[147] Freedom was defined by the Stoics as the authority to act on one's own, cf. DIOGENES LAERTIUS, *Lives*, VII, 121-122; EPICTETUS, *Discourses*, IV.I, 1ff.

Third, for the Stoics to act in accordance with the demands of nature was the law of life[148], the only principle for appropriate action. Only the one who lived according to nature was truly virtuous[149] and was truly free[150]. The free and virtuous man was the true wise man (*sophos*)[151]. The wise man alone possesses the knowledge or insight[152] that allows him to judge what is truly according to nature and what are only matters of indifference, viz., things «that are independent of the moral purpose»[153] neither contributing to happiness or misery. Under things morally indifferent the Stoics include all bodily things and most external things[154].

The Stoics believed that the wise man alone was truly «rich» and truly a «king»[155]. Further they held that all wise men would enjoy worldly benefits and would at all times enjoy a happy, perfect and praiseworthy life[156]. The wise man's life is a happy life because it is a moral life and in this he can boast[157]. The Stoics could even claim of wise men that they «alone even if they be hideous are handsome, if poor they are still rich; if slaves they are still kings[...] The wise man surmises nothing, repents nothing, is never wrong»[158]. Furthermore, the Stoics say the wise man is free of passions[159]. He alone is a king fit for office. Moreover he is infallible, not being liable to sin or error[160]. The Stoic wise man does everything well;

---

[148] «We must make it our aim neither to avoid that which nature demands, nor to accept that which is in conflict with nature», EPICTETUS, *Discourses*, I.XXVI, 2; cf. also MUSONIUS, Frag. 17 (all references to Musonius are from C. LUTZ, *Musonius Rufus*).

[149] Living according to nature was tantamount to living virtuously, cf. DIOGENES LAERTIUS, *Lives*, VII, 87

[150] On the Stoic understanding of freedom as a life lived according to nature, cf. S. VOLLENWEIDER, *Freiheit*, 28ff.

[151] To conform one's life to nature was wisdom, cf. CICERO, *De Finibus*, III.III, 21 and shows understanding of divine affairs, cf. EPICTETUS, *The Manual*, 53.

[152] Nature itself provides these resources, cf. EPICTETUS, *Discourses*, IV.I, 51.

[153] Cf. EPICTETUS, *Discourses*, I.XXX, 1ff; II.IX, 15; II.XIII, 9-15.

[154] Cf. DIOGENES LAERTIUS, *Lives*, VII, 105-107; CICERO, *De Finibus*, III.XV;XVI;XVII.

[155] CICERO, *De Finibus*, III,XXII, 75.

[156] CICERO, *De Finibus*, III.VII, 26.

[157] CICERO, *De Finibus*, III.VIII, 23. By moral life the Stoics mean a life according to nature.

[158] CICERO, *Pro Murena*, XXIX, 61.

[159] DIOGENES LAERTIUS, *Lives*, VII, 117.

[160] DIOGENES LAERTIUS, *Lives*, VII, 121-123. Cicero explains why this is so in *De Finibus*, III.IX, 32ff. Morality for the Stoics was a matter of intention not the deed or its results – the inverse of Paul's thought, cf. e.g. 1Cor 6,12-20; 8,1-13. Therefore, actions springing from the virtuous man are right from their inception because he can only intend what is right and good. The Stoic theory of sin is elaborated in J. RIST, *Stoic Philosophy*, c. 5.

everything belongs to him[161] and he possesses all virtues[162]. The picture of the ideal wise man is one of full attainment.

Could it be that Corinthian converts, brought up in a macro-society permeated with Stoic ideas and Stoic models, were influenced by these concepts in the micro-society of Christianity, especially if the gospel message was stated in language whose background was Greek philosophy?[163] If so, might some of them not have perceived Christian preaching as a variation on Stoic discourse? Might some even have fancied themselves, now that they were new creations, free, infused with wisdom and insight, along the lines of the ideal Stoic wise-man? Might some have unwittingly integrated the principles and goals of each, not realizing that any confluence between Stoic and Christian preaching and living ended at the level of semantic similarity? This blending of Stoic and Christian ideas and models for living was perhaps inevitable given the fact that Paul's evangelizing project and Hellenistic philosophical propagandizing were being carried on in the same social matrix. In addition, one must bear in mind that in the ancient world, teaching and preaching, moral exhortation, and the exegesis of texts were activities associated with philosophy, not religion[164]. In the mind of the average Corinthian convert, the scope and goals of both Stoicism and Christianity as preached by Paul and even the manner in which Paul's preaching was presented, may not have appeared to be linguistically, conceptually or even structurally as distinct as we might imagine[165]. The linguistic congruence, in all probability, eased the conversion of some Corinthians to Christianity. While this is positive, nonetheless there is the risk that the uniqueness of the Christian message and the goals of Christian living will be missed or, more problematically, that they will be transmuted or compromised. The Corinthian situation may represent just such a process. We are not suggesting by what has just been said that Corinthian converts to Christianity were necessarily orthodox Stoics, so to speak, but rather that their

---

[161] «*kai tôn sophôn de panta einai*», DIOGENES LAERTIUS, *Lives*, VII, 25.

[162] DIOGENES LAERTIUS, *Lives*, VII, 125. For the Stoics, one was either a total *sophos* or a total fool. Plutarch considered this absurd. With great sarcasm he mocks the Stoic claim that one can pass from a depraved fool to a completely virtuous wise man. With this instant virtue, «all will be yours. It brings wealth, comprises kingship, makes men prosperous and free from all wants [...] though they have not a single drachma» (cf. PLUTARCH, «On Stoic Self-Contradictions», esp. 1058b.

[163] Cf. F.C. GRANT, *Roman Hellenism*, 54ff.

[164] As pointed out by L. ALEXANDER, «Paul and the Hellenistic Schools», 60.

[165] Even the venues in which philosophical preaching and instruction took place are by and large identical with the settings in which Paul preached and ministered. Compare the comments of A. MALHERBE, *Moral Exhortation*, 13, with for example Acts 16,14-16; 17,16-21; 19,9; 20,20.

exposure to Stoic discussions and the Stoic ideas that permeated and dominated society may have provided the categories[166] through which some may have filtered the Christian message, at times with unfortunate results.

4.2 *Evidence for a Stoic self-understanding. 1Cor 4,8-13*

Here we could begin to point to the studies cited above[167] to show that in the text of 1Cor there are both Stoic arguments and Stoic language. In fact, the position Paul counters in 1Cor 6,12-14 accords well with Stoic ideas[168]. But the liability in doing so, as noted with regard to the theses expounding the influence of Hellenistic Diaspora Judaism[169], is that one is taking Paul's language for Corinthian language, expressing the Corinthians' self-perception. However, there is one place beginning at 4,8 where there may be reason to justify taking Paul's language as representing Corinthian self-perception, a self-perception decidedly in line with that of the Stoic ideal sage. In this instance we have the precise language used by Stoics to speak of the ideal sage found in their own literature and also in literature that summarizes their self-understanding. However as we shall argue, it is not the mere presence of the terms but rather how they are used that would justify taking them as true gauges of Corinthian self-understanding in the vein of the Stoic *sapiens*.

Starting in 4,8 Paul says *edè kekoresmenoi este, èdè eploutèsate, chôris hèmôn ebasileusate*. There is not much in the text section immediately preceding 4,8 that logically leads to this outburst about being rich or being a king. But earlier Paul had spoken about false wisdom and false pretensions to wisdom (1,18-3,1) and it is clear from what we have signalled above that wisdom along with riches and kingship were considered to be the prerogatives and hallmarks of the ideal Stoic sage. Plutarch, in the essay already cited[170] criticizes Stoic belief in instantaneous change from depravity to virtue using characteristic Stoic diction. He speaks of the depraved man who falls asleep demented, stupid, unjust, licentious etc., gets up and is now become «*kai basileus kai plousios*» and who, without showing even the normal biological signs of maturity, already has a «*noun*

---

[166] A. MALHERBE points out that Paul, too, appears to have appropriated Stoic categories for self-expression. But as the author notes, this was due to the milieu in which issues which engaged Paul and his converts were already being discussed in such categories (cf.«Determinism», 255).

[167] Cf. above n. 132.

[168] Cf. below § 4.3.

[169] Cf. above n. 55 and 56.

[170] Cf. above n. 162. Here we refer to 1058b.

teleion». In conclusion he repeats mockingly that this transformation brings «*plouton*» and includes «*basileian*». Plutarch is discussing the Stoics and obviously using their own language as the basis for his mocking critique. Paul, on the other hand, is talking to the Corinthian community and the fact that he uses these terms is no guarantee that Corinthians used them intending to express their self-perception as ideal wise men in the vein of the Stoic sages. However, the *way* Paul uses these terms may be an indication that they do mirror Corinthian self-perception and were part of the Corinthian community's lexicon.

Most commentators observe that in 4,8-13 Paul employs irony. The essence of the figure of irony is the «disparity between what is said, and what is intended or really thought»[171]. Now in order for Paul's irony to be an effective figure, in terms of its impact on the audience, the Corinthians must identify with, see themselves in the categories, or recognize their own idioms in what Paul is saying. In fact, as the irony continues in the contrast between what the Apostles are and what the Corinthians are, the irony can only be efficacious if the Corinthians do consider themselves, rich (v. 8), kings (v. 8), wise[172] (v. 10), strong (v. 10) and worthy of honor (v. 10). The fact that the efficacy of the irony turns on Corinthian self-identification with this language coupled with the fact that the terms «wise», «rich» and «king» constitute the linguistic triad used by both Stoics and their critics to describe the Stoic sage are two important considerations in light of which it can be reasonably suggested that the Corinthians, or at least some of them, probably did fancy themselves to be on an elite spiritual plane on par with the Stoic sage[173]. Here then we might have an example of Corinthian blending of the categories and models from Stoicism with those of Christianity. But did the Corinthians think and act like the Stoic sages? This is now the crucial question to answer if we hope to sustain our hypothesis. If we can show apart from abstruse lexical argumentation that the Corinthians thought or acted like Stoics, applying their principles while believing themselves to be reasoning or behaving in a manner consonant with Christianity, then it is no longer a matter of hypothesizing Stoic influence. Hence we must enquire whether Corinthian ethical practice shows signs of having been impacted

---

[171] W.J. BRANDT, *Rhetoric of Argumentation*, 157.

[172] Here Paul uses the term *phronimoi*. Among the Stoics *phronèsis*, i.e., the ability to distinguish between good and evil, distinguished the sage from the common man, cf. MUSONIUS, Frag. VI.

[173] Despite talk of equality and communion based on the sharing of the same *logos*, cf. above n. 146, the wise man and fool were considered incompatible and incapable of friendship, cf. DIOGENES LAERTIUS, *Lives*, VII, 124.

by Stoic conceptions. Before looking at 1Cor 5 we must first examine another text piece.

4.3 *Corinthian Principles for Ethical Action in 1Cor 6,12-20: Christian or Stoic?*

In the text piece, 6,12-20, to which 1Cor 5 is joined in an ABA' literary arrangement, a new discussion is introduced by the phrase *panta moi exestin* which most commentators consider to be a Corinthian slogan cited here by Paul in v. 12a.c.[174]. The concept of freedom and the belief that freedom was essentially manifested in acts according to nature was, as already noted, a key aspect of Stoic ethics. In a recent article T. Paige has argued that Paul was addressing people who were familiar with Stoic language, or thought in a Stoic manner or were impressed with Stoic ideas[175]. Paige reviews Stoic ideas pertinent to 1Cor 6,12-20, notes that the slogan quoted in 6,12 expresses the Stoic wise man's prerogative[176] and shows how the Stoic idea of mental choice as determining whether an action is good or bad as well as the Stoic category of *adiaphora* appear to play a major part in the Corinthian position here[177]. Of course the words are Paul's. However, in this dialogue[178] that Paul structures between himself and his dialogue partner[179],the partner's position accords well with Stoicism. What could have added conviction to Paige's thesis, but what he unfortunately did not highlight, is that as presented in the mouth of the dialogue partner[180] the argument for freedom is an argument to act according to nature. Here the partner cites a law of nature, «food is meant for the belly and the belly for food» (6,13). The implication, by analogy,

---

[174] Against the common view that *panta moi exestin* is probably a Corinthian slogan, see the recent article by B.J. DODD, «Paul's Paradigmatic 'I'», 39-58; it is argued, but unconvincingly, by R. KEMPTHORNE, «Incest», 568-574, that 6,12-20 is not a new discussion but continues with the incest case of 1Cor 5,1-13. But 5,1-13 is a concise literary unit with its own problem and a precise resolution.

[175] T. PAIGE, «Stoicism», 81.

[176] T. PAIGE, «Stoicism», 189; Cf. further, EPICTETUS, *Discourses*, I.I, 21-22.

[177] T. PAIGE, «Stoicism», 189.

[178] Dialogic exchange was a feature of what has been termed a diatribe. On the definition, characteristics and *Sitz im Leben* of the diatribe cf. D.E. AUNE, *The NT in Its Literary Environment*, 200-202; S.K. STOWERS, *The Diatribe*; ID., «The Diatribe», 71-84; J.L. KUSTAS, «Diatribe», 1-15.

[179] Who may be imaginary, cf. D.E. AUNE, *The NT in Its Literary Environment*, 201.

[180] J. MURPHY-O'CONNOR assigns the dialogue pieces based on syntactic parallelism (cf. «Corinthian Slogans», 394). To the dialogue partner belong the phrases in 12a.c; 13a; 13b; and to Paul 12b.d; 13c and 13d-14a. The author also considers v. 18b as representing the dialogue partner's views while most scholars consider it Paul's (cf. the survey in J.C. HURD, *Origin*, 68).

is that the sexual organ is for sex and sex for the sexual organ[181]. And all this is of no account anyway, an *adiaphoron*, because as the partner says, both food and the belly are going to be destroyed (v. 13b). For a Stoic, or a stoic-minded person, this was a perfectly coherent argument. The corruptibility of the body which is in accord with nature is being set forth as the ultimate context in which one decides comportment. In other words, nature, which, for the Stoic is interchangeable with the term god, will destroy the food and belly and sex organs: in sum, the body is of no account morally speaking; its end is destruction and this testifies to its insignificance[182]. But Paul's counter statement in v. 13c. implies that the body *is* of moral account and must not be used as an instrument of immorality. Against nature which destroys, Paul establishes the power and purpose of God who raised Jesus and who will raise us[183] (v. 14), i.e., our bodies, as the ultimate context for this ethical decision[184]. Here Paul finds himself arguing against nature which for the Stoic is the only principle for appropriate action[185], and is in fact the only principle on which the freedom to go to prostitutes is being established. This is by all counts a totally un-Christian argument based on the principle of nature alone. Hence it would be difficult to concede that the dialogue partner's position results from a radicalization of Paul's own freedom preaching. On the contrary, the argument Paul counters derives from totally different principles by which one could reason along the lines set out in 6,12-14 and, based on this reasoning, justify behavior such as going to prostitutes. This is coherent with the principle of acting in accordance with nature. But neither the principle nor the behavior it could justify have any connection

---

[181] In *The Manual* 33, Epictetus discusses what is necessary for the maintenance of the body. The mention of food and drink in v. 7 is followed by the mention of sex, in which, according to Epictetus, even the unmarried can be engaged. In the context it is clear that Epictetus considers sex to be a biological necessity of the same order as food and drink.

[182] The Stoic wise man could say, «my paltry body is nothing to me; the parts of it are nothing to me. Death? Let it come when it will, whether it be the death of the whole or some part». For what happens in death the Stoic asks? «Nothing but the separation of the paltry body from the soul», cf. EPICTETUS, *Discourses*, III, 22,21-24. If such expressed Stoic disregard for the body were influential within the community at Corinth it becomes easier to explain their views on sex and to imagine that they would have had no difficulty in denying the resurrection of the body, cf. 1Cor 15.

[183] In v. 14 *hèmas* replaces *sôma*. The use of *hèmas* does not broaden the meaning of *sôma*. Rather it is a stylistic variation. Cf. R. JEWETT, *Paul's Anthropological Terms* 262; R. GUNDRY, *Sôma*, 24, 29, 53.

[184] To this theological-teleological argument that begins 6,12-20, Paul adds Christological (6,15-17), and Pneumatological (6,19-20) arguments against going to prostitutes.

[185] Cf. EPICTETUS, *Discourses*, I.XXVI, 2.

to Christianity or to the claims of Christianity with regard to one's comportment. This is why, as we said earlier, to highlight the concept «freedom» and suggest that the Corinthian understanding of freedom at the root of their behavior was a radicalization of Paul's freedom teaching is too simplistic. As presented here the only recourse for determining ethical action is nature. Acting according to nature is an exercise of freedom but it has nothing to do with Christian freedom. As Paige has aptly stated, «only a Stoic could behave in such an individualistic, community destroying way – from a Christian perspective – while believing himself to be pursuing a virtuous life according to nature and based on the divine right of free choice»[186].

In conclusion, to return to the concern we mentioned above, it seems that the Corinthians were doing more than borrowing labels or categories from the Stoics with which to describe what they may have considered to be their own comparable elite spiritual status as Christians. Indeed the sloganizing Corinthian Christian with whom Paul dialogues in this passage would seem well-equipped and quite ready to argue from Stoic principles to behavior[187] totally incompatible with the claims of Christianity. Here, at least, a residue of Stoic ideas and influence is undeniably present in Corinthian reasoning along with behavior held to be permissible based on that reasoning.

4.4 *1 Corinthians 5*

In 1Cor 5, unlike what we have just seen in 6,12-20, there is no explicit mention of a rationale for the incest or boasting. On what evidence then might we begin to stake a claim that Stoic influences are to be reckoned with here? First we have to reconsider a point made above[188], viz., that bodily things were accounted indifferent in Stoic ethics. The body's func-

---

[186] T. PAIGE, «Stoicism», 189. This resonates well with Colish's statement cited above n. 146.

[187] Though some, e.g. G. FEE, *1 Corinthians*, 250, and A.C. WIRE, *Corinthian Women*, 72, consider Paul's discussion in 6,12-20 to reflect an actual situation wherein community members at Corinth were frequenting prostitutes, the fact is, from the text information, we cannot be certain that the discussion reflects actual practice. If not reflective of actual practice, then the question arises as to the motive for Paul's introduction of this discussion and its relation to its present context. Beyond partitioners' suggestions that 6,12-20 was inserted by a redactor, there are some recent attempts to explain the connection of 6,12-20 to its context, cf. e.g. A.C. WIRE, *Corinthian Women*, 72ff. and B. BYRNE, *Paul*, 18-19. Though differently conceived, both authors relate the discussion in 6,12-20 with the issue/problem of sexual asceticism under discussion in 1Cor 7. Cf. also the recent discussion in W. DEMING, art. cited n. 1.

[188] Cf. above, p. 72.

tions were nature's functions and no moral value could be imputed to them. Second, the Stoics apparently endorsed all forms of carnal conjunction, hetero or homosexual. They felt that sexual needs should be taken care of in any way seen fit and were not opposed to incest[189]. In fact, for the wise and liberated, perfect reason, their hallmark, enabled them to recognize that all those societal conventions which had no apparent basis in reason should be rejected. A lone voice dissenting from this rationalized brand of nothing less than gross immorality was Musonius Rufus[190] who considered not just adultery but all sexual relations outside of marriage disgraceful, unlawful and dissolute. The fact that Musonius, a Stoic himself, inveighed against all these forms of sexual immorality may indicate its prevalence and also make it clear that Stoic talk of virtue and lofty morality could be quite divorced from sexual morality as a Christian would understand that term.

The case of sexual immorality in 1Cor 5 and the community's response to it could very well fit into the framework of Stoic influence. First of all, Stoically influenced people would not consider incest a sin. On the contrary they could boast of such a relationship as an indicator of the attainment of perfect reason, *nous teleios*, by which one was able to judge correctly between the good, the bad and the morally indifferent. Incest, like all other forms of sex, fell in the sphere of the morally indifferent. To recognize this and to act against social convention was an act of true freedom. For an informed Stoic, incest might have been considered less an act of promiscuity and more as the prerogative of those with an illuminated *nous*. The question now is: did the Corinthians see and boast of this incestuous relationship with the Stoic-like intention of flouting societal norms as an act of freedom? Paul does not expressly say. However there is a peculiarity to note in his argument which may point to an affirmative answer for our question. In Jewish tradition, as is well known, the pagans were depicted as the epitome of moral depravity, especially in sexual matters[191]. In Paul's own writing, echoes of this same conventional view of pagans are found at Rom 1,18-31. Elsewhere at 1Thess 4,1, Paul exhorts Christians to act in a manner that is specifically contrasted to the manner in which «pagans who do not know God» conduct themselves (v. 5). Here in 1Cor 5 however, Paul begins with a most unusual statement, viz., that this behavior is of a «kind that is not even found among the pagans» (5,1b). We will discuss this statement more fully below, but here

---

[189] Cf. SEXTUS EMPIRICUS, «Against the Ethicists», 3.190-92.

[190] Cf. MUSONIUS, Frag. 12.

[191] A discussion of texts which reflect this view of pagans is found in O.L. YARBROUGH, *Not Like the Gentiles*, 8-29.

we wish to observe that with this mention of the pagans, Paul is essentially referring to moral reasoning and practice that is beyond Christianity, beyond Israel; it is the moral reasoning and practice of society at large. The implication is clear. This much vaunted incestuous relationship transgresses not just a religious norm but a societal norm, i.e., a value held in common by all decent people. The fact that Paul would make this atypical reference to pagans and moreover make it his opening comment after the brief statement of the issue (v. 1a) may indicate that the incest and the boasting had something to do with a desire to manifest one's freedom from the constraints of societal norms. This behavior, if a manifest act of rejecting society's norms, would be in line with Stoic ideas and may indicate that some Corinthians Christians influenced by these ideas thought such behavior could give expression to their freedom. Obviously what they did not realize is that such conceptualizations and behavior had nothing to do with Christian freedom. This may be another indication of how the Christian concept of freedom could have been combined by people conversant with Stoic ideas or impressed by them and used to reason to the kind of behavior discussed in c. 5 and perhaps also to the evaluation that the incestuous relationship was good! If what we have just suggested in terms of Stoic influence could account for the behavior of c. 5 then we can again, with reason, emphasize the inadequacy of views that see radicalized versions of Paul's freedom preaching as the basis for Corinthian behavior in c. 5. Rather, it seems that parallel ideas with a decidedly Stoic imprint were being interwoven with the ideas of the Christian proclamation with unfortunate results *vis-à-vis* the community and its status as holy. Here there is no need to ask who introduced these ideas to the Corinthians. Adult Corinthian converts had had a life-time of exposure to such ideas and these were not eradicated by their conversion. The Corinthian converts stayed in Corinth and Corinth stayed in them. Even after conversion they never left that world behind, never even left the old haunts and habits[192] that constituted their formative environment.

There is perhaps one more element in the text of 1Cor 5 that may indicate that Paul may have been dealing with Stoically minded or Stoically influenced persons. Here we refer to Paul's remark to the community, «ought you not rather to mourn» (5,2b), with specific reference to the verb *epenthèsate*[193]. In general[194], *penthein* denotes affective reactions: to

---

[192] Cf. esp. 1Cor 8,10 and 10,25-26.

[193] Cf. R. BULTMANN, «*penthos, pentheô*», 40-43.

[194] In the NT the term is infrequent, occurring just 10x. However in the majority of cases it is juxtaposed with *klaiô*, to cry or weep, and seems to be added as a reinforcement of the same idea rather than indicating something altogether different.

grieve, lament or express sorrow[195]. What it connotes here in 5,2b, is often determined by how the *hina* clause which follows in 5,2c[196] is understood. When understood as a purpose clause, the emphasis is not on *penthein* in contrast to *physioô* as a comparison of feelings but rather on *pentheô*, as the impetus for taking action against the man. According to Bultmann[197] *pentheô* connotes «to acknowledge wrong» since acknowledgement of the wrong, not mere feelings of grief, will impel the community to act. More recently B. Rosner has argued that mourning in 1Cor 5,2b connotes the act of «confessing the sin of the erring brother as if it were their own», in accordance with Jewish custom[198].

In the LXX, the majority of the 54 occurrences translate some derivative of אבל. In Paul, *penthein*, is used only here at 1Cor 5,2 and again at 2Cor 12,21.

[195] Some suggest that the mourning is over the impending loss of a brother about to undergo destruction, e.g. J.J. MOFFATT, *1 Corinthians*, 54; V.C. PFITZNER, «Purified Community», 42. Fee remarks that *penthein* probably refers to the kind of mourning, frequently related to true repentance, that the righteous experience because of their own sins or those of others. To back up his claim Fee cites Matt. 5,4; 1 Esdr 8,69; Ez10,6; *T. Reub* 1,10 (cf. G. FEE, *1 Corinthians*, 202, n. 31). However if we look at Paul's own writing we discover that when he speaks of «mourning unto repentance», he employs different vocabulary, cf. e.g. 2Cor 7,9-11 *lypein*; *kata Theon lypè*. This godly grief produces repentance. If Paul meant to speak of grief unto repentance at 1Cor 5,2 it is curious that he did not express himself there as at 2Cor 7,9-11 where the grief and repentance spoken of are related to an ethical matter.

[196] M. ZERWICK, *Biblical Greek*, § 415, considers this an example of the imperatival *hina*. H. CONZELMANN, *1 Korinther*, 96, suggests that the clause is better understood as explicatory and translates it as a result clause. C.K. BARRETT, *1 Corinthians*, 122, also translates the phrase as a result clause. However, he admits that it makes sense as a purpose clause and could also be taken as an imperatival *hina*. G. FEE, *1 Corinthians*, 198, circumvents the problem by inserting the conjunction «and» thereby producing a compound verb, «shouldn't you rather have been filled with grief and have put out [...]». Besides ignoring *hina*, Fee has translated *arthè* as a 2nd per. pl. perfect. English translations vary: the REB and NNAB opt for the imperatival *hina*; the NRSV construes it as a result clause. Besides the grammatical possibility that we have here an imperatival use of *hina*, Paul may have intended a parallelism between the generic command of 5,13b, which concludes his comments to the community on identifying and dealing with the *ponèros* in their midst and this command which concludes his opening comments to the community about the particular situation at hand and dealing with it. If so, the parallelism would weigh in favor of taking 5,2c as an independent imperative.

[197] Cf. R. BULTMANN, «*penthos, pentheô*», 42. This connotation is possible but the dichotomy between cognitive and affective with regard to what impels action may be overstated.

[198] B. ROSNER, «*Ouchi mallon epenthèsate*», 470-473 has attempted to explain the meaning of *penthein* in function of his overall thesis that the OT notion of corporate responsibility underlies Paul's exigency to expel the incestuous man. The author relies for the most part on a parallel with Ezra 10,6, interpreting Ezra's mourning as equal to an act of confessing the sins of others as if they were his own. But the verb, *exagoreuein*, used 11x in the LXX in contexts where one confesses his own sin, or

Except for an *a priori* rejection of the possibility[199], no one has considered whether *penthein*'s significance in philosophical discourse, particularly Stoic, enters in any way into Paul's usage here. There are two aspects to consider: 1) In Stoic thought *penthein* had pejorative connotations. It was associated with defective reason and judgement and was to be avoided by the wise man. Only the fool mourned[200].   2) *penthein* as any *pathos* was considered to be a judgement[201]. As pointed out by Inwood[202], for the Stoics *pathos* and judgement are mental events, always occurring together. With this latter point in mind, it should not be unreasonable to entertain the possibility that by using *penthein*, Paul is essentially suggesting to the community that it ought to judge the incest as evil, which judgement would have as its concrete manifestation, mourning. But wise men, the Stoics held, are *apathè*[203]. A wise man mourned over nothing since he had insight to know what was according to nature. Moreover, the wise man's insight, his *nous teleios*, allowed him to discern that sex and other bodily related matters were *adiaphora*. Hence, there was no reason to consider a matter such as incest something to judge as evil. As a sex-body event, incest was an *adiaphoron*, therefore not susceptible to moral evaluation. Such a perspective may explain why no action was taken against the offending brother by the community. Indeed, if an incestuous relationship was testimony to a man's perfect insight, to his understanding that this was simply acting in accordance with nature and hence an exercise of his freedom, then all the more reason to boast in that man's wisdom reflected in his choice to flout societal conventions and act in accord with nature. If this were the Corinthian approach, which would by all counts appear to be quite Stoically conditioned, could it be that in using *penthein*, Paul is intending to insert, in a subtle way, a bit of

---

those of others as his own (cf. e.g. Lev 5,5; 16,21; 26,40; Num 5,7; Neh 1,6; 9,2.3; LXX Ps 31,5), is used at Ezra 10,1 (*exègoreuse*), referring to Ezra's confessing the people's sins as his own. So why take *epenthei* in 10,6 with essentially the same meaning as *exègoreuse*? It is clear from 10,6 that Ezra mourned. It is also clear from 9,5-15 that Ezra confessed the people's sins as if they were his own. But from these two facts one cannot necessarily conclude that the term *penthein* in Ezra 10,6 is reducible to confessing the sins of others as if they were one's own, as Rosner claims. If it cannot be proven that *penthein* has this connotation in Ezra it somewhat precarious to suggest that by using *penthein* in 1Cor 5 Paul is effectively advocating the confession of the offender's sin as if it were that of the whole community. In sum, Rosner's interpretation of *penthein* in 1Cor 5 is not convincingly established.

[199] Cf. R. BULTMANN, «penthos ktl.», 41.

[200] Cf. EPICTETUS, *Discourses*, IV, 4,32; III, 3,1ff.; III, 22,32-36; II, 24,1ff.

[201] DIOGENES LAERTIUS, *Lives*, VIII, 3, referring to the Stoics, says, «*dokei d'autois ta pathè kriseis einai*».

[202] B. INWOOD, *Ethics*, 131.

[203] Cf. DIOGENES LAERTIUS, *Lives*, VII, 117; CICERO, *De Finibus*, III, 35.

irony, counseling the Corinthians to a course of action that wise men would eschew? It is at least worth considering, especially since just thirteen verses earlier in c. 4, Paul had engaged in an ironic contrast between the sated, rich and reigning wise and the Apostles. It may be that here in 5,2 Paul purposely used *penthein* to strike another chord relating to the wise-fool contrast already in play in cc. 1-4. Granted the terms *sophia, sophos, môria, môros* are not used explicitly in 1Cor 5,1ff, as in 1Cor 1-4. However, if the arrogant of 1Cor 5,2 are related to the arrogant of 4,18 who strive after wisdom[204], boasting wrongly in men, in false conceptions of wisdom and in their own presumed elite status, whom Paul is taking to task in cc. 1-4, then it may be possible that here in c. 5,2, but indirectly and under a different aspect, Paul alludes to the same categories that he challenged and redefined by inversion in cc. 1-4[205]. After dealing with the issue of what is true wisdom, and who is truly wise and in what one should and should not boast, Paul states in 4,18, «if any one among you thinks himself wise in this age, let him become a fool that he might become wise». For a Stoic wise man, to mourn over incest would be tantamount to defective judgement, the sign of an imperfect *nous* by which he would be exposed as a fool! Did Paul have this role reversal in mind when he advised the community to mourn over the incest? We cannot say for certain. However, it is rather curious that Paul proposes «mourning», a *pathos* connected in the Stoic conceptual world with the unwise, to the Corinthian community as the right course of action, expressing right judgement. Regardless of the Stoic assessment that the one who mourns is a fool, for Paul this is the only right judgement and proper response to this incest. For Christians, to mourn this situation would be no act of false judgement. On the contrary, it would signify that the incest will have been finally judged as evil. Based on such a judgement appropriate action can be taken against the offender.

5. Conclusion to Chapter 3

In this chapter we have followed the course delineated at the outset, noting the salient points of main hypotheses advanced to explain the

---

[204] The linkage suggested is intended to connect the boasters of 1Cor 5 with the dominant *ethos* of cc. 1-4 and not necessarily to factionalism. Paul does not specify in cc. 1-4 that being rich «in all speech and knowledge», the basis on which everyone in Corinth could presumably claim to be a *sophos*, or that the posture of arrogance, is the exclusive prerogative of factionalists.

[205] E.g. the kerygma of the crucified Christ is the opposite of *sophia*, that is, it is *môria*, 1,18; God continually turns the wise of this world into fools and their wisdom into folly, 1,19-25; God chooses what is foolish in this world to shame the wise, what is weak in this world to shame the strong, 1,27-28.

historical-religious background of 1 Corinthians and focusing particular attention on how adequately these hypotheses account for the background to 1Cor 5. With the exception of Schmithals' hypothesis, which could perhaps be rejected because of unacceptable points of departure for his investigation[206], the other hypotheses can only be evaluated in terms of more or less probable. Some of these did not deal directly with 1Cor 5, and those that did, have problems, some of which we have attempted to signal. The unsatisfactory nature of these hypotheses as they relate directly to the background of 1Cor 5, along with insights gained from other studies, lead us to ask whether the behavior under discussion in 1Cor 5 may betray Stoic influence. To answer the question we looked first at 1Cor 4,8ff. and then at 6,12-20. With regard to the former we argued that the *way* in which Paul uses decidedly Stoic terms seems to indicate that at least some in the Corinthian community developed their religious self-perception in line with Stoic conceptions about the ideal wise man. With regard to 1Cor 6,12-20, we noted that here Paul dialogues with a partner who begins with a Stoic principle, reasons like a Stoic and proposes behavior that would be consonant with Stoic conceptions. In light of the possible Stoic self-conception and Stoically influenced reasoning and behavior reflected in these text pieces we turned to look at 1Cor 5. The behavior and the attendant boasting discussed in this chapter can not be proved beyond doubt to be due to Stoic influence. However, we attempted to show that the behavior could accord well with Stoic conceptions. In addition, we noted two elements in the text of 1Cor 5, usually overlooked, that may weigh in favor of admitting a Stoically influenced background for the behavior under question. The first was Paul's atypical reference to the pagans (5,1). The second was Paul's counsel to mourn (5,2) which may resonate with Stoic ideas, although in a subtly ironic way. With regard to Paul's use of *penthein,* the insights we have offered are speculative and, admittedly, attain significance only in light of the rest of our argument. In fact, there is no way of knowing with certainty if Paul intended *penthein* along the lines we have suggested. On the other hand, Paul's atypical reference to the pagans stands peculiarly on its own and emphasizes how this behavior runs counter to societal, and not simply religious, norms. This emphasis raises suspicions about Stoic influence. In fact, when we considered Stoic notions about wisdom, the purpose of life, freedom, sexual behavior and enlightened attitudes regarding social conventions, we saw that the incest discussed in 1Cor 5 could have been intended as a convention-defying act testifying to the

---

[206] Cf. our discussion above § 2.2.

freedom to act in accordance with nature understood in a typically Stoic way.

Admitting a Stoically-influenced background for the behavior in 1Cor 5 has certain advantages. A Stoic context explains how such behavior could be considered good, or at least unobjectionable, and this may further explain why the community did not feel any exigency to take action against the man. Moreover, it provides a reasonable alternative to the two possibilities that have been advanced so far with regard to the provenance of ideas that influenced community behavior: 1) the behavior was influenced by ideas introduced into the community from outside – a possibility that does not accord with the text information, or 2) the behavior is rooted in ideas which were a direct radicalized outgrowth of Paul's own teaching.

We have argued that the ideas that influenced Corinthian behavior in 1Cor 5 were based on notions and principles other than Paul's. These other ideas and notions with which the Corinthians would be familiar by virtue of their exposure to the philosophical talk of the day, especially Stoicism, may have appeared to the Corinthians to have some affinity with what Paul was preaching. However, beyond semantic overlap, Christian and Stoic concepts of freedom and their respective principles for guiding the choice of ethical actions diverged[207]. A Corinthian Christian who would hear the Christian proclamation in the key of Stoicism may not have even perceived the great dissonance that lay beneath the apparent harmony. But concrete ethical choices would make such dissonance apparent, as 1Cor 5 seems to illustrate. It was Paul's task to bring Corinthian sexual practice in line with the demands of Christianity. 1Cor 5, we suggest, may be an indicator of how some in the community confused the *telos* of Christian living which was holiness (cf. 1Thess 4,3; Eph 2,21), with the ideal Stoic sage's *telos* of living in accordance with nature.

If what we have established is a reasonable reading of the situation of 1Cor 5, then we can answer the question whether the Corinthian behavior discussed in c. 5 was intended to defy Paul or challenge his authority in the negative. If anything, the behavior was more likely intended to challenge social convention as a testimony to freedom as understood by some Corinthians. As contemporary Christian readers, uninfluenced by 1st century Stoicism and with an all together different *Weltanschauung*, we recognize this behavior as a perversion of Christian freedom and consider it as wrongful or sinful. However, the Corinthians may not have

---

[207] It is on the level of principles of ethical action that any illusions of similarity between Stoicism and Christianity dissipate, cf. A. JAGU, «La morale d'Epictète», 2195.

perceived the behavior as wrong and may not have intended it as an intentional act of defiance directed against Paul's authority. In fact, in c. 5, Paul's effort seems in no way related to quelling challenges to his authority but rather to rectifying the situation and introducing the criteria which must guide Christians so that their behavior and judgement are congruent, not with Stoically conditioned ideas or claims but with the claims of Christianity. While some Corinthians were apparently interested in the rational life, a life in accord with nature, Paul was interested in the sanctified life, a life pleasing to God. This becomes clear in 1Cor 5, where Paul's center of concern, as we shall see below, was the sanctified life of the community.

In the next chapter we will define the limits of the rhetorical unit, consider the ABA' rhetorical pattern[208] according to which 1Cor 5,1-13 is composed and consider whether and to what extent this pattern can and should be considered a guide to interpretation.

---

[208] Here we use the term rhetorical as intended by J. MUILENBERG, «Form Criticism», 1-18. By rhetorical pattern Muilenberg was essentially referring to surface literary patterns. The author coined the term «rhetorical criticism» (8), to refer to the study of these patterns.

CHAPTER IV

Establishing the Unit of Text. 1Cor 5,1-13

1. 1Cor 5,1-13. Rhetorical and Literary Dimensions

A rhetorical unit[1] corresponds to the pericope in Form Criticism or the literary unit in Literary Criticism. That 1Cor 5,1-13 forms an independent literary unit is clear both from the introduction of three new sets of vocabulary[2] that mark the unit off from what precedes and follows[3] and also by the repetition in v. 13 of the expulsion call announced in v. 2, which repetition forms an *inclusio* that brackets the discussion and defines the limits of the unit. Though at first glance vv. 9-13, where mention of the «previous letter» is made, may appear to be the start of a new section[4], as we shall see below, these verses, which are formally bracketed into the discussion by the *inclusio*, are integrally related to the discussion in 5,1-8. Hence, we can speak of 1Cor 5,1-13 as a self-contained literary unit.

---

[1] See the description in G. KENNEDY, *New Testament Interpretation*, 33-34.

[2] 1) *porneia, pornos. Porneia* occurs 2x in 1Cor 5,1 and signals the new topic under discussion. It recurs at 6,13 and 18 and only once more in this letter at 7,2. *Pornos*, appears again in 5,9.10.11 and only once more in the Pauline corpus at 6,9, heading the vice list; 2) *ponèros, ponèria. Ponèria* occurs here at 5,8 and nowhere else in 1 Cor. *Ponèros* occurs in 5,13 as part of the formula cited from Dt., cf. Dt. 17,7.12; 19,19; 21,21; 22,21.22.24 and 24,7; 3) *airô* and the compound *exairô. Airô* is used only here in 5,2 and again in 6,15. *Exairô* is part of the formula cited in 5,13. With the exception of *pornos* which comes up once in 6,9, the vocabulary introduced by Paul recurs only within 6,12-20 and only once again in 1Cor at 7,2.

[3] But the text is not without lexical links to what precedes and follows: e.g. *krinô* at 5,12 and 13 and 6,1.2.3; likewise 5,1-13 is lexically related to c. 4 through *physioô* whose seven NT occurrences are limited to Paul with six of these occurring in 1Cor. Of the six, four are concentrated in cc. 4 and 5 at 1Cor 4,6.18.19 and 5,2.

[4] In fact, the chapter has been susceptible to partitioning here at v. 9 with vv. 1-8 assigned to one hypothetical letter and vv. 9-13 to another, cf. e.g. R. PESCH, *Paulus Ringt*, 138-139; 154-155.

This particular literary unit can also be designated and treated as a rhetorical unit. Such a designation and treatment is justified by the fact that in 1Cor 5,1-13 an argument is discernible within the limits of the *inclusio*[5]. In broadest strokes, for the moment, it can be said that in 1Cor 5,1-13 Paul states the problem and the action to be taken (vv. 1-5), argues against the posture the Corinthians had adopted *vis-à-vis* the incest, supplies an argument for why the action he advises should be taken (vv. 6-11), and then recaps his argument (vv. 12-13). Hence we can also speak of 1Cor 5,1-13 as a complete, independent rhetorical unit.

This point would seem to appear rather obvious and in the rhetorical studies of both Mitchell[6] and Witherington[7], both authors treat the text as an independent unit of rhetoric within the larger rhetorical structure of the letter. However, in his recent study, Probst[8] has effectively challenged this view by suggesting that 1Cor 5-7 was a separately occasioned, independent letter, dealing with *porneia* and having at stake the issue of who is competent or authorized to judge. Though Probst's assertion that 1Cor 5-7 originally constituted an independent letter lacks substantiating proof[9], we must still consider his rhetorical analysis of these chapters because, as it has already been shown, some sections within larger epistles while composed according to a concentric, ABA', rhetorical pattern[10] also[11]

---

[5] An action or argument which connects the beginning and end is essential in order for a unit to be defined as a rhetorical unit, cf. G. KENNEDY, *New Testament Interpretation*, 34.

[6] Cf. Introduction n. 19.

[7] Cf. Introduction n. 19.

[8] Cf. H. PROBST, *Paulus und der Brief*, 314-321.

[9] Most notably, as already mentioned (cf. above c. 1 n. 6), Probst has not established an occasion for this alleged independent letter that is substantially different from the occasion established for the whole of canonical 1Cor, cf. *Paulus und der Brief*, esp. 319.

[10] Scholars have long noted the surface literary patterns in the bible, cf. the survey in R. MEYNET, *L'analyse rhétorique*, 1-120. The concentric pattern was one of three conventional compositional models of antiquity along with the dramatic model and the *dispositio*, cf. B. STANDAERT, «La rhétorique ancienne», 86. «Chiastic» is incorrectly used by some authors as interchangeable with «concentric», e.g. A. DI MARCO, «Der Chiasmus», 22 or J. BRECK, «Biblical Chiasmus», 70-71. On the differences between concentric and chiastic patterns cf. I. THOMSON, *Chiasmus*, 25.

[11] More than one model can be present even in the same literary unit. Standaert remarks, «la schéma concentrique s'imposera de plus en plus sur toute composition, qu'elle soit rhétorique ou dramatique». He further states, «Une bonne composition ancienne se servira le plus souvent de deux modèles, les équilibrant adroitement en maintenant une tension qui est toute la vie du sujet» (cf. B. STANDAERT, «La rhétorique ancienne», 87). Thus it would be short-sighted to maintain that a NT text obeyed a single compositional model at a time (cf. J.-N. ALETTI, cf. «La *dispositio* rhétorique», 389).

display a rhetorical *dispositio*[12]. Thus while Probst's assertion regarding the original independent status of cc. 5-7 may be wrong, we must reckon with the possibility that his rhetorical analysis may still be correct. A number[13] of authors recognize that 1Cor 5-6 is composed according to a concentric pattern[14]. If these chapters do display the rhetorical *dispositio* that Probst suggests then 1Cor 5,1-13 loses its independent unit status and should be treated in terms of its functions within the *dispositio* that the author claims is discernible throughout 1Cor 5-6 where a larger argument is being unfolded. If so, this will necessarily affect the interpretation of 5,1-13.

The *dispositio* which the author proposes for cc. 5-6 is the following: *Exordium* 5,1-5; *Narratio* 5,6-11; *Confirmatio* 5,12-6,1-20 (Proof 1 = 5,12-6,10 and is developed around the *topos* of competence; Proof 2 = 6,11-20). What the author designates as the *Peroratio* is not clear. He mentions that 5,11 is the transition to the *peroratio*, from which we should assume that 5,12-13 is the *peroratio*. This *peroratio* must be *Peroratio* I, since the letter does not conclude here. But Probst does not say what constitutes *Peroratio* II, viz., the conclusion of the whole letter. As for c. 7, Probst considers this a paraenetic appendage, the kind of un-arranged paraenesis typically following a major epistolary arrangement in ancient letters[15].

On close examination Probst's proposed rhetorical structuring evidences a number of problems. First, 5,6-11 do not fulfill the function of *narratio*. The *narratio* consists in the persuasive exposition of that which either has been done or was supposed to have been done; its purpose is to instruct the audience in the nature of the case and prepare for the proofs[16]. The verses designated by Probst as *narratio* do not perform these functions[17]. Moreover, if 5,12-13 constitute a *peroratio*, which they do, then 5,6-11 cannot be a *narratio* as claimed since the *peroratio,* by definition a

---

[12] For example, 1Cor 12-14, composed according to the ABA' pattern, viz., A = 12,4-30 B = 12,31-14,1 A'= 14,2-40, also displays a rhetorical *dispositio* as shown in the analysis of B. STANDAERT, «Analyse rhétorique», 23-34. In Rom 9,6-29 it has been argued that there are three models: the rhetorical *dispositio*, the concentric and the midrashic are discernible (cf. J.-N. ALETTI, «Argumentation», 41-56; ID., *Comment Dieu*, c. 7).

[13] Cf. e.g. C. TALBERT, *Reading Corinthians*, 12; J. MURPHY-O'CONNOR, *1 Cor*, 30; J. WEISS, *Der erste Korintherbrief*, 145.

[14] A = 5,1-13; B = 6,1-11; A' = 6,12-20.

[15] Cf. H. PROBST, *Paulus und der Brief*, 318.

[16] Cf. QUINTILIAN, *Institutio*, IV.II, 1

[17] Probst seems to realize that his designated *narratio* is problematic (cf. *Paulus und der Brief*, 315).

summing up of the arguments already advanced[18], must logically follow the argumentation, not the *narratio*. Second, Probst suggests that the confusion in the community due to a misunderstanding of the previous letter, about which Paul has been informed, leads him to take up the question of the community's competence to judge[19]. Competency to judge, a *topos* usually taken up in forensic rhetoric, is, as alleged by Probst, the point of the argument in 6,1-10. However, on closer reading it is clear that competency to judge ceases to be the concern at 6,6. Even more difficult to accept is Probst's assertion that this same issue is at stake in 1Cor 5. This does not appear to be the case. Rather, competency and the right to judge are assumed in 1Cor 5. In fact, the problem in c. 5 is precisely that this community has failed to discern both the evil and the identity of the evil-*doer*, and in consequence failed to do what it is competent to do, viz., judge and expel the offender. Third, as far as we can determine, Probst does not indicate of what 6,11-20 is the *confirmatio*. If the issue at stake is who has the right or who is competent to judge and 6,1-10 takes this up, what does 6,11-20 prove *vis-à-vis* this issue? Beyond the problems regarding arrangement, there are others questions which cannot detain us here[20]. In sum, Probst's rhetorical analysis of these chapters cannot be endorsed. Moreover, it is difficult to avoid the conclusion that his rhetorical analysis was unduly conditioned by the presupposition that 1Cor 5-7 was an original, independent letter. This presupposition apparently lead Probst to force on this text unit a rhetorical schema which simply does not fit.

1Cor 5-6 is one of the macro units that comprises canonical 1Cor. Attention to Paul's preference for unfolding his thoughts in smaller units[21] and also to the rhetorical pattern according to which the macro-unit cc. 5-6 is composed, would have made it clear to Probst that a) the macro-unit, 1Cor 5-6, is not an independent letter needing to be schematized as such and b) 1Cor 5,1-13 is a self-contained unit of text dealing with incest and the community's failure to discern the evil and take appropriate measures[22]. Moreover, attentive study of 1Cor 7 reveals that this is hardly, as Probst claims, an un-arranged block of paraenesis appended to a rhetorical *dispositio*[23]. Rather it is a self-contained literary unit arranged according

---

[18] Cf. ARISTOTLE, *Ars Rhetorica*, III.XVIII, 19.

[19] Cf. H. PROBST, *Paulus und der Brief*, 315.

[20] Cf. above c. 1 n. 6.

[21] Cf. above c. 1 n. 17, 18.

[22] Probst's attempt to force on 1Cor 8,1-13, another independent literary and argumentative unit, the function of *exordium* in a larger rhetorical schema has been noted in J. MURPHY-O'CONNOR, *Paul et l'art épistolaire*, 124.

[23] Cf. H. PROBST, *Paulus und der Brief*, 318.

to the ABA' model[24]. In sum, we can conclude this section by re-stating what was already indicated above, viz., that 1Cor 5,1-13 is an independent self-contained unit, both from a literary and rhetorical perspective.

2. The «ABA'» Pattern and Its Interpretive Significance

In the preceding section, and earlier, in chapter 1, we have referred to the rhetorical compositional arrangement[25] known as ABA' or the concentric model[26]. This pattern is especially prevalent in 1Cor[27] and 1Cor 5,1-13 is considered to be the «A» or first section of the concentrically arranged macro-unit, 1Cor 5-6. Moreover, on further examination one notes that 1Cor 5,1-13 is itself arranged concentrically. This is especially evident in the distribution of vocabulary[28]. According to the aba' patterning 1Cor 5,1-13 can be schematically presented as follows:

> a 5,1-5 Failure of Discernment: Identifying and reacting to porneia
> b 5,6-8 Negative ramifications for the community
> a' 5,9-13 Failure of Discernment: Identifying and reacting to pornos/ponèros.

Apropos of such a compositional pattern, there are a number of scholars[29] who would hold, in light of the axiom that form determines meaning,

---

[24] A=7,1-16; B=7,17-24; A'=7,25-40; On the chapter's ABA' pattern and the structure of each of the sub-units see the excellent treatment in G. BARBAGLIO, *La prima lettera ai Corinzi*, 325-364.

[25] To avoid equivocation, here we use the term «arrangement» not «structure» to refer to the compositional pattern. On the distinction cf. J.-N. ALETTI, «Problèmes de composition», 213.

[26] The ABA' pattern is characterized by an oscillation between a topic introduced in A/a, an apparently unrelated topic introduced in B/b followed by a return in A'/a' to the original topic introduced in A/a, even if in A'/a' it is treated under a different aspect or more broadly. See the discussion in J.J. COLLINS, «Chiasmus, ABA' Pattern», 579ff.

[27]

1Cor 5-6	1Cor 7	1Cor 11,17-34	1Cor 12-14
A - 5,1-13	A - 7,1-16	A - 11,17-22	A - 12,4-30
B - 6,1-11	B - 7,17-24	B - 11,23-26	B - 12,31-14,1
A' - 6,12-20	A'- 7,25-40	A'- 11,28-34	A' - 14,2-40

[28] In a = vv. 1-5, key terms are *porneia* and *pornos*. *Porneia* occurs 2x in 5,1 and *to praxas* (5,2), *ton katergasamenon* (5,3) and *ton toiouton* (5,5), are all synonyms for *pornos*. In b = vv. 6-8, key lexemes are *zymè/zymoô*, *azymos*. The noun *zymè* is found at 5,6.7.8; the verb *zymoô* at 5,6; the adjective *azymos* at 5,7.8 Note also, in «b», the contrast terms *palaia* at 5,7.8 and *neos*, at 5,7. In a'= v. 9-13, the term *pornos* reappears (5,9.10.11), returning the discussion, but on a broader level, to *pornoi*.

[29] Cf. e.g. N.W. LUND, *Chiasmus*, esp. 145-196; A. DI MARCO, «Der Chiasmus» esp. § 3.10.3; R.E. MAN, «The Value», 146-157; J. BRECK, «Biblical Chiasmus», 70-74; A. BRUNOT, *Le génie littéraire*; C. TALBERT, «Artistry», 362-366.

that an ABA' pattern, whether notable in macro-units as for example 1Cor 5-6, or micro-units as for example 5,1-13, is a guide or key to the interpretation of the text[30]. Note is taken of the fact that in an ABA' arrangement, the unit pivots around a center, or B section. Based on spatial logic it is then held that this center is the conceptual center[31]. It is also noted that this center or B section often has no ostensible thematic link[32] to the discussion in the adjacent units. Scholars explain this phenomenon by asserting that far from being an interruption, the center section is always the high plane[33] or summit[34] to which Paul moves the discussion in order to discuss general principles which illuminate his whole discussion. According to Brunot, it is precisely here in the B section, often perceived as a digression or erraticism, that one finds « la clef de voûte »[35] of Pauline literary architecture. He insists further, that the strictest link of internal logic unites these B sections to the adjacent text segments[36]. B. Standaert essentially concurs with these views and, adding insights culled from the classical handbooks of rhetoric about *digressio*, in the technical sense of the term, he affirms that in the *digressio*, one arrives at the summit of Paul's exposé which subtly becomes the true center of his discourse[37]. Greater familiarity with this ancient rhetorical technique is essential for understanding how persuasive discourse was set out in the New Testament and, in particular, in the letters of Paul[38].

---

[30] «Der Chiasmus ist keine einfache künstleriche Verschönerung, sondern ein Schlüssel zur Bedeutung [...]» (A. DI MARCO, «Chiasmus in der Bibel», 55).

[31] J. BRECK comments, «Because of the central focus, genuine chiasm is able to set in relief the central idea or theme the writer wishes to express», (cf. «Biblical Chiasmus», 73). In a similar vein cf. R. MAN, «The Value», 147-148. Note that for these authors «chiasm» includes concentric patterns.

[32] Attempts to impose thematic unity on an ABA' unit are misguided, cf. e.g. P. RICHARDSON, «Judgement», 337-357; ID., «Judgement in Sexual Matters», 37-58. Richardson's working assumption, that if an ABA' pattern represents literary unity, thematic unity can also be expected, is incorrect. Cf. above n. 26, 27.

[33] Cf. A. SABATIER, *L'apôtre Paul*, 77.

[34] Cf. A. BRUNOT, *Le génie littéraire*, 50.

[35] A. BRUNOT, *Le génie littéraire*, 50.

[36] A. BRUNOT, *Le génie littéraire*, 50.

[37] Cf. B. STANDAERT, «1Cor 13», 127.

[38] «La *digressio* recoupe l'argument à un niveau plus sublime et plus fondamental tel que ne fait toute l'argumentation qui l'entoure[...]. Plus on se familiarise avec toute la rhétorique ancienne, plus on découvrira combien le discours persuasif religieux, tel qu'il joue dans les écrits du Nouveau Testament, et notamment dans les lettres de Paul, emprunté des stratégies propres à la culture ambiante qui sont parfois fort différentes des nôtres» (B. STANDAERT, «Lecture rhétorique», 190-191).

The use of this methodological approach[39] to the text would appear to allow for easy access to the interpretive key of a passage and therewith guarantee accuracy in interpretation. However, caution needs to be exercised. The method is avowedly heuristic[40], has potential for eisegesis, and its key assumption regarding the importance of the center is questionable. As Murphy-O'Connor asks, «L'element central est-il en fait l'énoncé clé dans l'unité littéraire délimitée par la structure concentrique?»[41]. We can only agree with his response, «il serait difficile, sinon impossible, de fournir une réponse affirmative convaincante en ce qui concerne la grande majorité des chiasmes publiés». Spatial arrangement does not, of itself, necessarily signal which segment of the schema is more important and sometimes attempts to show the logical connection between this alleged high point of the discourse and the adjacent units are not all together convincing[42]. Moreover, what happens when different centers are proposed? For example, W. Beardslee[43] has recently suggested that 1Cor 5 is composed of two main sections: 5,1-8 and 5,9-13[44]. He claims that 5,1-8 is arranged in the aba' pattern as follows: a = 5,1-2 Paul rebukes his hearers for arrogant toleration of the wrongdoing; b = 5,3-5 Paul shows how he and the church will jointly deal with the problem; a'= 5,6-8 Paul returns to boasting. If we were to use Beardslee's proposed center of 1Cor 5, i.e., vv. 3-5 (which appears to be

---

[39] The study of surface or stylistic structures may be called «rhetorical criticism» as proposed by Muilenberg (cf. above, c. 3 n. 208). It is also referred to as «Analyse structurelle» in contradistinction to «Analyse structurale» which is concerned with syntax. Cf. M. GIRARD, *Les psaumes*, 13-14.

[40] This method presupposes a literary theory about which, «on n'en sait rien» (M. GIRARD, *Les psaumes*, 15).

[41] Cf. J. MURPHY-O'CONNOR, *Paul et l'art épistolaire*, 138.

[42] For example, it is asserted that 6,1-11 is the interpretive key of the macro-unit 1Cor 5-6. However, a convincing demonstration of whether and how this unit contains principles that illuminate the discussions in the adjacent passages is still lacking. Curiously, despite his own skepticism, Murphy-O'Connor has recently asserted that 6,1-11 is the key to this whole concentric unit (cf. *Paul et l'art épistolaire*, 140-141). Unfortunately, the author does not explain how what he alleges to be Paul's point in the B section, i.e., «la puissance réconciliatrice de l'amour en résolvant elle-même ses problèmes plutôt que de recourir à des procès», does in fact illuminate what is said in A = 5,1-13 and A'= 6,12-20.

[43] W. BEARDSLEE, *First Corinthians*, 47.

[44] Beardslee gives no compelling reason to consider vv. 9-13 a separate section nor any explanation of how, if at all, vv. 9-13 are related to vv. 1-8. Moreover, he later contradicts himself saying that, «the A [...] A' pattern also rounds off the whole chapter, as v. 13 repeats the command of v. 2 in the words of a biblical quotation [...]» (47-8). Having noted the *inclusio* created by vv. 2 and 13 and having stated that v. 13 is part of A', it is curious that Beardslee divides c. 5 at v. 8 and claims that the aba' arrangement only extends through vv. 1-8.

incorrect), then Paul's judgement pronouncement would be the most important aspect of the passage rather than his instruction in vv. 6-8, the verses which we, and others[45], recognize as the central section. This discrepancy in identifying the center section is just one more indication that one needs to proceed with caution in applying this method and making claims based on it.

To prescribe caution is not to deny any value to this approach. In fact, the recognition of the surface compositional pattern is a necessary and valuable preliminary step in approaching a text. The arrangement underscores the artistic quality with which macro- and micro-units were composed, manifests the ABA'/aba' unit's coherence on the literary level, indicates the extent of a unit and helps to determine the original text sequence. This latter is especially important for saving perfectly valid text sequences from the imputation of incoherence which can and has lead to partitioning. These are all positive and important insights to be gained from studied attention to the compositional pattern. However, one must keep in mind that the concentric pattern «describes primarily the movement of thought but not the thought itself»[46]. Hence, it would be more appropriate to say that «form enhances meaning»[47] rather than determines it.

In light of these considerations, one is led to admit that the concentric pattern is not a sufficient sole guide to the interpretation of the text and to look to corroborating evidence to determine what Paul's central concern is. Though the interpretive key to a concentrically arranged unit may be shown, at times, to coincide with the spatial center of such an arrangement, it does not seem advisable to make this a starting assumption.

3. Conclusion to Chapter 4

In this chapter we have defined the limits of the rhetorical unit which turn out to be co-extensive with that of the literary unit. Thus 1Cor 5,1-13 can be examined as a self-contained argumentative unit. Further, we asked if the particular literary arrangement by which this chapter is composed is a sufficient guide to its interpretation. As we believe to have shown, though rhetorical compositional techniques need to be taken into consideration, a rhetorical pattern such as the ABA' model is, by itself, an insufficient basis on which to posit the interpretation of a unit. As we go

---

[45] Cf. e.g. G. FORKMANN, *Limits*, 140.

[46] I. THOMSON, *Chiasmus*, 25. According to the author, this holds true for the chiastic pattern as well (cf. 38).

[47] I. THOMSON, *Chiasmus*, 39.

forward with our rhetorical analysis of 1Cor 5, other factors may emerge which may contribute to affirming that in 1Cor 5, what can be considered its «b» or center section, vv. 6-8, bears the import of the passage. If this is so however, it must be established, not assumed, as we have already noted.

We are now ready to turn to the analysis of 1Cor 5 where attention will be focused on the way Paul unfolds his argument, the relationship of its parts and the types of proofs which he sets out to persuade the Corinthians to recognize the evil and take action.

CHAPTER V

Rhetorical Analysis of 1Cor 5,1-13

1. Introduction

Various studies, to which we have already referred, have convincingly shown that in his letter writing Paul adopted and adapted the strategies, features and some of the *topoi* of rhetoric in order to guide, mold, instruct and persuade the communities he founded and continued to pastor through his written discourse. However, this does not mean that in order to argue persuasively this or that point or teaching Paul restricted himself to writing according to a rigidly defined rhetorical *dispositio*. In fact, as we saw earlier in chapters 2, 3 and 4, rhetorical analysis aimed at showing how texts conform to predictable patterns can be carried out at the expense of the text which may have forced upon it an ideal schema to which it does not configure. To avoid abusing the text and to take advantage of rhetorical analysis in a way that can produce more profitable results, our analysis will focus on the types of proof[1] Paul sets out in order to argue persuasively and on how the parts of the argument are logically related. In this way we hope to comprehend as accurately as possible what Paul's argument and aims are here in 1Cor 5.

2. The Time Frame of 1Cor 5,1-13

If we wish to avoid hasty judgements about exactly what Paul is hoping to accomplish in 1Cor 5 and what his expectations for his audience may

---

[1] According to ARISTOTLE, *Ars Rhetorica*, I.II, 3-7, proofs were of three kinds: those based on *ethos, pathos* and *logos*. The first two constituted appeals to the emotions and were crucial for molding and transforming attitudes and behavior; *logos* refers to the logical arguments, whether inductive or deductive, used to persuade the audience, cf. QUINTILIAN, *Institutio*, VI. c. 2.

have been, it would be well to keep in mind from the outset that there are three time frames that converge in this one passage.

There is the past in which an incestuous marriage has been contracted and is presumably still going on at the time the Corinthian community receives Paul's letter calling for the termination of the man's[2] affiliation with the community. No proviso[3] accompanies the call for expulsion and the suggestion that the offender's obduracy was the reason for the unconditional call for expulsion appears unlikely[4]. Recently, W. Deming[5] has suggested in view of the discussion in 6,1-11, that a community member, representing a «morally indignant» segment of the community, brought court proceedings against the incestuous man[6]. The author further speculates that the accuser/s lost the case and also hypothesizes on what grounds the case was probably lost[7]. In Deming's reconstruction of events, the offender's court victory becomes the alleged basis for the boasting by the offender's partisans whom Paul takes to task in 1Cor 5[8].

---

[2] On whether the offender of 1Cor 5 is identifiable with the one to be reconciled to the community mentioned in 2Cor 2,5ff., see the discussion in V. FURNISH, *II Corinthians*, 163-166. The growing scholarly consensus, to which Furnish adheres, is that the individuals are not identifiable.

[3] *Pace* B. ROSNER, «Corporate Responsibility» 473, it cannot be said that Paul «demanded the expulsion of the sinner unless he separate from his illicit partner». Such a condition is not even insinuated in 1Cor 5. Rosner is paralleling 1Cor 5 with Ezra 10 where dissolution of mixed marriages and repentance were the conditions set for rectifying the situation. While it is true that both passages concern illicit marriages prohibited in the Torah, with regard to incest, the Torah states no provision for repentance or separation to avoid punishment. Cf. also Jub 33,1-17 where it is expressly stated with regard to Reuben's sin of incest that «there is no forgiveness for it but only that both of them shall be uprooted from the midst of the people» (cf. 33,17).

[4] *Pace* G.W.H. LAMPE, «Church Discipline», 345.

[5] Cf. W. DEMING, «The Unity», 289-312.

[6] Deming hypothesizes charges that could have been levelled against the offender (295). These go beyond the text information. However, Deming justifies this by claiming that «5:1 reflects the manner in which Paul chooses to address the situation, not the original, unsuccessful charges that may have been made by the Corinthians» (295 n. 51). While it must be admitted that 5,1 represents Paul's presentation of the issue, still there are no text grounds to support Deming's speculations that a group or its representative charged the offender. On the possibility of charges relating to a dowry, Deming draws on the studies of J.K. Chow and A. Clarke (both cited above c. 3 n. 6) but again there is no text support for such a conclusion.

[7] One reason suggested is that «the man could have been an adopted son, confusing the issue of adultery or incest» (295). Reasons with this degree of speculation do not contribute to the credibility of Deming's argument.

[8] Deming's reconstruction leads to his identification of two factions: a) the offender's partisans, i.e., the boasters of 1Cor 5 and b) the accuser/s of 1Cor 6,1-11. According to Deming, Paul takes the former to task in 1Cor 5 for vaunting the offender's alleged court victory and castigates the latter in 6,1-11 for having recourse to pagan courts. While Paul does denounce recourse to pagan courts still it can be

This study is a clever attempt to explain the logical connection of 1Cor 5-6, a connection which some scholars deny and others have explained unsatisfactorily according to Deming[9]. Nonetheless, his six-part[10] reconstruction of events is built on a series of speculations[11] for which the text offers little support. These speculations do not compel in this reader the confidence that Deming seems to believe is warranted. The text gives us no indication that the offender had been previously reproved by Paul or the community or taken to court by some of the community. In fact, there is no indication that the community was even grieved by this case of incest[12]. On the contrary, what can be reasonably inferred from the text is that the community allowed the offender to live openly with impunity[13].

In this same past time, the community[14] had obviously rendered a positive judgement about this relationship, not only approving it, but making it

---

objected against Deming that there is nothing to suggest that the legal proceedings in question in 1Cor 6,1-11 involve the offender of 5,1-13 (cf. below n. 11). Moreover, in 6,2 Paul uses the phrase *kritèriôn elachistôn*. If Paul intends that the *pragma* of 6,1 is just one of these «trivial cases» – and this appears to be the implication – then it is difficult to concede that *pragma* refers to incest, which judging by the response in 5,1-13, Paul hardly considered trivial. Second, there is nothing to suggest that Paul was scolding a particular faction, the «morally indignant» in 6,1-11. Moreover, there is a certain incongruity in postulating that a segment of the community was morally indignant enough, presumably from a Christian standpoint, to go to court over this sexual offense but not morally sensitive enough from a Christian standpoint to realize that pagan courts were no place for Christian affairs to be settled.

[9] See Deming's brief but essential and up-to-date review of scholarship on this subject, 289-293.

[10] See Deming's outline, 294. Based on the text information, we can be certain of only elements one and six in Deming's reconstructed scenario: 1) a community member committed an offense; 6) this matter was referred to Paul for his response.

[11] Key to Deming's whole argument is to show that the case of 6,1-11 is a case against the incestuous man of c. 5 and this involves establishing the referent of the term *pragma* in 6,1. Deming touches only lightly on this issue (cf. 297 n. 30) and has not convincingly established the connotation of *pragma*.

[12] *Pace* G. FORKMANN, *Limits*, who states, «the community is criticized for not driving out the sinner from their midst when they were grieved by the case of fornication» (139). However, six lines later he appears to contradict himself, stating: «The Corinthians have winked at the fornicator, and they have not been grieved by his behavior». Based on the text information, the latter appears to be correct.

[13] Reproof was the first step in dealing with offenders at Qumran. If reproof failed, the obdurate offender underwent partial expulsion, and then, as a last resort, full expulsion, cf. G. FORKMANN, *Limits*, 46-68. Forkmann sees Paul operating within such a process, though he denies that Paul was influenced by Qumran (cf. 181). However, nothing in 1Cor 5 suggests that the expulsion came as the end of a process. Even though at 2Cor 13,1-2 warnings are mentioned, we do not know if this passage relates to the offender of 1Cor 5. Hence, there is no hard evidence that the offender was reproved prior to the expulsion announced in canonical 1Cor.

[14] Paul uses the 2nd person plural throughout the chapter.

the object of boasting. Subsequent to the «past» of the initiation of the relationship and prior to the «present» of canonical 1Cor 5, there was an intermediate time frame in which Paul, apprised of the relationship between the community member and his step-mother, made a judgement about the situation, and issued an expulsion[15] sentence. In canonical 1Cor, Paul now intervenes to correct the matter[16]. He communicates his decision to the community and outlines some type of disciplinary process (cf. 5,3-5).

Some questions emerge from these observations which will be addressed in the course of the following treatment of c. 5. What is the role Paul is expecting his audience to perform[17]? In 1Cor 5, is Paul asking the community to judge the *pornos* in its turn? Are they simply to execute the pre-determined sanction? If the community is called on to make a judgement what criteria are proposed? On what criteria did Paul make *his* judgement against the individual? Since a judgement is contained in these 13 verses, one might conclude 1Cor 5 is a unit of judicial rhetoric. However, this may be a premature assumption[18]. The matter of the incestuous relationship was referred to Paul presumably for his judgement, which, in any event, he gave. This is certain from the text. But this does not necessarily mean that in 1Cor 5, which represents a new moment of reflection on the situation, Paul is presenting the community with the task of judging the offender. On the other hand, that Paul has judged does not necessarily preclude that the community, too, is being called on to discern and render a judgement. Determinations have to be made in light of the text.

---

[15] The expulsion is variously expressed: *arthè* (5,2); *paradounai* (5,5); in symbolic language, *ekkatharate tèn palaian zymè* (5,7); *exarate ton ponèron* (5,13).

[16] It has been claimed that Paul wrote 1Cor 5 because «the congregation had chosen to follow the lead of other prophets» and had, at the instigation of the latter, resisted Paul's previous attempt to clear this matter up (cf. P. MINEAR, «Christ», 342-343). However, there is no evidence that prior to canonical 1Cor Paul had intervened in this case of incest and met community resistance.

[17] The rhetorical genre adopted by the writer follows from the role the writer expects the readers to perform, cf. W. WUELLNER, «Paul as Pastor», 55.

[18] It is also premature to take 5,1-13 as a piece of deliberative rhetoric on the assumption that 1Cor as a whole is deliberative. In line with M. Mitchell, B. Witherington has recently suggested that 1Cor is deliberative – with the exception of c. 9, which has a semi-forensic cast, and c. 13 which is epideictic – and considers 5,1-13 as a piece of deliberation in which Paul would have engaged had he been in Corinth in person (Cf. B. WITHERINGTON, Conflicts, 46).

3. Addressing the Issue

Paul begins his treatment in 5,1a with the remark, «*holôs akouetai*[19] *en hymin porneia*». Curiously he does not begin with, «it is heard that a man is living with his father's wife», which one might reasonably suppose to have been the contents of the report. By stating the issue as he does, Paul already indicates that his attention is directed to the level of community[20] and the problem of unchecked immorality within its confines to which the case of incest attests. Paul's concern for the ultimate redemption of the individual offender may be discerned in 5,5, if *to pneuma* is understood as an anthropological designation[21]. However, apart from this, Paul has nothing more to say about the individual, and this adds weight to the conviction that the community, and not the individual, was his primary focus here[22]. This is further confirmed by the terms of the *inclusio* in which the twice-stated goal is to rid the community of this sinful presence. Moreover, the concern of vv. 6-8, i.e., the purity and holiness of the community reinforces this claim that Paul's primary concern is for the community whose sanctified life is threatened by the continued presence of this evil in its midst[23].

Apropos of the threat posed to the community by the incest, we must consider M. Mitchell's recent proposal that the incest case threatened the community's social-political unity which Paul is allegedly attempting to preserve through his deliberating response to the issue in 1Cor 5[24]. The author brings to bear on her reading of 1Cor 5 an impressive amount of information about Greek political theories, including discussions on political unity and factionalism and the function of expulsion from the *polis* as a way to secure the unity of the political body. Mitchell reads 1Cor 5 against the background of political factionalism and considers this a unit of deliberative rhetoric with the issue at stake the unity of the community and the key question for deliberation: is the man/his deed good for the unity of the community or not? For text evidence Mitchell relies essentially on the occurrence of the terms *pephysiômenoi* (5,2), and *kauchèma* (5,6) to support her reading. In view of Paul's use of these terms in 1Cor 1-4 which Mitchell, in light of Greek parallels, takes as

---

[19] This is an example of the perfective present, equivalent in meaning to *legetai*, cf. Blass – Debrunner, § 322. At times it is translated, «it is actually reported» (cf. e.g. RSV, NRSV, NAB).

[20] Correctly noted in G. HARRIS, «The Beginnings», 5.

[21] Cf. below n. 82.

[22] *Pace* C.K. BARRETT, *1 Corinthians*, 127.

[23] Cf. G. FORKMANN, *Limits*, 141 and C.J. ROETZEL, *Judgement*, 118.

[24] Cf. M. MITCHELL, *Paul*, 112-116.

lexical proof that Paul was referring to political factionalism, the author argues that the recurrence of these terms in 1Cor 5 requires that this chapter also be read against the background of political factionalism. Mitchell's working assumption that parallels in vocabulary point to parallel situations, which brings her to read all of 1Cor against the background of political factionalism, is seriously flawed as noted by Pogoloff[25]. Moreover, even if it were proven beyond doubt that the vocabulary in cc. 1-4 points to a discussion of political factionalism, it would have to be proved, not assumed, that all recurrences of this vocabulary in other parts of the letter also refer to political factionalism. Hence claims to the effect that the offender's incestuous relationship exacerbated the factionalism[26] or that his expulsion was aimed at securing the unity of the Corinthian church, understood as a new political group[27] are circular. Based on the text there is little to suggest that Paul is engaged in deliberating over whether it is expedient to expel the man because his incestuous marriage constitutes a point of contention in the community, understood as a new political group. The problem, as we learn from the text (cf. 5,6), is that the incestuous man is a source of contamination. It is precisely because he is a source of contamination that he is to be expelled from the community[28]. Whether he is a creator of *discordia* or bad for the proper «mix» essential to *homonoia* is beside the point[29]. Were there no dissension and were the community unanimous in the conviction that this incestuous relationship was a good thing, this expulsion would still be necessary and justified because this evil has negative ramifications for the sanctified life of the community. Finally, even when lexical parallels are notable, it is short-sighted to fail to consider that Paul may have employed all of these rhetorical terms in a transferred sense[30], concerned not with the political *homonoia* of a *miktè politeia*[31] but with the community's corporate sanctity. Understanding the discussion in c. 5 in purely political terms unfortunately obscures the religio-ethical character of the issue and the concern for the holiness of the community expressly understood as *hè*

---

[25] Cf. S. POGOLOFF, *Logos and Sophia*, 90.

[26] Cf. M. MITCHELL, *Paul*, 112.

[27] M. MITCHELL, *Paul*, 115.

[28] Correctly noted by J. NEYREY, *Paul*, 91, 151. See also, R.F. O'TOOLE, *Who is a Christian?*, 44.

[29] Mitchell's understanding of *phyrama* at 5,6 and *synanamignysthai* at 5,9 in political terms obscures this point. A similar observation is made by W. SCHRAGE, *1 Korinther*, 368.

[30] As observed by B. WITHERINGTON, *Conflicts*, 75. Meeks suggests that the political terms in 1Cor 12,12ff. should also be taken in a transferred sense (cf. W. MEEKS, *The Moral World*, 131).

[31] Cf. M. MITCHELL, *Paul*, 114.

ekklesia tou theou (1Cor 1,2; 10,32; 11,22; 15,9). As we continue our study this will become increasingly evident.

4. The Reference to the Pagans

Before specifying that the *porneia* in question is incest Paul inserts the phrase, *«kai toiautè porneia hètis oude en tois ethnesin»*. Some scholars take the mention of the pagans as an indication that Paul was concerned with scandal[32]. It is then alleged that the scandal to the pagans is the motive for Paul's severe judgement[33]. Though initially this may sound reasonable, further considerations point up both the improbability of this view and the inconsequence of scandal to Paul's response. First, if scandal to the pagans were the motive for Paul's severe response it is curious that beyond this one mention at 5,1, pagans or pagan sensibilities are not mentioned again in this chapter. Second, to read the mention of the pagans as a reference to scandal assumes that Paul was referring to an actual historical situation in which pagans, aware of this one community member's incestuous marriage with his step-mother, were actually scandalized. We do not know this. Moreover, the phrase is used rhetorically[34], as we will argue below, and does not necessarily provide a window on to the actual historical situation confronting Paul. Third, even though it cannot be denied absolutely that scandal accompanied this situation, still, to make it the motive for Paul's severe response is to establish a logical cause and effect connection between the two which is not supported by the text. Whether there was scandal or not, Paul's severe response would still be forthcoming because of the sin's contaminating effect on the community[35]. The issue of scandal is, in a manner of speaking, beside the point here. As we shall now see, the mention of the pagans plays an important role in Paul's rhetorical strategy in relation to the reaction he wishes to provoke in the community.

---

[32] Cf. e.g. I. HAVENER, «A Curse», 335, 341; D. DAUBE, «Pauline Contributions», 224; C. TALBERT, *Reading Corinthians*, 19; F.F. BRUCE, *Corinthinas*, 54; B. ALLO, *Première épître aux Corinthiens*, 122.

[33] Havener speaks of the sin's «particularly scandalous nature» which calls for a «harsher punishment upon the offender» (I. HAVENER, «A Curse», 341). It has also been suggested that Paul was especially concerned that the scandal would have negative ramifications *vis-à-vis* his evangelizing efforts among the pagans; hence his severe response (Cf. C. TALBERT, *Reading Corinthians*, 19).

[34] C. Spicq considers the phrase an example of those hyperbolic phrases, current among contemporary moralists and lawyers, used to stress the enormity of a fact (cf. C.SPICQ, *Théologie morale*, II, 818).

[35] Cf. above § 3.

5. Proof by *Pathos*

The reference to the pagans in 5,1 functions as an appeal to the emotions of the Corinthians for the purpose of inducing shame[36] which becomes a motivation for change[37]. According to the handbooks of ancient rhetoric, appeals to the emotions were rightly placed and most effective at the beginning or conclusion of the argument[38]. Such appeals were an important part of argumentation since, as Aristotle noted, «the emotions were all those affections which cause men to change their opinion in regard to their judgements»[39]. In fact, a person could deliver quite different judgements depending on which emotion influenced him[40]. Moreover, ancient rhetors perceived that among the emotions, shame was one of the more powerful to tap in order to induce change. As Cicero observed, the desire not to be disgraced was a very strong incentive to change one's thoughts or behavior[41].

Employing what appears to be good rhetorical strategy and in keeping with good rhetorical *taxis*, Paul begins his argument in 1Cor 5, capitalizing on the shame that this comparison with the pagans could arouse in order to move the community to change. Among the pagans, a notoriously immoral segment of society, such a *porneia* is not heard[42], (5,1b) but it is heard of among Corinthian Christians, among the ones called holy[43]! The implicit comparison[44] between what Corinthians do, tolerate and are puffed up about[45] and what pagans do not do[46] or tolerate[47], suffices as

---

[36] On the definition of shame and what evokes it, cf. ARISTOTLE, *Ars Rhetorica*, II.VI, 1-27.

[37] Cf. above n. 1.

[38] Cf. e.g. CICERO, *De Oratore*, II, 77.310-11; QUINTILIAN, *Institutio*, Bk 8, preface, 6. Quintilian adds elsewhere at IV.II, 116 that it is advisable to avoid waiting until the *peroratio* to appeal to the emotions, for then the appeal may be too late to be effective.

[39] ARISTOTLE, *Ars Rhetorica*, II.I, 8.

[40] ARISTOTLE, *Ars Rhetorica*, I.II, 5

[41] CICERO, *De Partitione*, XXVI, 91.

[42] The phrase «kai toiautè porneia hètis oude en tois ethnesin» lacks a verb, as attested by the best MSS evidence, P46 A ℵ B C D F. In cases of ellipsis when the preceding verb makes good sense it should be taken up to supply for the omission, cf. Blass – Debrunner, § 479. In the present case, *akouetai* makes perfect sense and reinforces the negative comparison, «heard that there is among you such *porneia* which is not *heard* of among the pagans».

[43] Cf. 1Cor 1,2 «hègiasmenois en Christô Iesou, klètois hagiois»; cf. also 6,11.

[44] One of the functions of comparison in an argument is to serve as a quick proof, cf. W.J. BRANDT, *The Rhetoric of Argumentation*, 109.

[45] Cf. 1Cor 5,2 «pephysiômenoi este». The perfect periphrastic, indicating a continuing condition, is often employed for rhetorical purposes to add force, cf. Blass – Debrunner, § 352. It could be possible then to translate the phrase, «and you are still puffed up».

proof that the brother is guilty of grave transgression and that the community's moral reasoning, whatever may have guided it, is defective and its behavior reprehensible. To vaunt in what even pagans know and consider to be wrong is simply shameful.

Here Paul sets up no formal judicial process whereby he directly indicts the offender nor does he argue for the man's guilt and punishment based on an accumulation of facts deriving directly from this particular case. Rather, Paul first allows the community to be confronted with the fact of its own bad judgement and comportment with regard to a matter that even pagans acknowledge to be wrong. The shame induced by the comparison should disturb and create a sense of dissatisfaction within the community sufficient to put the first crack in its patina of arrogance and move it to see that change of opinion and action is needed if for no other reason than to efface this disgrace. This is hardly the highest or most noble stimulus for change. In fact it is a negative stimulus. However, what matters is that it is sufficient to motivate the audience to be willing to change its opinions and behavior. This is the function and ultimate purpose of the appeal to emotion[48]. Thus Paul paves the way toward achieving his ultimate aim which is to move the community to assume its responsibility to take appropriate action.

Though Paul has judged the matter as evil, still on the level of text argumentation we can observe how he sets to work to create the condition necessary for rendering the community amenable to changing its attitude toward its own judgement and comportment relative to this matter. Paul does not bother to consider and refute the criteria by which the community came to its evaluation of the incest and deemed it a cause for boasting. It does not matter how they reasoned[49]. Their judgement is simply wrong. Once the community acknowledges that its judgement and comportment is by societal standards unsatisfactory and is motivated by

---

[46] That incest was not to be found, or was not done among pagans is no doubt an exaggeration. The exaggerated comparison proves the point without need for enthymatic argumentation, cf. ARISTOTLE, *Ars Rhetorica*, II, 24,4; QUINTILIAN, *Institutio*, VIII.IV,II.

[47] Officially pagan law proscribed incestuous marriages, cf. *Institutions of Gaius*, «De Nuptius», § 56-64. Included among the banned unions was marriage with one who was his father's wife (cf. § 63); cf. also CICERO, *Pro Cluentio* 5,14; 6,15; Roman law and punishments for incest are discussed in A. CLARKE, *Secular and Christian Leadership*, esp. 77-79.

[48] Cf. e.g. DIO CHRYSOSTOM, *Discourses*, 4.77-78. In Diogenes' speech to Alexander the aim was to arouse the emotions of the latter in order to move him to change; cf. also C. PERELMAN – L. OLBRECHTS-TYTECA, *The New Rhetoric*, 47.

[49] Schmithals claim that Paul was unable to understand Corinthian reasoning would appear to be incorrect, cf. above, c. 3 n. 4.

this shame to change, then Paul can take up the issue on another level, viz. why the sin is a peril to the community. On level one, vv. 1-2, Paul takes up the issue in respect to a broader social context, drawing on an emotional appeal that puts the spotlight on the boaster's deficient moral reasoning and deplorable deportment. On the second level, vv. 6-8, Paul will deal with the issue in a theological context, setting out reasons which show why this situation is incompatible with the community's sinless status and how the sin negatively affects the whole community. After this, Paul will return to the ineptitude of the community in regard to identifying and judging who is bad for the community.

6. Medial Summary

Thus far we have attempted to show that the cause and effect logic which connects the notion of scandal, allegedly suggested by the reference to the pagans, to the issue of Paul's judgement and its severity is incorrect. The text pieces are not logically related in this manner. Rather, this reference to the pagans constitutes an argument by comparison in which the «holy ones» are shown to come up on the short side *vis-à-vis* the pagans with regard to judgement and behavior. This is shame-evoking and this shame becomes for the community the incentive for change. Logically then, the reference to the pagans relates to the change of mind and willingness to act that Paul is hoping to generate in the Corinthians and not to his own judgement or to the severity of the sanction he announces.

Though a negative stimulus, the evocation of shame is a positive rhetorical strategy. Through it Paul gains access to the community's emotional lever which must be pushed in order to dispel its arrogance and open it up toward change. That Paul begins with a rhetorical tactic that aims at establishing a willing and cooperative spirit within the community betrays his rhetorical skill. But more importantly, it betrays his concern for the community which he brings forward step by step in what is ultimately a process of conversion and recommitment to the values and behavior consonant with the reality of its new mode of being in Christ. Such a process cannot be effected through force but through skillful persuasion.

7. Shaming and the Alleged Polemic Over Authority

Before leaving the discussion of this reference to the pagans we want to enquire whether there is anything further to observe in its regard relative to whether 1Cor 5 needs to be read under the lens of polemic about authority. In this vein we will examine the dynamic of shame. How does it work? Does it imply anything about the relationship between the speaker/writer and the audience? If so, what significance may this have regarding the alleged polemical relationship that 1Cor 5 is said to reflect?

Regarding the first question we begin by noting that by referring to pagan behavior and moral reasoning, Paul essentially insinuates that there exists a societal consensus that incest is wrong. If the pagans consider this wrong then everyone must hold this to be wrong. This universal moral value is set out as a standard against which Corinthian judgement and behavior is initially critiqued. In other words, it is not Paul's behavior or moral reasoning, but that of a collectivity which is first cited as a critical standard. In starting this way, Paul situates himself within a larger sphere of moral discerners. As such, we do not encounter a situation of Paul versus the Corinthians[50]. It is not Paul as an individual figure of authority who reproaches the community. Instead, he cleverly exploits the convergence of the world's values and Christian values with regard to incest, using the concurrence as a point of departure for his argument. Thus, looking at the reference to the pagans from the vantage point of rhetorical strategy, one observes that Paul has set up the situation in such a way that the Corinthians are confronted by something much more comprehensive than just his own authoritative voice[51]. Now if Paul did perceive the situation reflected in 1Cor 5 as posing an intentional threat to his authority then it would appear rather curious that here, at the outset, he should risk underplaying his personal authority by introducing a universal norm of decency as the first critical voice raised against the Corinthians rather than his own. Of course Paul's own voice of criticism is one with that of society here. However, by that very fact, it does not predominate[52]. Based on these observations, one could deduce that: a) if Paul is not exigent about asserting his authority here, the probability is high that its contestation was not at issue and b) the incest and boasting should probably not be read as intentional challenges to Paul's authority. These seem to be reasonable deductions which, added to the many observations made in the preceding chapters, continue to suggest that it is misleading and unfounded to read this chapter through the lens of polemic over authority. A consideration of the second question, regarding the dynamics of shame, will, we believe, further support this suggestion.

---

[50] Cf. above Introduction n. 17.

[51] Calling upon universal values or opinions to form a kind of testimony or critique is good rhetorical strategy. Such testimony is supplemental, supports but does not necessarily constitute the basis on which a judgement is rendered, cf. QUINTILIAN, *Institutio*, V.XI, 36.

[52] Paul's emphatically placed «I» is reserved until 5,3.

In discussing shame, Aristotle observes that two elements are necessary in order to induce this emotion[53]. The first is material; the second is relational. Succinctly stated, this means that we feel shame not only *over a matter*[54] but *in front of someone*. Now the kind of relationship that exists between two persons or an individual and a group will determine whether and to what degree shame will be evoked. For example, while men will not feel shame before another «whose opinion about truth is greatly despised»[55] they will feel shame before those whose opinions they value[56], those whom they esteem and admire[57], and those who are themselves reproachless[58]. In *breve*, a positive relationship is necessary in order for shame to be evoked. The implications of this for our discussion should be apparent. It is highly unlikely that Paul was so rhetorically unsophisticated as to have begun 1Cor 5 with an emotional appeal, manifestly aimed at evoking shame, if the Corinthians were hostile, had no esteem for him and were, as it has been alleged, acting out their defiance and disdain for his authority through their boasting. Why would a group which so opposed Paul be moved to shame on account of what he thought or the critical standard he set before them? If Paul adopted a shaming strategy whose effectiveness depends on a positive relational dynamic, then the relationship between himself and the community was probably more positive than has been alleged. It would appear then that the dynamics at work, at least so far in this passage, did not involve opposition to Paul's authority.

In sum, in this section we have attempted to show that attention to Paul's rhetoric here can give us insights into the dynamics of this opening reference to the pagans and the strategy of shaming which invite the reconsideration of some fixed views on the alleged polemical character of the relationship that obtained between Paul and the Corinthians as it is understood to be manifested in 1Cor 5. Paul does begin by shaming the Corinthians. This is good rhetorical strategy requiring for its persuasive efficacy positive relations. It is because of both the shameful matter and the positive relationship that Paul can arouse Corinthian emotions for the

---

[53] Cf. ARISTOTLE, *Ars Rhetorica*, II.VI, 1-27.

[54] Both the incest and the boasting over it classify as matter over which to feel shame. See Aristotle's discussion of shameful matter, II.VI, 1-13. A shorter discussion on shameful matter and the persons in front of whom one should feel shame is also found in Sir 41,14-24.

[55] ARISTOTLE, *Ars Rhetorica*, II.VI, 23.

[56] ARISTOTLE, *Ars Rhetorica*, II.VI, 16.

[57] ARISTOTLE, *Ars Rhetorica*, II.VI, 15

[58] ARISTOTLE, *Ars Rhetorica*, II.VI, 20.

purpose of generating the willingness needed to move the Corinthians to consider changing their opinions and adopt appropriate action.

What we have learned by this attentive look at Paul's rhetorical strategy in these opening verses, at least as we have interpreted it so far, raises the positive suspicion that continued attention to the rhetoric will help to achieve a more accurate understanding of Paul's concerns and aims in this chapter.

8. The Judgement Pronouncement: 5,3-5

The brief shaming reference is followed by Paul's counsel to the community to mourn[59] and remove the offender, 2c. Paul belabors none of these points. Then in vv. 3-5, without having made a direct formal case against the offender, stating reasons or giving voice to any possible defense, Paul delivers his judgement and pronounces a sentence, sealing the man's fate. The rapid pace and omission of a developed case against the offender could suggest that Paul was in a great hurry to pronounce his judgement and impose his orders. In comparison to vv. 1-2 where Paul rapid-fires the statement of the issue, shaming comparison and counsel to mourn and expel, all in thirty-eight words, here his pronouncement is enunciated in fifty two words. The length, coupled with the undeniably solemn tone, could suggest that what is of utmost importance is precisely *his* judgement and sentencing.

The impression one could gather is that whatever good rhetorical strategy Paul may have adopted in vv. 1-2, he seems now to have abandoned it, reverting instead to the exercise of power and exchanging what could be considered good persuasive technique for strident, authoritarian, straightforward talk. Seen this way, it is easy to imagine how some scholars[60] could translate these impressions into allegations about the authority-polemic represented by 1Cor 5. Paul could indeed be perceived to be maximizing his power[61], intending to turn this issue into a «face-off» to test whether or not the community will obediently acquiesce to his

---

[59] It is possible but perhaps inadequate to translate *epenthèsate* ingressively, «going into mourning», as in D. DERRETT, «Handing Over to Satan», 170. *Penthein* is not simply the response that Paul is asking for now as a result of his letter, but rather the appropriate response that the community should have adopted and ought to adopt whenever such a situation arises within the community. «You ought to have gone into mourning» (REB); or «should you not have mourned» (NRSV) render the aorist as a perfect, implying continuity where it may not be intended (cf. B. FANNING, *Verbal Aspect*, 260). The indefinite, «should you not rather mourn» is perhaps preferable.

[60] Notably I. HAVENER, «A Curse», 334 and G. FEE, *1 Corinthians*, 195ff.

[61] «This paragraph [i.e. 5,1-5] is a bold expression of his apostolic authority in the church, calling them to conform to his way» (G. FEE, *1 Corinthians*, 199).

authority[62] and carry out his orders[63]. However initially understandable such a reading may appear, it does not mean it is an accurate or valid view of this segment. Granted, in vv. 3-5, Paul introduces performative language[64] and this may create the impression that he has moved out of the realm of persuasive discourse. However, two considerations need to be kept in mind as we proceed. First, vv. 3-5 are only one segment of the larger argument being unfolded in 1Cor 5 and must be considered within that total argumentative context. Second, the introduction of performative language may not necessarily indicate the abandonment of persuasive strategy, for however prescriptive these verses may appear, the execution of what is being prescribed ultimately rests with the community which must be persuaded to act. Hence, though prescriptive, these verses may still be seen, as we intend to argue below, as part of Paul's rhetorical strategy and need not be immediately translated into assertions of authority. Before we look at the pronouncement under the aspect of rhetoric we must first examine the *crux interpretum* in 5,3-5 and then briefly rehearse the scholarly positions on what the sentence could signify in concrete terms.

8.1 *The Crux Interpretum: 5,3-5*

Verses 3-5 constitute a major NT *crux interpretum* which entails the following difficulties: a) specifying what *en tô onomati* qualifies; b) specifying what *syn tè dynamei* qualifies; c) determining whether *paradounai* is to be understood as an independent infinitive or as dependent on *kekrika.*

Translations reflect the range of possible syntactic combinations but no one rendering of these verses is dominant[65]. Among commentators the

---

[62] Cf. G. FEE, *1 Corinthians*, 195.

[63] The community's only role according to I. HAVENER, «A Curse», 335 and H. CONZELMANN, *1 Korinther*, 97, who follows E. KÄSEMANN, «Sentences», 70.

[64] Cf. the definition below, n. 115.

[65] The following are possible:

  a. *en tô onomati* qualifies *synachthentôn*; *syn tè dynamei* qualifies *paradounai* (JB, REB)

  b. *en tô onomati* and *syn tè dynamei* BOTH qualify *synachthentôn* (NEB, NJB)

  c. *en tô onomati* and *syn tè dynamei* BOTH qualify *paradounai* (TOB)

  d. *en tô onomati* qualifies *paradounai*; *syn tè dynamei* qualifies *synachthentôn*. (BJ, Vulgate)

  e. *en tô onomati* qualifies *kekrika*; *syn tè dynamei* qualifies *synachthentôn*. (NAB, AB, NRSV)

  f. *en tô onomati* qualifies *ton katergasamenon*; *syn tè dynamei* qualifies *synachthentôn* (cf. J. MURPHY-O'CONNOR, «1Cor V,3-5», 239-45).

same situation prevails[66]. Various arguments are advanced to support one rendering over another but they are not always built on incontrovertible evidence[67]. The difficulty in resolving this *crux* turns on two points: 1) Every one of the proposed translations is syntactically possible; 2) The criteria used for ruling out possibilities are themselves arbitrary[68]. Moreover, at times ideological considerations weigh heavily in proposed resolutions. For example taking *kekrika* with *en tô onomati* may have more to do with a desire to maximize Paul's authority than with the syntax[69]. In reference to the combination of *katergasamenon* with *en tô onomati*, one can ask whether the conviction that Corinthian spiritualists could perpetrate, in the name of the Lord, sins as outrageous as incest is more responsible for this combination than the grammar[70]? Dealing with this *crux*

---

[66] E.g. G. FEE, *1 Corinthians*, and W. ORR – J. WALTHER translate in accord with e); H. CONZELMANN lists possibilities but only insists that *paradounai* depends on *kekrika*; C.K. BARRETT translates in accord with a); J. Moffatt, with regard to *en tô onomati*, accords with e); E. FASCHER, *Erste Brief an die Korinther* and H. KLAUCK, *1 Korintherbrief*, accord with b); G. FORKMANN, *Limits*, 141-2, argues for d). The solutions of other commentators are noted in B. ALLO, *Première épître aux Corinthiens*, 121.

[67] E.g. 2Thess 3,6 is used by G. FEE, *1 Corinthians*, 207, n. 51, to argue that *en tô onomati* qualifies *kekrika* and by J. MURPHY-O'CONNOR, «1 Cor V,3-5», 240, to argue that *en tô onomati* qualifies *katergasamenon*. Fee connects *en tô onomati* with *kekrika*, citing 2Thess 3,6 in support of this construction. Yet in this occurrence *en tô onomati* comes after *parangellomen*, but also precedes the verb *stellesthai* and could conceivably qualify it. So 2Thess 3,6 is not an example of an open and shut case of verb + *en onomati* anymore than is *kekrika* + *en tô onomati*. Moreover, it should be noted that the only unambiguous case where what Paul does is connected with the name of the Lord Jesus Christ is at 1Cor at 1,10, where he makes his opening appeal, «dia *tou onomatos tou kyriou hèmôn Ièsou Christou*». Murphy-O'Connor, on the other hand, relies on 2Thess 3,6 to illustrate the verb + modifier pattern with the stress on the proximity of the antecedent verb to the modifier. Based on this, he argues that in 1Cor 5,3-4 the proximate antecedent, *katergasamenon* is qualified by *en tô onomati*. But in 1Cor 5, the prepositional phrase is preceded by not one but TWO verb forms which it could theoretically modify. To argue conclusively for the qualification of *katergasamenon* by *en tô onomati*, an example would have to be cited where, despite the presence of TWO antecedent verbs, it could be shown beyond doubt that the prepositional phrase necessarily qualifies the verb which is immediately antecedent to it. 2Thess 3,6 does not provide this type of example.

[68] E.g. to rule out that *en tô onomati* may modify *synacthentôn* on the grounds that it goes without saying that the community meets in the name of the Lord, cf. J. MURPHY-O'CONNOR, «1 Cor V,3-5», 240. No less arbitrary are some of the ruling out criteria offered in e.g., G. FEE, *1 Corinthians*, 206 n. 47; A. ROBERTSON – A. PLUMMER, *Handbook*, 98; C.K. BARRETT, *1 Corinthians*, 124.

[69] Cf. e.g. G. FEE, *1 Corinthians*, 195, 207; J. J. MOFFATT, *1 Corinthians*, 54.

[70] Cf. J. MURPHY-O'CONNOR, «1 Cor V,3-5», 240-41; Collins also accepts this syntactic arrangement on the assumption that we have here a «bold ideological act» (A.Y. COLLINS, «The Function» 252-253). In homily XV, John Chrysostom consid-

implies dealing with syntactic combinations, all disputable to some extent. Of those proposed, the following arrangement[71] seems preferable:

en tô onomati tou Kyriou....	prepositional phrase
synachthentôn	verbal form
syn tè dynamei tou Kyriou....	prepositional phrase
paradounai	verbal form

Apart from whether Havener's arrangement may or may not be used to sustain his views regarding Paul's autocratic intentions here, this proposal, based on structural parallelism, provides what appears to be the best resolution of the *crux*. Its adoption here does not necessarily include an endorsement of Havener's reading of the situation[72].

This still leaves the question of whether *paradounai* is dependent on *kekrika* without a verb supplied, with a verb supplied, or is best taken as an independent infinitive[73]. All three are possible. On the one hand, *kekrika* + *paradounai* with no additional verb introduced, could be taken to accent Paul's authority and action, independent of the community. He has judged and decided that the offender is to be handed over. The community just executes the orders. On the other hand, supplying the verb *chrè* or *dei* tempers the accent on authority, as if to imply that Paul was simply suggesting a course of action[74]. Adoption of one of these alternatives can also be conditioned by ideological concerns. For example, it has been suggested that *kekrika* governs *paradounai* because «it makes better sense in terms of Paul's argument[...] where he is underscoring *his* [au. ital.] decision»[75]. Even if taking *kekrika* as governing *paradounai* were

---

ered but rejected this syntactic combination as unlikely. Cf. JOHN CHRYSOSTOM, *Homilies*, 84.

[71] Proposed by I. HAVENER, «A Curse» 336-337.

[72] A reading which acknowledges Paul's exercise of power but not to the exclusion of the community has more support in the text which shows Paul at work to move the community to assume its role. Cf. C.K. BARRETT, *1 Corinthians*, 125 and J. MURPHY-O'CONNOR, «1Cor V,3-5», 234,

[73] According to Blass – Debrunner, § 196, the imperatival use of an infinitive is limited to two NT passages, both in Paul at Rom 12,15, *chairein* and *klaien*. In other passages a governing verb, *chrè* or *dei* can be supplied.

[74] Barrett holds that *paradounai* depends on *kekrika*, but renders the phrase, «we should, with the power of the Lord Jesus hand over [...]» (cf. C.K. BARRETT, *1 Corinthians*, 124). This rendering is particularly effective in underplaying Paul's authority.

[75] Cf. I. HAVENER, «A Curse» 338. He adds that in the face of the community's failure to act in regard to this «singularly scandalous situation», Paul felt it necessary «to exercise his apostolic authority completely, leaving nothing to chance. He is very definitely not sharing in a collegial exercise [...]» (338).

the best option (which it seems not to be), the rendering of a syntactic combination should not be settled in view of ideological concerns. That Paul acts with authority is undeniable. However, there are a number of other factors to consider[76], not least of which is the fact that Paul is engaged in argumentation[77] and the argument extends through thirteen verses. Since these verses form a complete rhetorical unit in which Paul unfolds one self-contained argument, assertions about Paul's argumentative aims ought to be based on a consideration of the whole argument. Likewise, the addition of *dei* or *chrè* should not be admitted simply on the basis of ideological considerations where the concern is to temper Paul's tone so that he is depicted as only recommending action[78].

Of the three possibilities, 1) *kekrika + paradounai*, 2) *paradounai* as independent infinitive and 3) supplied verb + *paradounai*, the first is the least preferable but not for ideological reasons. *Kekrika* has a direct object. Furthermore, it is considerably removed from *paradounai*. The second option is possible. However, given the infrequency with which the independent infinitive is used with imperatival force in the NT[79], there seems to be no compelling reason to take *paradounai* as an independent infinitive with imperatival force. The third option seems preferable. However, the introduction of the verb *dei* into the text, should be admitted in view of the frequency with which the *dei* + accusative + infinitive construction occurs in the NT[80] rather than the concern to temper Paul's tone.

In light of the preceding considerations the following interpretation is adopted:

a) *en tô onomati* qualifies *synachthentôn*
b) *syn tè dynamei* qualifies *paradounai*
c) the verb *dei* should be supplied before *paradounai*

---

[76] For example, a) Paul's judgement would have been purely formal had the community not chosen to assume responsibility; b) unless the sanction meant death (not likely, cf. the discussion below), the fencing-out of this member from the community had to be a continual voluntary act of the community; c) imposing a sanction may be, but is not always or necessarily, a testimony to high handed authoritarianism.

[77] Argumentation ought to be taken as an indication that one has renounced resorting to high-handed imposition and coercive tactics (cf. C. PERELMAN – L. OLBRECHTS-TYTECA, *The New Rhetoric*, 55).

[78] Cf. e.g. J. MURPHY-O'CONNOR, «I Cor V,3-5», 242-244; ID., *1 Cor*, 41.

[79] Cf. above n. 73.

[80] The NT occurrences are too numerous to cite. Suffice it to say that within the Corinthian correspondence alone, the *dei* + infinitive construction occurs 8x at 1Cor 8,2; 11,19; 15,25.23; 2Cor 2,3; 5,10; 11,30 and 12,1.

Thus, the English rendering:

> For I, absent in body but present in spirit, have already judged as present the
> one who has done such a thing. When you are assembled in the name of the
> Lord Jesus and with my spirit, with the power of our Lord Jesus you should
> hand this man over to Satan for the destruction of the flesh, so that the spirit
> might be saved in the day of the Lord.

8.2 *The Concrete Significance of the Sanction*

How to understand vv. 3-5[81] and the significance of what is being
prescribed in v. 5. have been the subject of much scholarly debate. In fact,
as we mentioned in the introduction, the larger part of scholarly literature
dealing with 1Cor 5 concentrates on these enigmatic verses. Here we will
attempt to summarize the issues and opinions.

In the main scholars agree that the twofold purpose of the sanction, as
the text indicates, is: the removal of the offender from the community and
his ultimate salvation, *«hina to pneuma*[82] *sôthè en tè hèmera tou
Kyriou»*[83]. Beyond this, there is no consensus about what *«paradounai
ton toiouton tô satana eis olethron tès sarkos»* means concretely. Most
agree that handing over to Satan[84] means, on a primary level, to excom-

---

[81] As a solemn execration formula? So A. DEISSMANN, *Light*, and A.Y. COLLINS,
«The Function» 251-263. However, critics point out that execration texts cited as
parallels are late, ca. 4th c. and are not as verbally parallel as claimed. As a charismatic announcement of divine Law? So, E. KÄSEMANN, «Sentences», esp. 70-72. As
the announcement of the penalty of *Karet*? So, P.J. TOMSON, *Paul*, 101-102.

[82] For a concise summary of main views on the connotation of *to pneuma* cf. J.
GUNDRY VOLF, *Paul and Perseverance*, 114. *Pneuma* is probably intended as an
anthropological designation, i.e., the man's *pneuma*, as contended by the author. Cf.
further, R.T. ETCHEVARRIA, «A proposito», 133.

[83] «In the day of the Lord» is taken by most to refer to the day of eschatological
judgement. It is been recently suggested that the phrase should be taken non-escha-
tologically as a reference to a day of grace when the offender is offered a possibility of
a new beginning and return to the spiritual circle of the community from which he was
excluded (cf. N. BAUMERT, «Frau und Mann», 142-143).

[84] In the OT and Jewish literature Satan is depicted as God's agent, the inflicter of
His destruction, cf. e.g. Job 1,21; 2,10; Ex 12,23; CD 8,2. In the main, commentators
take the mention of Satan at 1Cor 5,5 to mean an agent of destruction, though what
that entails concretely is debated. It has also been suggested that Satan is equal to the
secular authority to which the offender would have been handed over since incest
cases required the penal authority of the state (cf. D. DERRETT, «Handing Over», 167-
186). One major problem with this thesis is the incoherence it forces on Paul. Derrett
deals with the problem by distinguishing between criminal and civil cases, the former
applying to 1Cor 5 which would require the intervention of secular authority, the latter
to 6,1-11 where the Corinthians should have handled the case intramurally (cf. 179-
80). The distinction may be valid. However, given the fact that Derrett emphasizes in
view of 5,9 that confusion reigned in the community (cf. 172-174), why would Paul

municate the man[85]. Some would say that along with excommunication the phrase announces a curse[86] under which the offender is placed, therewith effecting his consignment to the realm of Satan. The realm of Satan has been taken to mean the place where sin reigns[87] or the realm of the *orgè theou*[88] or simply outside of the spiritual shelter and loving context of the community[89]. Fee rejects the curse interpretation but maintains that the excommunication also entailed the offender's transference from the realm of Christ to that of Satan[90]. Still others claim that the phrase announces excommunication, a curse[91] signifying consignment to Satan's realm, and ultimately physical death[92].

Further, there is notable division over the significance of *eis olethron tès sarkos*, particularly the meaning of *sarx*. When *sarx* is taken to refer to the physical body the punishment is understood either as: a) the actual death[93] of the sinner or b) less drastically, physical suffering and

---

have risked adding to it by recommending both recourse to and avoidance of secular courts in contiguous units of text without specifying any distinction?

[85] C. TALBERT considers *«paradounai ton toiouton tô satana»* a synonym for «let him be removed from among you» v. 2c; «cleanse out the old leaven» v. 7 and «Drive out the wicked person [...]» v. 13, all of which refer to excommunication (cf. *Reading Corinthians*, 16); On excommunication understood as «status transformation ritual» cf. J. NEYREY, *Paul*, 91.

[86] Cf. e.g. A. DEISSMANN and A.Y. COLLINS, both cited above n. 81; also G. FORKMANN, *Limits*, 143-144.

[87] Cf. e.g. C.K. BARRETT, *1 Corinthians*, 126;

[88] Cf. E. KÄSEMANN, «Sentences», 71. Following Käsemann are H. CONZELMANN, *1 Korinther*, 98 and C.J. ROETZEL, *Judgement*, 122 n. 4.

[89] Cf. e.g. J. CAMBIER, «La chair», 226; N. BAUMERT, *Frau und Mann*, 142; J. MURPHY-O'CONNOR, *1 Cor*, 42.

[90] Cf. G. FEE, *1 Corinthians*, 208-209.

[91] In rabbinic practice curse and exclusion were a substitute for the execution of covenant-breakers, probably in continuity with pre-rabbinic custom (cf. W. HORBURY, «Extirpation», 29-31).

[92] Cf. e.g. I. HAVENER, «A Curse», 341; H. CONZELMANN, *1 Korinther*, 97; C.J. ROETZEL, *Judgement*, 121; G. FORKMANN, *Limits*, 143-146; E. KÄSEMANN, «Sentences», 71-72.

[93] The most common arguments for the curse/death interpretation are reviewed in J.T. SOUTH, «A Critique», 539-61. In this article (extracted from his book, *Disciplinary Practices*), South concludes that the evidence points away from a 'curse/death' understanding of 1Cor 5,5. Four additional considerations strengthen this conclusion: 1) On a theological level, if Paul were intending actual physical death of the body for the salvation of the soul, this would signify a dualistic approach to body/soul in Platonic fashion. 2) On the socio-political level one must consider that cases involving capital punishment were the competence of the Roman authorities (cf. above n. 84). 3) Though in theory cases involving prohibited sexual relations were punishable by death, this may not have been practiced, especially in the Diaspora. For the background on Jewish practice cf. P.J. TOMSON, *Paul*, 101-102. 4) As noted by Tomson, the sentence pronounced by Paul was not arrived at according to the process

affliction[94]. *Sarx* has also been taken in a moral/ethical sense to refer to one's lower or sinful nature, with the punishment understood as the destruction of base and carnal desires[95]. Just how these desires or the «tendency which binds the offender to the sin»[96] are destroyed and what Satan's role would be in the process has not been fully explicated, leaving unanswered, *inter alia*, the objection that if Satan is viewed as the instrument of the destruction of this evil he would effectively be operating against his own interests[97].

Among scholars who take the moral/ethical view of *sarx*, some do not exclude the possibility that some physical affliction may have also been intended in the process[98]. Barrett takes *sarx* both ethically and physically and understands the destruction as aimed at both levels[99]. With regard to the physical, Barrett sees at least some affliction in view and probably death[100]. According to Tomson, who sees in vv. 3-5 the application of the *karet*[101] penalty[102], the aims of the disciplinary process prescribed here,

---

for trying capital cases, cf. Dt 17,6; hence it is unlikely that Paul was arguing for capital punishment (cf. 103).

[94] Cf. G.W.H. LAMPE, «Church Discipline», 354; C.K. BARRETT, *1 Corinthians*, 126; G. FORKMANN, *Limits*, 145-146. This general line of interpretation is often connected with a) 1Cor 11,30-32 which has in common with 1Cor 5 the motifs of sin, punishment and salvation and b) the notion that the physical punishment was for remedial purposes. Apropos of point a) both G. FEE, *1 Corinthians*, 211 and more recently J. GUNDRY VOLF in *Paul and Perseverance*, 115, have shown that these texts are less comparable than previously thought. Regarding point b) C.K. BARRETT, *1 Corinthians*, 126, points out that the text does not support the claim that physical suffering was for remedial or expiatory purposes. Of the same view is I. HAVENER, «A Curse», 341.

[95] Cf. J. CAMBIER, «La chair» 221-232.; also C. TALBERT, *Reading Corinthians*, 16; W. BAIRD, *The Corinthian Church*, 66; N.G. JOY, «Is the Body?», 429; C.J. ROETZEL, *Judgement*, 124.

[96] N.G. JOY, «Is the Body?», 436.

[97] Cf. I. HAVENER, «A Curse», 340.

[98] Cf. e.g. J. MURPHY-O'CONNOR, *1 Cor*, 41-42; A. ROBERTSON – A. PLUMMER, *Handbook*, 99.

[99] Cf. C.K. BARRETT, *1 Corinthians*, 126.

[100] Ibid, 126. Barrett does not say who would carry out the execution.

[101] A penalty distinct from e.g. חרם, ארר, בער (cf. G. FORKMANN, *Limits*, 16-28).

[102] The *karet* formula occurs 36X in the OT. In Lev 18, e.g., the offenses that Israel must avoid, vv. 6-23, including the *porneia* type of 1Cor 5,1 are listed, followed by general exhortation to avoid these. Then the penalty is announced: «Everyone who does any of these abominations shall be cut off (נכרתו= LXX *exolothreuthèsontai*), from among his people», v. 29. The *karet* punishment was inflicted by God, although there is no agreement on the means, cf. B. LEVINE, *Leviticus*; J. MILGROM, *Numbers*; N. SARNA, *Exodus*. As pointed out by Milgrom (cf. 406), the punishment was understood as a divine prerogative because a) offenses incurring *karet* were violations of religious law and considered deliberate sins against God and b) the cardinal postulate

viz., to deter the offender from backsliding and move him to repentance, were achieved exclusively through excommunication[103].

This brief exposé of scholarly opinion showing divergences, and nuanced overlaps, reveals that nothing of a definitive nature has been established with regard to what exactly the pronouncement means. There does seem to be sufficient reason to set aside the death interpretation and affirm the view that expulsion from the community was intended. What such excommunication entailed beyond physical separation cannot be known with any certainty. This non-conclusiveness will undoubtedly appear to some to be unsatisfactory. However, if Thiselton's[104] insight is accurate, perhaps we need to acknowledge the non-specificity of the pronouncement and refrain from attempts to delineate what Paul may have intended to leave unspecified. This insight is not mere capitulation to the enigma of these verses, nor is it a clever attempt to circumvent the issue. Rather, it is a positive attempt to respect the text and focus on the essential point rather than specifics which, in any case, Paul does not supply. Moreover, for understanding Paul's argument, the specifics of what is being prescribed, are, in the long run, less important than recognizing what kind of speech we are dealing with and what the function of these verses is in the argument. It is to these considerations we now turn our attention.

8.3 *The Rhetorical Function of the Judgement Pronouncement*

To appreciate the rhetorical[105] significance of the judgement pronouncement in vv. 3-5, we will have to consider the aspect of timing and placement in the argument and also take account of Paul's pedagogy. As we already noted in our opening comments about vv. 3-5, Paul seems to introduce the judgement pronouncement into the argument with great haste. To consider this simply as proof of Paul's intent to champion his

---

of priestly legislation was that sins against God are punishable by God. The priestly certainty of this was institutionalized in the *karet* penalty, unique to P texts. While the divine punishment could take the form of the offender's premature death, it was not synonymous with capital punishment at the hands of men (cf. J. MILGROM, *Numbers*, 408).

[103] Within the Jewish community extirpation was mostly carried out by way of disciplinary flogging, a prerogative of the Jewish community to which the Christians were not entitled (cf. P.J. TOMSON, *Paul*, 102).

[104] Cf. A.C. THISELTON, «The Meaning» 204ff. Thiselton's basic argument is that here in 1Cor 5, as well as at 6,14-18 and 7,14 Paul makes statements intended to communicate the idea that something happens in the physical/material domain which affects the spiritual. To grasp this is to grasp the essential point.

[105] On the sociological significance cf. G. HARRIS, «The Beginnings», 18.

authority, lay down the law and test the Corinthians' obedience is to overlook his rhetorical strategy and to risk misconstruing the function of these verses. Here we will first focus on the element of timing and placement of this pronouncement in the argument. A brief rehearsal of what has taken place so far on the level of text will be helpful.

Through his reference to the pagans, which we said allows Paul to insinuate that a societal moral value has been transgressed, he has already passed a comment on the sin, the sinner and the community's judgement and behavior which cannot be negatively augmented. Indeed it would be hard to place the matter in a worse objective light. The step-son is necessarily inculpated as the sin's gravity is set in relief and the community is shown to be deficient in discernment and behavior. No further argument is necessary. But this is not because Paul was intent only to rush to impose his judgement and assert his authority. On the contrary, all that needed to be said for the moment was said. The brevity of the reference to the pagans should not cause us to miss its multiple implications, which the Corinthians, whom Paul considered *phronimoi*[106], were presumably quite capable of apprehending. The whole situation is shameful and incest is evil, a fact which everyone, not just Paul, recognizes. The community has been confronted with this wider perspective and, from this vantage point, cannot now disagree with Paul's response. Thus, the potential for a meeting of minds between Paul and the community is taking shape[107]. The judgement and sentence prescribed for what should now be perceived as nothing but an egregious moral transgression would probably, from this vantage point, appear to the community to be warranted.

The multiple implications of the reference to the pagans all contribute to the evocation of shame. However, as already noted, the arousal of emotion is not an end unto itself. Rather, its ultimate aim or function in the argument is to create a willing disposition toward action[108]. When this willing disposition is induced, the time is propitious and, from the point of view of the unfolding of the argument, speech concerned with action is appropriate. Indeed it is crucial that the speaker capitalize on the willingness he has labored to create[109] by indicating what ought to be

---

[106] Cf. 1Cor 4,10; 10,15.

[107] It has been proposed that Paul pronounced the judgement because he assumed the consensus of the community (cf. W. MEEKS, *The First Urban Christians*, 124). This seems inaccurate given what the text reveals about the Corinthian attitude and also because Paul appears to be arguing to create a consensus.

[108] Cf. C. PERELMAN – L. OLBRECHTS-TYTECA, *The New Rhetoric*, 47.

[109] Taking advantage of the created emotion to move the community to act, while considered by many to be consonant with the goals of deliberative rhetoric, can also be considered consonant with those of epideictic (cf. C. PERELMAN, *The Realm*, 20).

done or pointing toward a direction that a course of action may take. When the dynamic relation between arousal of emotion, willing disposition and speech focused on action is understood, then the function of vv. 3-5 in the unfolding of the argument becomes self-evident. Paul's apparent exigency to arrive at this pronouncement is thus best understood as linked to the exigencies of the rhetorical strategy and not to any polemically derived necessity to champion his authority. In other words, having aroused the emotions of the community for the purpose of inducing a willingness in the community to consider changing its judgements, behavior and course of action, Paul moves to the next rhetorically strategic step of directing the community's focus to a course of action.

To some extent the case would now appear to be closed. All the community need do is obey Paul and execute the sentence. Despite appearances, this is not so. Thus far the community has reason to see that its judgement and behavior is shameful and, in consequence, has acquired a motivation for opening itself to other considerations and opinions, other behavior, and the adoption of another course of action. However, this attitude-molding is preparatory to vv. 6-8[110], where Paul sets out reasons that should actually compel the Corinthians to execute the sentence. But one could ask, why would Paul provide the reasons for expulsion only after he has already made his severe judgement pronouncement? What good is post-factum reasoning? If Paul were not intending to impose his orders and wrap this case up undemocratically, as Havener has claimed, would he not have set out all the reasoning and let the community discern?

We believe we have already sufficiently shown in view of the dynamics of the text strategy that Paul's quick introduction of his directives for action ought to be considered in terms of what the rhetorical strategy requires. Paul wants the community to act and this is the right time to bring up the actions. However, the fact that the rhetorical strategy makes the introduction of speech directed to action appropriate at this point does not allow us to conclude from its placement in the argument, antecedent to the reasoning, that the action will be performed by the community merely as a response to a command, or that a reasoned judgement and response by the community is inessential or, at any rate, subordinate to shame-motivated obedience to Paul. Nor can it be concluded that the written order establishes a hierarchy of importance. It is true that Paul's pronouncement comes first, but is it more important than the reasoning, and does its placement confirm views that Paul's intent here was to

---

[110] This is why it is insufficient to study only this first preparatory phase of Paul's argument in 1Cor 5 and draw conclusions about his aims based only on vv. 1-5.

champion his authority? A consideration of Paul's pedagogy will be helpful here.

Paul addresses the community at Corinth not merely as one *paidagôgos*
among many but as father and founder and hence, among evangelizers,
the community's preeminent *paidagôgos* (cf. 4,15)[111]. Paul says that the
meaning of the advent of faith for Christians is that they are no longer
under the pedagogy of the law (cf. Gal 3,24-25), but having been set free
(cf. Gal 5,1.13), now live and are led by the Spirit (cf. Gal 5,18.25). Paul's
intervention could appear to contravene the Spirit's guiding role and the
community's freedom. But, the Spirit's guiding role is not limited to
interior monitoring. Rather, the Spirit also works actively in and through
outer exhortation that can take the form of apostolic admonitions[112].
Within this perspective Paul can be understood as assisting the Spirit, who
«needs (and *uses*) the Apostolic commands»[113]. Furthermore, Christian
freedom is not suppressed because, along with corrective directives here
in c. 5, Paul provides the proper criteria by which the community should
judge. In other words, he enables the community to arrive at an informed
judgement that should issue in appropriate action. In 1Cor 5 we can
observe how correction (vv. 3-5), and reasoning (vv. 6-8) go hand in
hand, the latter complementing the former; two components of what has
been termed Paul's «autorité pédagogique»[114]. By stating the sanction
first, Paul is able to dispose with the obvious and necessary. Since there is
transgression, a sanction is in order. That Paul expects the community to
cooperate in what is essentially the defense of its own well-being by
applying the sanction is beyond question. We have referred to the
language Paul uses in vv. 3-5, as performative speech[115]. When used by
one with authority who introduces imperatives, performative speech does
more than describe and promote action, it creates a new situation[116]. In
vv. 3-5 Paul sets the responsibility squarely before the community and
raises its level of accountability. All know what ought to be done.
However, Paul does not stop here. To assist and enable the community to

---

[111] Apropos the father-children metaphor, it has been pointed out that this metaphor
is associated with school instruction in technical and moral matters where exemplary
qualities, and not obedience, are central (cf. B. FIORE, *The Function of Personal
Example*, 167).

[112] Cf. W. SCHRAGE, *Die konkreten Einzelgebote*, 86.

[113] Cf. T. DEIDUN, *New Covenant Morality*, 219. Parentheses and italics are the
author's.

[114] Cf. J.-N. ALETTI «L'autorité», 243.

[115] Performative speech, whether literal or metaphorical, is speech which is
concerned with action or whose main point is «to do something» (cf. P.W. MACKY,
The Centrality, 247).

[116] P.W. MACKY, *The Centrality*, 247.

think through this matter and assume its responsibility to correct the situation, Paul directs the community in a reasoning process so that all can understand why this action ought to be taken as well as what it ought to be. For Paul then, reason accompanies the call to action. In the laying out of the criteria what will become evident is why the community is not only in error but in danger and hence why the man has to expelled.

In vv. 6-8, posterior to the disclosure of his own judgement, Paul does not advance reasons why the community should unquestionably submit to his will or obey him, something which Paul never demands[117]. Rather, he advances persuasive reasons through which he effectively enables the Corinthians to reason correctly for themselves. Not by force but by persuasive reasoning Paul exercises his authority[118], creating the possibility for the Corinthians to join with him in the defense of their own common sanctified life. Based on this reasoning the community will be able to take stock of the situation from a new perspective from which there should issue a new evaluation that will undoubtedly lead to appropriate action. It could be said then that the ultimate impetus for the community's action will have been its own discernment on the matter, a discernment which Paul guides.

The community action that should issue from this new evaluation of the situation could properly be described as an act of obedience[119]. Here the obedience is ultimately to the gospel and its claims on Christians which Paul sets before the community in vv. 6-8[120]. But a qualification is necessary. Obedience to the gospel does not exclude obedience to Paul[121] since he, as Apostle, sent to announce and advance the gospel (cf. 1Cor 1,17; Rom 1,15) does not announce his own will but the demands of the gospel (cf. Gal 1,11). These demands impinge not only on matters of faith but ethics as well[122]. When the demands of the gospel are unheeded or transgressed as in the case of 1Cor 5, then the Apostle, as the community's

---

[117] See the discussion of Paul's use of *hypakouô, hypakoè* and *parakoè* in J.-N. ALETTI, «L'autorité», 231.

[118] Cf. J. MURPHY-O'CONNOR, *L'existence*, 123.

[119] Cf. Phl 1,21. Philemon's «obedience» is also conceived as the fruit of interior discernment, cf. v. 14.

[120] Likewise at 2Cor 2,9.

[121] Cf. Phl 1,21. Though not specified, it is likely that the response of Philemon, whose obedience will bring him «to do even more» than Paul says, is an obedient response to the gospel though clearly obedience to Paul is included.

[122] The approach to the offender whose sin and its tolerance perverts the gospel and threatens the community is no less exigent than Paul's anathemizing of promoters of circumcision (cf. Gal 1,6-9) who pervert the gospel, threatening the community's essence and existence.

guardian, must not only correct but also redirect the community to a new level of understanding and a new level of commitment to these demands.

The reasoning process through which Paul guides the community in vv. 6-8 attests to the fact that while the sanction may have been pronounced, the community's own valuative process is just beginning and the action is still to come. After the criteria have been unfolded and the community is brought to a new level of understanding, then Paul will repeat the call for expulsion again in v. 13b. When the dynamic relationship between sanction and reasoning is considered then it becomes apparent that the sanction, while occupying a precedent place in the unfolding of the argument, is not logically antecedent to the reasoning[123] nor does it indicate that persuasive tactics have been abandoned. The sanction and the community's decision to execute it depends on and issues from the reasoning.

From the perspective of Paul's pedagogy one has another viewing angle by which to interpret his apparent haste in vv. 1-5. The exigency that accompanies the pronouncement of the sanction is real yet it derives not from an urgency to assert or impose authority over the community but rather from the urgency to correct a bad situation. However, that correction must be carried out by the community and Paul must help the Corinthians to see why. Reasoning is not an appendage here, a last resort, or change of tactics, so to speak, in case the command should go unheeded[124]. One is not a substitute for the other. Both are necessary and Paul has the responsibility to shame/commend, correct, sanction and command, which he does according to the exigencies of the situation[125]. The reasoning set out in 5,6-8 complements the authoritative pronouncement in vv. 3-5. In this pedagogic process, the reasoning enables the now shamed and presumably willing community to evaluate anew and adopt a new course of action. As the enabling factor, the reasoning takes on a role

---

[123] Cf. J.-N. ALETTI, «L'authorité», 243.

[124] E. SCHÜSSLER FIORENZA suggests that the key problem Paul faced in 1Cor was the challenge to his authority (cf. «Rhetorical Situation», 394-395). She then claims that Paul, finding himself speaking to a situation which would not tolerate coercive force – his ordinary approach, as the author seems to imply – adopted a strategy of deliberation (cf. 398). What appears to be insinuated is that Paul employs reason *in extremis* when he realizes that strong-arming the community will not produce the effects/response he wants. The danger of such an insinuation is that one could construe 1Cor 5 in such terms and assume that Paul's introduction of reasoning in vv. 6-8 was a concession rather than an integrated part of his pedagogy.

[125] Cf. e.g. 11,2 where Paul first commends, then begins the reasoning in v. 3; apropos of abuses at the Lord's supper, again Paul first shames, 11,17-22 then in vv. 23-26 instructs; in Gal 1,8.9 anathemizing precedes the explication of why the other gospel is a perversion of the gospel of Christ.

of major significance in the unfolding of the argument[126]. Recognition of this pedagogic process and its dynamics is important to the task of interpreting Paul's aims here especially with regard to the role of the community[127].

In sum, shame is evoked to induce in the community a willingness to change its opinions, behavior and course of action; the sanction points them in the direction they must go but the reasoning will enable them to understand why the expulsion must be carried out and presumably move them to do it. When the action takes place, they and Paul with them in Spirit, will pass sentence and put it into effect, acting with the power of the Lord Jesus (cf. 5,4)[128].

9. Proof by *Logos*[129]: 1Cor 5,6-8

In the preceding section we have suggested that in vv. 6-8 Paul guides the Corinthians through a reasoning process in which he sets out considerations that will effectively enable them to understand for themselves how it is that they are in error and why taking action is necessary and in

---

[126] This reasoning is located in the center of c. 5, constituting the «b» section of this concentrically arranged unit. The importance of the reasoning derives from its function and this importance is «enhanced» by its central location, cf. above c. 4.

[127] Käsemann takes no account of this process or the larger argument being unfolded in 1Cor when he argues that vv. 3-5 constitute a «sentence of Holy Law» (cf. «Sentences», esp. 70-72). In Käsemann's thesis the emphasis is on Paul's role as charismatic prophet and the pronouncement's divinely derived absolute character. All authority is poised in Paul; the community can only assent and execute the sanction (cf. 71). In these verses Paul does speak with an authority that is undiminished by his absence (cf. R. FUNK, «The Apostolic Parousia», 263-265). Paul knew himself to be Spirit-endowed (cf. e.g. 1Cor 3,12; 7,40) and used prophetic imagery of himself (cf. Gal 1,15) – whether this betrays Paul's actual self-understanding is another question. Moreover in 5,5 the judgement has an eschatological orientation. To say that Paul speaks prophetically and that something more than a purely human judgement is being communicated cannot be denied. But are vv. 3-5, which lack the formal elements of a sentence of holy law, as outlined by Käsemann (cf. 67), really to be regarded as such? We are not convinced and find the implications of this claim, especially with regard to the community's role, not in accord with what appear to be Paul's overall argumentative aims or with the aims of the pedagogic process at work in vv. 3-5 and 6-8. Others, dissatisfied with the role accorded to the community in Käsemann's proposal, readily accept his view that vv. 3-5 are a sentence of Holy Law (cf. e.g. G. HARRIS, «The Beginnings», 10) but cite H. CONZELMANN as the originator of the view that the community is only a vehicle for action (cf. G. HARRIS, «The Beginnings», 15). But, in fact, Conzelmann follows Käsemann and is simply accepting what the latter proposes as the implications for the role of the community *vis-à-vis* the status of vv. 3-5 as a sentence of holy law.

[128] The *ekklesia* as a whole is the ultimate authority. Cf. O. MICHEL, *Das Zeugnis*, 67; Of the same view cf. G. FORKMANN, *Limits*, 142 and end note 145.

[129] Cf. above n. 1.

their own interests. Now we need to take a look at these reasons, how they are presented and in what way they function as a stimulus for action.

In v. 6a Paul declares, *«ou kalon to kauchèma hymôn»*. As already noted[130] *to kauchèma* refers to the object of, or grounds for boasting. It is the incest which Paul describes as *ou kalon*[131]. Having declared this, Paul moves immediately to help the community understand why incest is not simply bad, but bad for *them* and therefore should be no source of a boast.

A single assertion, *«mikra zymè holon to phyrama zymoi»*, couched in the form of a question[132], is Paul's starting point. This proverb enunciates what is common knowledge drawn from simple observation about which everyone would agree. Since, in this instance, Paul is going to use the concepts, language and images contained in this proverb as a basis for reasoning[133], this agreement about the proverb's truth or reliability is important and obviously enhances the possibility of persuasion[134]. By employing this particular proverb, Paul is able to set before his audience three important notions. First, the proverb conjures the notion of proportion, i.e., a small cause can produce great effects. Second, through the proverb Paul is also able to vividly image for his listeners the notion of infectiousness. *Zymè* is something dynamic. It moves and penetrates its environment. Third, the proverb allows Paul to introduce the notion of total permeation and corruption of which *zymè*[135] is emblematic. Thus the effects of even a little *zymè* can never be isolated or benign. These

---

[130] Cf. above c. 3 n. 5.

[131] Some commentators consider *to kauchèma* as referring to an attitude, claiming that it is parallel to (H. CONZELMANN, *1 Korinther*, 98) or a synonym (G. FEE, *1 Corinthians*, 215) for *physioô* in v. 2. Understood this way *ou kalon* negatively qualifies an attitude or posture of arrogance (G. FEE, *1 Corinthians*, 215) or self-glorying (H. CONZELMANN, *1 Korinther*, 98) that Paul considers bad. However, these suggestions disregard Paul's 8 other uses of *kauchèma* where the term clearly means the grounds of boasting. Moreover, in Paul, boasting, as an attitude, assumes a negative or positive value depending on whether its *object* is negative or positive. In 1Cor 9,15-16 or 1,31 boasting is obviously good because what is boasted in is good. Here in 1Cor 5,6 because incest is *ou kalon*, then obviously so is their boasting posture.

[132] As generally recognized the question *«ouk oidate hoti»* usually introduces information with which the audience is familiar, cf. Rom 6,16; 11,2; 1Cor 3,16; 6,2.3.9.15.16.19; 9,13.24.

[133] Cf. Unlike the usage at Gal 5,9.

[134] Cf. C. PERELMAN – L. OLBRECHTS-TYTECA, *The New Rhetoric*, 65.

[135] Yeast, something good and wholesome, was distinct from leaven/*zymè*, a piece of old moldy dough, held back before being placed in the new dough to make it rise. Hence *zymè* came to connote corruption and was eventually associated with moral evil, cf. C.L. MITTON, «New Wine», 339-340. In Philo's allegorized interpretation of Ex 23,18, «leaven» connotes sensual pleasure and lust. It cannot be set on the altar with blood, the sign of souls consecrated to God, because *«mignynai de ta amikta ouk hosion»* (it is not right to mix the unmixed), cf. *Q. Exod*, ad loc.

aspects: proportional effects, permeation and corruption are key and point up Paul's concern to impress on the community one fact, viz., the negative effects of this incest for the whole community.

Paul does not articulate the analogy[136] that emerges when the terms of the proverb are considered metaphorically and applied to the community situation. Instead, based on its implications, he moves immediately to prescribe action, *ekkatharate*. But now, as the metaphor is expressly continued in v. 7, we note that Paul introduces a new set of qualifications: *palaia*[137] qualifies *zymè* and *neon* qualifies *phyrama*, and the latter is equated with *azymoi,* which introduces a new concept. By a metaphoric leap, Paul moves to a new level of consideration where the emphasis shifts from proportional effects, *mikra/holon,* to absolute incompatibilities, *zymè/azymoi* (v. 7b *kathôs este azymoi*). With the introduction of the term *azymoi* there seems to be a break in the logic. «Bad yeast» and its effects have been the gist of what Paul has been discussing so far and one might expect Paul to continue with a discussion of good/new yeast[138], but «without yeast» is something different altogether. This is precisely the point. The verbal and logical discontinuity reflect the reality. The community needs to cleanse out the *palaian zymè* because it is totally incompatible with what it is and must continue to be, viz., *azymoi.* This term stands for a reality, a condition that is totally dissociated from all that is *palaia zymè*[139]. Here Paul sets before the community a consideration of its own quality and underscores the incompatibility of *zymè* with this new condition. The community cannot BE *azymè* and at the same time BE *zymè,* which it would necessarily be even if only a little *zymè* were in its midst. This fact is validated by the proverb. The incompatibility demands resolve and Paul has proleptically stated what it is to be, *ekkatharate tèn palaian zymèn, hina ète neon phyrama,* v. 7a.b[140].

---

[136] As a little leaven (*mikra zymè*) is to the whole loaf (*holon phyrama*) so is the community member's *porneia* = (*mikra zymè*) to the community (*phyrama*).

[137] Old yeast is bad yeast and so far can be considered ethically neutral, though in v. 8 it will be associated with *kakia* and *ponèria* and explicitly imbued with negative ethical value.

[138] As one finds for example in IGNATIUS, *Ad Magnesios,* 10,2, where evil leaven which corrupts is contrasted with the new leaven, Jesus Christ.

[139] *palaia/neon* are antithetical categories that Paul uses to express the contrast between Christian and pre-Christian existence, cf. Rom 6,3-6 old/new self; Col 3,9-10 and Eph 4,22-24, old/new nature,

[140] This is an example of Paul's characteristic imperative/indicative (more often the inverse order is used) construct. Bultmann's proposed understanding of the relationship of these statements, viz., that the imperative is grounded in justification and derives from the indicative was a major attempt to move beyond the contradiction in need of resolution approach (cf. R. BULTMANN, «Das Problem», 126). However, it was

Why *azymè* is the quality of new Christian existence and why cleansing is necessary is grounded by Paul in one brief statement in 7c, *kai gar to pascha hèmôn etythè Christos*. This is the core[141] of Paul's reasoning, functioning as a hinge[142] which a) explains and qualifies the apposite statements in 7b and 7a which in turn illumine and ground the command in 7a[143] and b) grounds the exhortation that will follow in v. 8. The term Paul uses here is *pascha*. If taken metaphorically[144] the translation becomes «Christ our Paschal Lamb has been slain». Understood this way, the emphasis is on one aspect of the Passover, i.e., the sacrifice of the lamb. But with the introduction of *azymoi*, Paul has already alluded to the Feast of Unleavened Bread, which he will pick up again in v. 8. It would seem reasonable then to entertain the possibility that *pascha* may have

---

hardly the last word on the subject. Post-Bultmann proposals are too numerous to list. Some of the more significant ones are reviewed in W. SCHRAGE, *Ethics*, 167-172. Apropos of 5,7, our immediate concern, some have adopted the pithy «become what you are» to express the relationship of these terms, cf. e.g. R. LE DÉAUT, «The Paschal Mystery», 209; also G. FEE, *1 Corinthians*, 217. V. 7 seems to lend itself to this conceptualization. However, caution is in order. «Become what you are» can imply self-realization, which is un-Pauline, and diminish the indicative which is the new, redeemed, sanctified condition (cf. 1Cor 6,11; Gal 3,27-28) of which believers already (cf. Rom 8,4) partake through Baptism (cf. Rom 6,4). In Paul, this condition is not contingent on the realization of imperatives, but only on faith (cf. Rom 3,25, 4,16, 5,1; Gal 2,16, 3,8). Any solution that would purport to be adequate must respect both the imperative and the indicative in their full integrity. For a qualified understanding of «become what you are» that seems to do justice to Paul's thought cf. J. MURPHY-O'CONNOR, *L'existence*, 100-101.

[141] Central both in terms of its significance and its placement in the center of two parallel constructions which reinforce each other:

A ekkatharate *tèn* palaian zymè 5,7a
   B *kathôs este* azymoi 5,7b
      C kai gar to pascha hèmôn etythè Christos 5,7c
A heortazômen *mè en* zymè palaia 5,8a
   B *all' en* azymois 5,8b

[142] In her study of 1Cor 5 (cf. the discussion above § 3), Mitchell makes no reference at all to this key phrase, its hinge function and how it serves to qualify ethically the terms *azymoi* and *phyrama*. In light of 7c, *phyrama* stands for the community as an indivisible moral entity, not a political unit.

[143] This is denied by L. NIEDER, *Die Motive*, 32-33. He maintains that the *kai gar-satz*, 7c, is not the reason for the purification of the old yeast. Rather, he argues that v. 7b, *kathôs este azymoi*, is the reason for the cleansing while the *kai gar-satz* must be taken as the answer to the question, «Why are Christians *azymoi*?» Both O. MERK, *Handeln*, 90 and H. CRUZ, *Christological Motives*, 69 follow Nieder in maintaining that Paul's paraenesis in vv. 6-8 is built on two separate motives. Even if such a distinction is valid it is superfluous since in the chain of logic in v. 7, Christ's death is ultimately the reason for purifying the old yeast.

[144] As a number of commentators do, cf. e.g. H. CONZELMANN, *1 Korinther*, 99.

been intended to stand for the whole event[145] of the Jewish Passover which included the combined rites of the slaying of the lamb and unleavened bread[146]. In fact, it is this combination which provides a paradigm for Paul's uniting of the death of Christ/his blood and cleansing.

By a symbolic reinterpretation of these cultic rites[147], reset in the moral sphere, Paul explains how it is that Christians are *azymoi* (v. 7b,a); why the cleansing is a necessity (v. 7a), and grounds the exhortation to unleavened living (v. 8). Again, Paul leaves the analogy unarticulated[148] but the implications are clear: Christ's redemptive act creates the condition of new life[149], a cleansed/without leaven condition which for Paul is the condition of *hagiasmos*[150]. Hence, to be *azymoi* is to be holy/clean[151], a condition willed by God[152] and effectuated through the death of Christ. Here the death of Christ is put forward as the key event for the community's self-definition as *azymoi*.

Moving forward from these implications[153], Paul continues with paschal imagery, exhorting, *heortazômen*[154], the community, now conceived through a new shift in metaphor as celebrators, to celebrate the

---

[145] In which case *pascha* might be considered as the rhetorical figure metonymy which expresses a relationship of part to a whole, e.g. the sail for the ship, or an intrinsic association, e.g. the White House for the President. Metonymy differs in function from metaphor in that it is not predicative. See the definition in W.J. BRANDT, *The Rhetoric of Argumentation*, 143.

[146] Cf. Ex 12,21-36; 13,6-10;

[147] A detailed examination of Passover imagery and discussion of how it informs these verses is presented in R. LE DÉAUT, «The Paschal Mystery» IV, 202-210; V, 262-69. These rites were also symbolically interpreted by PHILO, cf. *Q. Exod*, I, 4,1ff.; 15,1ff.

[148] As Israel, through the power of God was redeemed from the bondage of slavery, set apart by the blood of the lamb to be protected and brought forth as his people, so are Christians saved by the power of God through the redemptive historical act of Christ, purified by his blood and established as God's people.

[149] Cf. 1Cor 1,30 «*hos egenèthè* [...] *hymin dikaiosynè te kai hagiasmos kai apolytrôsis*»; cf. also Eph 5,25.

[150] *Hagiasmos* is a *nomen actionis*. Hence to be in the state of sanctification implies to be in a continual process of sanctifying (cf. O. PROCKSCH, «*hagiasmos*», I, 113).

[151] Cf. 1Cor 7,14, the opposite of holy is *akathartos*; Holiness without a moral connotation is translated by the Greek, *hieros*. *Hagios*, possibly under the influence of the Greek *hagnos*, pure or chaste, came to include moral ideas and was understood as equivalent to *to katharos* (cf. N.H. SNAITH, *The Distinctive Ideas*, 45).

[152] Cf. 1Thess 4,2. «*touto gar estin thèlema tou theou, ho hagiasmos hymôn*».

[153] Here *hôste* is inferential, «therefore».

[154] This is the only example in the NT of *hôste* followed by the subjunctive. According to Blass – Debrunner, § 335, the hortatory subjunctive can be considered as a substitute for the imperative.

festival[155] *en azymois*[156]. Since they are unleavened bread, this can only mean that the community must celebrate the feast with its very life. The seven-day ritual of unleavened bread is now replaced by the perennial[157] living of unleavened lives. In other words, the material is replaced by the personal[158]. Hence holiness is now transferred to the sphere of the personal and is linked with the ethical. That their lives must make tangible the reality of new life gives insight into Paul's choice of the words[159] *eilikrineias* and *alètheias* to characterize unleavened life. From the etymology[160] of *eilikrineias* comes the derived meaning purity, which also points to transparency. By combining this term, taken in a moral sense, with *alètheias* Paul lays stress on the authenticity and transparency that must characterize Christian life so that the reality of the new life feasted is made visible in and through the moral life of the community[161]. Without a new way of living, «new life» would remain an abstract conviction. For Paul, Christian life is meant to attest to the acceptance of the truth and claims of the gospel and make the reality of new life tangible. Here, as

---

[155] According to H. CONZELMANN, *1 Korinther*, 99 the feast was definitely not a Christian Passover. Others see this as a possible allusion to the celebration of the Eucharist, cf. e.g. G. FEE, *1 Corinthians*, 218.

[156] *en azymois* has been translated «with unleavened bread» cf. e.g. NRSV; NAB. Forkmann takes *en* locally, links this phrase with Pauline expressions relating to walking *in* an old/new context of life and then suggests that by this expression Paul has given a fundamental motivation for expulsion, viz., by walking in the old, the brother has, in fact, removed himself from the community which the expulsion simply confirms (cf. *Limits*, 149). Even if one were to take *en* in the local sense, whether one can infer from this all that Forkmann claims is questionable.

[157] The present tense, *heortazômen*, implies duration and is preferred to the aorist in cases where general precepts regarding behavior are set out, cf. Blass – Debrunner, § 336.

[158] Similarly in Rom 12,1 the material offering as something distinct from the giver is replaced by the personal offering of the body. Hence the community is both presenter of the sacrifice and the holy and acceptable sacrifice itself.

[159] G. FEE's suggestion (cf. FEE, *1 Corinthians*, 219) that the choice of words may be related to a polemic about Paul's own behavior seems far-fetched.

[160] Cf. F. BÜSCHEL, «*eilikrinès, eilikrineia*», 397-398. Recently, D.A. RENWICK has suggested that *eilikrineia* ought to be translated here at 5,8 in the cultic sense of purity which the author considers «more appropriate in the context of Paul's argument» (cf. *Paul*, 64-65). The author relies on Newton's disputable claim (see the discussion below), that Paul frames 1Cor 5 within a cultic not moral perspective. Based on the alleged cultic meaning of *eilikrineia* at 5,8, Renwick further claims that this same cultic sense is maintained at 2Cor 1,12 and 2,17, the only other occurrences of this term in Paul. But in neither of these occurrences is it indisputably clear that Paul intends a cultic meaning.

[161] Cf. Phil 2,15; Christians must «shine as lights in the world [...]»; cf. further the comments in G. THERRIEN, *Le discernement*, 181.

elsewhere[162], the manifestation or verification of the reality of new life is linked by Paul with ethical action[163]. Hence, the necessity of renouncing and separating from *palaia zymè*, that is *kakia* and *ponèria*, vice and wickedness, which, taken together, imply a renunciation of all evil deeds. By way of this general exhortation Paul urges the community to live in a manner consistent with its own moral *ethos*, which is holiness. On a particular level, apropos of the matter at hand, this implies the necessity of expelling the offender, which in the final analysis is not an obligation imposed from without, but derives from the intrinsic nature of the community as *azymoi*/holy, a term that is at once both descriptive and prescriptive. In this light, Paul's command to remove the man can be understood as an explicit articulation of an implicit obligation that derives from the condition of new life in which the Corinthians as Christians exist[164].

M. Newton[165] has argued that this command to cleanse is a cultic not moral injunction since Paul envisions the community as the temple of God with the cultic obligation to keep purity within its precincts. But this argument is not especially compelling[166]. First, the language of cult purity referred to in 1Thess and Phil and mustered as evidence for Paul's concern with cultic purity is, with two exceptions, not found in 1Cor[167]. Moreover, the term *naos*[168], which one would expect to be linked with language of cultic purity is entirely absent from 1Thess and Phil. The fact that Paul encourages the communities in 1Thess and Phil to be pure by employing language of cult purity without ever referring to them as the *naos tou theou*, while he refers to the Corinthians as the *naos tou theou* (1Cor 3,16; 3,17 bis)[169], but without using the expression in combination

---

[162] Cf. Rom 12,2; 13,13; Gal 5,22-25; Eph 4,25-31; 1Cor 6,12-20.

[163] Moreover, in Paul «l'éthique[...], elle est aussi le lieu de progrès dans la sanctification, dans la mesure où nous laissons la grâce de Dieu produire ses effets» (J.-N. ALETTI, «Ethicisation», 131). However, as Aletti emphasized, in Paul, ethical action is not what saves, 128-131. Cf. further A. HIEBERT, «The Foundations», esp. 59.

[164] Another way to express this would be to say that for Paul, community limits are oriented from the fact of its holiness, cf. G. FORKMANN, *Limits*, 193.

[165] M. NEWTON, *The Concept*, esp. 86-97.

[166] Objections to Newton's thesis as a whole are raised in L.W. COUNTRYMAN, *Dirt*, 98 and passim.

[167] For example, *amemptos* (1Thess 3,13), *amemptôs* (1Thess 2,10; 3,13; 5,23) and *amômos* (Phil 2,15) are not found in 1Cor. *Aproskopos* is found only in 1Cor 10,32. *Eilikrinia*, not *eilikrinès* as in Phil 1,10, is the only term of those cited by Newton which actually appears in 1Cor 5 at v. 8.

[168] In the entire Pauline corpus this term occurs only 8x at 1Cor 3,16.17(bis); 6,19; 2Cor 6,16; Eph 2,21; 2Thess 2,4.

[169] The expression *naos theou*, as a designation for the community is found only one other time at 2Cor 6,16 for a total of 4 occurrences in the Pauline corpus. Once, at

with language of cult purity, is hardly incidental. The dissociation of these terms within these letters[170] is no doubt intended to reflect and underscore the fact that for Paul cult was spiritualized[171]. This is made explicit in Rom 12,1. Personal purity, i.e., moral cleansing, replaces cultic/material purity. Second, if Paul understands the community as the new temple of God with purity obligations that are cultically not ethically conceived, then Paul would have to insist on the community's total separation from the world with its polluting possibilities[172]. But Paul did not advocate segregation. Rather, he expected Christians to live in the world and there, in the midst of a crooked and perverse generation, to «shine as lights» (cf. Phil 2,15). In fact, unlike the Qumran covenanters[173], Paul manifested a great openness with regard to social intercourse, though he insisted that the holiness of the community also demanded great discipline and vigilance. Third, there is no explicit mention of the temple in 1Cor 5. B. Rosner[174] recognizes the latter as an obstacle which he tried to overcome, but it appears without success, in order to sustain his own thesis that 1Cor

---

2Thess 2,4 it refers to the concrete reality. In light of this, it is hard to understand what Ellis intends when he says: «the designation *naos theou* is fairly common in Paul» (E.E. ELLIS, *Paul's Use*, 90).

[170] The only time in the entire Pauline corpus that the term *naos theou* as a designation for the community is combined with a cultic purity term, *akathartou*, is at 2Cor 6,16-17. But even here, there is a transferred spiritual meaning. Cf. the discussion in B. GÄRTNER, *The Temple*, 50-56.

[171] The notion of spiritualized cult is also found in the Qumran community, cf. 1 QS VIII, 5-6; 4QFlor 1,6ff. Some assume Paul's dependence on Essene ideas (cf. e.g. B. GÄRTNER, *The Temple*); others argue for independent development (cf. e.g. J. MURPHY-O'CONNOR, «Christ» 123 n. 7; ID., «Qumran», 63-65).

[172] Paul does not prohibit, for example, mixed marriages (cf. 7,13), eating with non-believing persons (cf. 10,27), eating what is being sold in the pagan meat markets (cf. 10,25) – all polluting things.

[173] The Qumran community also envisioned itself as a new spiritual temple in which new spiritual sacrifices were offered (cf. 1QS 8.4-10; 9.3-6), but it also maintained the principle of physical separation as testimony to the holiness of the community (cf. 1QS 5,1). Detailed rules regarding intercourse with gentiles so as not to profane the holy are listed in CD XII, 12-20. Christians remained un-segregated as did the Pharisees although for the latter cultic rules dominated daily existence (cf. J. NEUSNER, *The Idea*, esp. 66-71).

[174] Cf. B. ROSNER, «Temple», 137-145. The author's solution is to take 1Cor 3,16-17 as the theological background against which to read 1Cor 5. He offers a few observations to justify this proposal but these start with the author's claim to know that Paul's starting presupposition in his discussion in 1Cor 5 is that the community is a temple (cf. 141). Among the difficulties of associating the discussion of 3,16-17 with that of 1Cor 5 in order to show that the holiness of the temple is the issue in 1Cor 5 is that one must take the term *phtherein* in the protasis of 3,17 with a moral connotation, i.e., «if someone makes God's temple unholy». But the context does not support this connotation.

5 should be read against the OT temple motif. In any event, apropos of Newton's proposal, it would appear that the stress on the cultic over the ethical is unwarranted.

In sum, we have seen that in vv. 6-8, Paul walks the community through a reasoning process in which he presents and integrates a series of ideas and images which are ultimately rooted in the fact of Christ's redemptive act. By now the minds of the Corinthians should be sufficiently illuminated so as to bring them to say: yes, we understand why this is a bad situation for us, we see who we are[175], and we know what we must do. While this section aims at the minds of the community, nonetheless it contains a certain emotional appeal as well since Paul's reasoning sets in evidence the community's own noble sinless and sanctified state. Now along with, but even more than, the need to efface its disgrace, the community has acquired sound and positive reasons why a change of judgement and comportment is necessary and why the offender must be expelled.

10. Proof by Pathos: 1Cor 5,9-13

In the five concluding verses of chapter 5, Paul wends his way back to the issue of the community's failure in discernment through the mention of a previous letter[176] which obviously included a warning about relations with immoral persons[177]. A number of scholars[178] maintain that a misunderstanding of Paul's instructions in the previous letter had led to confusion within the community which allowed the incest issue to get out of hand and the brother to live in this relationship with impunity. This would explain Paul's apparently abrupt mention of the previous letter here and the subsequent clarification. Some take the misunderstanding as deliberate but give varying motives[179]. According to Fee the misinterpretation was intended as a blatant challenge to Paul's authority and explains Paul's

---

[175] Cf. On the importance of the question, Who are we? in moral argument (cf. W. MEEKS, *Moral World*, 12).

[176] Beyond this warning the contents of the «previous letter» are irretrievable except hypothetically. Cf. above c. 3 n. 61.

[177] The phrase *mè synanamignysthai pornois* (5,9) presumably only summarizes what Paul had written.

[178] Cf. e.g. W. SCHRAGE, *1 Korinther*, 386; ID., *Die konkreten Einzelgebote*, 39; C.J. ROETZEL, *Judgement*, 115-116; C.K. BARRETT, *1 Corinthians*, 130; G. FEE, *1 Corinthians*, 220-221.

[179] Hurd claims that it was an intentional misunderstanding affording a pretext to act badly, «out of a deliberate desire to make him [Paul] appear ridiculous» (cf. J.C. HURD, *Origin*, 152). Unless one accepts Hurd's reconstruction of events this suggestion has little foundation. Others consider the community's behavior as «in part deliberate» (cf. e.g. C.K. BARRETT, *1 Corinthians*, 130).

need to reassert his authority in c. 5[180]. It is also hypothetically possible, although it has not been suggested, that Paul inserts the mention of the previous letter as a way of anticipating and heading off any possible Corinthian recourse to it for apologetic purposes to excuse their behavior which Paul's letter is now revealing to be reprehensible. What Paul shows is how such misinterpretation, whether actual or as he may be anticipating it to be, is absurd since the community would need to go out of the world (cf. 5,10) – an impossibility[181]. Then in 5,11 Paul reasserts what he did say. Whether the mention of the previous letter is taken to be necessitated by actual or feigned confusion over it or is introduced by way of anticipating and proleptically thwarting a community recourse to it for apologetic purposes, what is implied is the same: the community failed to discern the evil that corrupts the community and to judge and discipline those inside[182], *tous esô* (cf. 5,12) who perpetrate evil.

Based on the text before us we know what Paul claims he did not intend by his remarks, viz., a prohibition of all social intercourse with the immoral *tou kosmou toutou* (cf. 5,10), i.e., society at large. What he intended he now makes explicit in 5,11[183] viz., separation from *tis adelphos onomazomenos*, if he falls into the category of vice-doers listed in v. 11. Our concern now will center on the rhetorical function of the vice list[184] that Paul introduces in v. 11.

By classing[185] the «one calling himself a brother» with the other perpetrators of evil mentioned in the vice list, Paul is, in effect, arguing[186] that

---

[180] Cf. G. FEE, *1 Corinthians*, 221.

[181] A condition contrary to fact is expressed in the imperfect *ôpheilete*, before which *an* should be supplied, cf. Blass – Debrunner, § 358,1.

[182] Paul's thought, as reflected here, is that corruption can proceed only from within the community. Evil perpetrated by outsiders was no less evil but it had no corrupting impact on the community; hence it was not the community's but God's competence to judge these.

[183] Most commentators take *egrapsa*, v. 11, as an epistolary aorist, in contrast to the simple aorist *egrapsa* at v. 9. Conzelmann regards *nun* v. 11, as logical, not temporal, and takes *egrapsa* as a simple aorist, as in v. 9. He translates *nun de egrapsa*, «But in actual fact I wrote you» (H. CONZELMANN, *1 Korinther*, 102). Conzelmann's translation stresses that Paul is not introducing a new idea but only specifying what he meant in the previous letter. Taking *nun* as temporal and *egrapsa*, v. 11, as an epistolary aorist does not necessarily undermine this point.

[184] For opposing views on whether the vice list is specific or extrinsic to the epistolary context of 1Cor with its unique ethical and theological concerns, cf. e.g. H. CONZELMANN, *1 Korinther*, 100 and W. SCHRAGE, *Die konkreten Einzelgebote*, 43-44 (extrinsic); P. ZAAS, «Catalogues», 623 and V. FURNISH, *Theology*, 84-86 (specific).

[185] Note the coordinating conjunction or (*ê*) used 3x in 5,11 by which Paul associates the so-called brother with a class of sinners.

[186] Classification is «rarely devoid of argumentative intent» (C. PERELMAN – L. OLBRECHTS-TYTECA, *The New Rhetoric*, 127).

the incestuous man is a rank sinner, identifiable with those sinners mentioned elsewhere cf. 6,9-10, who will not inherit the kingdom[187]. Thus Paul brings «brother», a term whose use has been reserved until now, under the common mantle of *ponèros*, establishing a connection between two terms which should otherwise be mutually exclusive. One cannot be brother participating in the same paschal condition in which the whole community partakes and at the same time *ponèros*. Through this classification Paul no doubt intends to create a negative attitude in the community toward the brother. In fact, «classes are indeed characterized not only by the features common to their members but also, and sometimes mostly, by the attitude adopted toward them, the manner of judging and treating them»[188]. Apropos of the particular case at hand, the classification is aimed at influencing the community to recognize and treat this brother who has married his step-mother as a sinner. Regardless of those reasons by which the community may have come to tolerate or boast of this marriage, Paul's classification makes it clear that it is still an act of *porneia* and the brother is a *pornos*. The vice list makes evident that there is no double standard for Paul nor does he expect one to operate within the community. A vice-doer who is a brother is still a vice-doer and hence a rank sinner[189]. This is the reality with which the community must deal. Here Paul draws the line not between Christians and pagans or Christians and Jews but between Christians and pseudo-Christians.

Rhetorically speaking, it seems clear that the function of this classification is to appeal to the community's *pathos*, i.e., to rouse the community's negative emotions, creating a sense of abhorrence for the brother and his

---

[187] According to J. GUNDRY VOLF, the difference between the incestuous man, considered by Paul, «a falsely professing Christian who is yet outside the kingdom and who belongs to the world» (cf. *Paul*, 116) and the «fornicators of this world» is that the latter merely await the final judgement when God judges outsiders, whereas for the former, ultimate destruction is not the final word since the discipline is intended to induce repentance and conversion, the «presupposition of his final salvation» (cf. 119). Though the author admits that Paul makes no mention of repentance and conversion, she insists that it is understood since for Paul the offender's «final salvation is unthinkable apart from repentance and conversion» (cf. 119). Similar views are found in G.W.H. LAMPE, «Church Discipline», 345; G. FORKMANN, *Limits*, 145-146 and R. HAMMERTON-KELLY, *Sacred Violence*, 86. For opposing views cf. e.g. H. CONZELMANN, *1 Korinther*, 98 n. 40; I. HAVENER, «A Curse», 338. Perhaps the most that can be said based on the text evidence is that the offender's ultimate salvation is intended.

[188] C. PERELMAN – L. OLBRECHTS-TYTECA, *The New Rhetoric*, 127.

[189] The implication is that neither the identity of the subject of the action nor his intention counts. Paul may be subtly intending to contradict Stoic claims to the effect that the wise man could not sin because sin was a matter of intention, cf. above c. 3 n. 160.

deed and a feeling of alienation toward such a one. This sense of abhorrence and alienation that the rhetorical use of the vice list was aimed at
provoking constitutes a further stimulus, again negative, which should
move the community toward formalizing the alienation through expulsion.

The use of the vice list itself[190], the feeling of abhorrence and the type
of negative evaluation that this classification was intended to elicit resonate with Jewish sentiments and negative evaluation of such *porneia*[191].
Of the practices characteristic of the heathen, specifically the Egyptians
and Canaanites named in Lev 18,1-3, the first to be listed as forbidden to
Israel was the practice of incest (cf. 18,6). This reference to incest extends
for nine more verses as every degree of relationship that could be considered incestuous is individually mentioned. Such incestuous relationships
were rejected by the law of Moses because as Philo claims, they were
regarded «with abhorrence, as alien and hostile to a commonwealth free
of reproach and as encouragements and incitements to the vilest
customs»[192]. Jewish renunciation of this and other such vile practices was
mustered as evidence of what distinguished Jews from pagans and touted
as testimony to the moral superiority of the Jews[193]. Paul's injection of the
Jewish perspective into this third unit of the chapter is subtle but clear
from v. 13b which contains an allusion[194] to the Torah. This allusion
functions rhetorically to confirm[195] and make explicit the Jewish perspective.

---

[190] In Hellenistic Judaism, the vice list enumerated sins which were considered patently pagan, cf. e.g. PHILO, *De Specialibus,* 4,84.87; *T Reub* 3,2-8; *T Levi* 14.5-8; *T
Jud* 16,1; *Jub* 21,21; *Syb Or* 2,255; 1,174-179. On the provenance of virtue and vice
catalogues see the concise discussion in H. CONZELMANN, *1 Korinther,* 100-101.

[191] This forbidden relationship with one's step-mother was frequently discussed in
Jewish literature, cf. e.g Jub. 33,1-17; PHILO, *De Specialibus,* III, 20; JOSEPHUS, *Cont
Ap* II, 200; *Ant.* III, 274; Ps. PHOC., *Sentences,* 179. On attitudes toward *porneia* in late
Judaism see the study by L. ROSSO UBIGLI, «Alcuni aspetti», 201-245.

[192] PHILO, *De Specialibus,* III, 22-25. Moreover in regard to incest, an impious
deed, Philo also says, «justice who watches over human affairs avenges unholy deeds
on the impious and the impiety extends beyond the perpetrator of the deed to those
who range themselves with the perpetrator», III, 19 Cf. also JOSEPHUS, *Ant..,* 3.12.1.
Incest, he remarks, was «abhorred» by Moses as «one of the greatest crimes».

[193] Cf. *The Letter of Aristeas,* 151-152.

[194] V. 5,13b may be classified as an allusion (cf. E.E. ELLIS, *Paul's Use,* 153).
More will be said on this below, § 12.

[195] P. ZAAS suggests that the citation functions rhetorically to introduce the original
ethos of the book of Deuteronomy (cf. «Cast the Evil Man» 259-261). It might be
more precise to say, v. 13b. confirms the perspective of Judaism since it is already
interwoven into this last unit of c. 5 starting with the vice list.

Paul's conclusion[196] to the whole argument begins at v. 12 where he personally disclaims judgement of outsiders and reminds the community that its responsibility is to judge insiders[197] i.e., those who can have a corrupting effect on the community. Then in v. 13b Paul introduces an expression which recalls an expulsion formula found in Deuteronomy[198], *exarate*[199] *ton ponèron ex hymôn autôn*. With this phrase Paul concludes the sub-unit vv. 9-13, and rounds off the whole argument, echoing v. 2c.

11. Rhetorical Strategy, Community Role and Rhetorical Genre

In the preceding pages we have analyzed each of the three segments attentive to the rhetorical features and strategy that Paul has employed. Now we must go back and answer the questions raised at the beginning of the present chapter with regard to Paul's aim/s in 1Cor 5 and the role of the community. We will also consider what these findings suggest with regard to the type of rhetoric Paul employed. Then we will consider and evaluate the criteria Paul sets out in this chapter. Before we begin these tasks it would be useful to schematize our analysis, which can be presented as follows:

Subsection a: vv. 1-5

Strategy	Argument based on Pathos
	Comparison of the community with pagans
	Negative emotional stimulus – *pathos*/shame
Criteria	Extrinsic (Secular society)
Objective	Move the community to change opinions and take a new course of action
Action	*arthè ek mesou hymôn*, v. 2; action elaborated vv. 3-5

---

[196] The conclusion of Paul's argument conforms perfectly to the paratactic style that is recommended for the epilogue, cf. ARISTOTLE, *Ars Rhetorica*, III.XIX, 5-6.

[197] The contradiction that 6,2, «*hoi hagioi ton kosmon krinousin*», poses with 5,12 is only apparent. In 5,12 Paul is not speaking about eschatological judgement but judgement and disciplining in the present.

[198] Cf. LXX Dt 17,7b.12b; 19,19b; 21,21b, 22,21c.22c.24d; 24,9b.

[199] While in the Deuteronomic formula the verb is always an aorist 2nd person singular, Paul uses an aorist plural. The change may signify Paul's awareness that «excommunication is not an apostolic prerogative» but necessarily the work of the «whole community, in whose hands (under Christ) authority lies» (C.K. BARRETT, *1 Corinthians*, 133).

Subsection b: vv. 6-8

Strategy	Argument based on Logos
	Analogical Reasoning (Grounded in Christ's death)
	Positive rational stimulus (contains positive emotional appeal)
Criteria	Intrinsic (new life in Christ)
Objective	Move the community to change opinions and take a new course of action
Action	*ekkatharate tèn palaian zymè*, v. 7a

Subsection a': vv. 9-13

Strategy	Argument based on Pathos
	Classification of the brother with sinners
	Negative emotional stimulus=*pathos*/abhorrence – alienation
Criteria	Extrinsic (Jewish)
Objective	Move the community to change opinions and take a new course of action
Action	*exarate ton ponèron ex hymôn autôn*, v. 13b

In each of the sub-units Paul's objective remains constant. He wants to move the community to change its own opinions about the incest and adopt a new course of action. The point of the action also remains constant; it is exclusion. To accomplish his aims Paul works both on the emotions and the mind of the Corinthian community. As we have seen, his strategy is to begin in the *a* unit and end in the *a'* unit with proofs based on pathos. In the center of these emotional appeals, he sets his argument based on logos. Some[200] would maintain that Paul casts the community in the role of decision maker about a future action and take the rhetoric as deliberative[201]. As far as we can see there are a number of difficulties attached to designating 1Cor 5 as exclusively deliberative rhetoric. Consider, for example, the following points: a) the *telos* of

---

[200] Cf. e.g. B. WITHERINGTON, *Conflicts*; M. MITCHELL, *Paul*, G. KENNEDY considers the letter largely deliberative with perhaps two judicial passages, 1,13-17; 9 (cf. *New Testament Interpretation* 87). J. MURPHY-O'CONNOR has recently come down on the side of deliberate as most suited to Paul's letters and considers 1Cor as deliberative (cf. *Paul et l'art épistolaire*, esp. 105-115). While he recognizes Paul's occasional use of judicial, he summarily dismisses the attribution of epideictic to Paul's discourses. However, the importance of the epideictic genre which was well-suited to the occasional nature of letters and, to which genre many types of letters listed in the handbooks correspond, should not be facilely dismissed (cf. S.K. STOWERS «Social Typification», 84-86).

[201] See the description in QUINTILIAN, *Institutio*, III, 8.2ff. A schematic summary of Quintilian's statement on the object, method, etc. of all three genre, is provided in J. MURPHY-O'CONNOR, *Paul et l'art épistolaire*, 104.

deliberative rhetoric is to decide one course of action from among possible courses. In essence then, deliberative rhetoric is occupied with the question, What shall we do? In 1Cor 5, there is no deliberation over possible courses of action. One and only one course of action is announced; b) the chapter is punctuated with imperatives[202] and not exhortations which are characteristic of deliberation[203]. If something is imperative then it is necessary, but necessity rules out deliberation[204]; c) in other passages in 1Cor where Paul is unambiguously deliberating he explicitly sets up advantage/*utilitas*[205] and then discusses possible courses of action from the vantage point of what is helpful[206], better[207] or can build up[208]. He does not do this here. Granted Paul states in 1Cor 5,6 «your boasting is not good». The use of the term «*kalos*» could be considered as introducing a deliberative element into the discussion. However, there really is no deliberating here about whether their choice to boast is good or not. Their boasting is simply pronounced «not good». Nor, it would appear, is Paul deliberating with the community over a course of action. There can only be one course of action taken against the offender and Paul announces it.

Based on the analysis presented above what Paul aims to do is to refocus the Corinthians' attention on the values from which right judgements and actions will issue. He does this in every way possible: by shaming (v. 2a,b), commanding (v. 2c,5,7,13), telling them to judge (v. 2b[209],12b), molding their attitude to the incest (v. 1b) and the sinning brother (v. 11), and by bringing them through a process of discernment through which they are confronted by and reminded of who they are and must be, vv. 6-8. In 1Cor 5, Paul primarily seeks to influence the minds, dispositions and opinions of the community[210]. In varied ways, the community is being called on to reconsider its identity, to what values it must be committed and then to render a new judgement about the brother in light of these values and go forward with the appropriate action that Paul has outlined. These aims and these tasks, in light of what has been advanced by

---

[202] Cf. 5,2c.5.7.13b; *heortazômen* in v. 8 is probably meant to stand for the imperative, cf. above n. 154.

[203] Cf. QUINTILIAN, *Institutio*, III, 4,1.

[204] QUINTILIAN, *Institutio*, III.VII, 21-25.

[205] Characteristic of deliberative oratory, cf. *Ad Her.*, II, 3.

[206] Cf. *sympherein*, 1Cor 6,12; 10,23; *symphoron*, 1Cor 7,35; 1Cor 10,33.

[207] Cf. e.g. *kreisson*, 1Cor 7,39; *kalon*, 1Cor 7,26.

[208] Cf. e.g. *oikodomein*, 1Cor 10,23b; 14,3ff.

[209] Cf. the discussion on *penthein*, above c. 3 § 4.4.

[210] This would appear to be the task of the whole letter as argued convincingly by C.B. COUSAR, «The Theological Task», 90-102.

Perelman and Olbrechts-Tyteca[211], coincide with epideictic, understood as rhetoric that seeks to strengthen adherence to values and create a sense of communion, not as a mere intellectual exercise but rather, to move an audience to perform a desired action[212]. Moreover, in epideictic oratory, the role of the speaker is that of educator whose primary concern is to speak in defense of the cause of his audience, in defense of the values that he and his audience hold in common[213]. In the course of the analysis we have seen that Paul has assumed such a role, speaking for the values of the community and persuading them, both through shame and reason, to defend these. If we have understood correctly the tasks of the community, the aims of Paul and the role he assumed, then it would be more accurate to designate 1Cor 5 as largely epideictic rhetoric.

12. The Criteria Employed in 1Cor 5

As Paul began by capitalizing on the convergence of Greco-Roman and Christian values to launch his argument, he concludes it, as pointed out above, with reference to the Jewish perspective. Neither perspective dominates the discussion but together form the framework for the argumentation. Paul can bring both to bear on the discussion because, with regard to incest, the moral standards of the secular world and those of Judaism are related positively to the moral demands of new life in Christ[214]. What pagans know naturally regarding incest[215] and Jews know by revealed law[216], comprises standards of behavior that Christians, living according to the Spirit, cannot simply abandon[217]. The Corinthians ought

---

[211] Cf. C. PERELMAN – L. OLBRECHTS-TYTECA, *The New Rhetoric*, 47-51.

[212] C. PERELMAN – L. OLBRECHTS-TYTECA, *The New Rhetoric*, 49. Even in antiquity the conception of epideictic rhetoric had undergone a certain degree of revisionism. By the 1st c. A.D., epideictic was no longer viewed as mere ornamentary rhetoric, but was considered as having a persuasive and pragmatic function related to praise and blame. See the discussions in B. VICKERS, *In Defense*, esp. 54-61 and J.R. CHASE, «The Classical Conception», 293-300.

[213] Cf. C. PERELMAN – L. OLBRECHTS-TYTECA, *The New Rhetoric*, 51.

[214] But when pagan and Jewish criteria and standards are in conflict with the demands of new life in Christ, Paul rejects these, cf. e.g. Gal 2,15; 5,2-4; 1Cor 2,6.13. At 1Cor 10,1-13 he warns against imitating Jewish immorality.

[215] Cf. Rom 2,14-15. Whether Paul was here referring to the Hellenistic concept «*nomos physikos*» (cf. e.g. EPICTETUS, *Discourses*, III.XVII, 6), or simply meant that pagans know and obey naturally God's law which is positively formulated in the Torah is debated, cf. V. FURNISH, *Theology and Ethics*, 48-49.

[216] Cf. Lev 17,8.

[217] See the comments of J. MURPHY-O'CONNOR, *L'existence*, 134, 137-138; E. LOHSE, *Theological Ethics*, 35-36. However, it is perhaps too much to claim that, in his moral teaching, Paul's «first concern was to inculcate Jewish behavior in his converts» (E.P. SANDERS, *Paul*, 95).

to have known as the pagans, among whom «such a *porneia* is not heard» (v. 1), that incest is an evil and not to be done or tolerated. Further they ought to have recognized that the one who lives incestuously is a *pornos*, and ought to be removed from their midst (v. 13b). Paul is able to invoke these standards as criteria against the toleration of incest and for the expulsion of the *pornos* and thereby reinforce his argument.

But continuity with the standards of the world and Judaism is not the ultimate motivation or the *telos* of Christian ethical living. Rather Christians must live and regulate their behavior because of a person and an event[218]. Christ's death is the only «because» (*gar*, v. 7c) in the entire chapter and as we observed in the analysis, it is the hinge which grounds Paul's affirmations and commands in vv. 6-8. In c. 5, the material instruction to remove the offender derives directly from this Christological argumentation and its derivation need not be sought in the Torah, as sometimes claimed. Recently, B. Rosner has studied 1Cor 5-7 to test his thesis that Paul is indebted to the OT for his ethics[219]. Apropos of 1Cor 5, Rosner takes v. 13b, which he considers a Torah citation[220], as a signal that the moral demands of the OT must somehow lie at the heart of Paul's ethical instruction in 1Cor 5. Operating out of this assumption, Rosner quarries through 1Cor 5 in light of the OT and argues, based on alleged parallels, that the OT motifs of corporate responsibility, temple holiness and covenant underlie and inform Paul's line of argument in c. 5. The first two motifs were the subject of independent articles by Rosner. In discussing these articles[221], we found that in neither instance had the author convincingly established his case and that there were indications of forced reading. Moreover, in chapter three of his book, a chapter entitled, «Ezra and Paul Excluding Sinners. 1Cor 5,1-13», the author verges on parallelomania as he seeks to bolster his argument for the scriptural basis of Paul's ethics by noting word parallels in the OT and 1Cor 5[222].

Rosner's attempt to redress what he considers to be unwarranted scholarly dismissing[223] of the OT with regard to Paul's ethics has perhaps

---

[218] Cf. P. GRECH, «Christological Motives», 549.

[219] B. ROSNER, *Paul*, This is a revision of the author's dissertation.

[220] B. ROSNER, *Paul*, 63. We are inclined to agree with Ellis' evaluation of v. 13b as an allusion (cf. above n. 194). A citation is usually preceded by an opening statement, then an introductory formula. Moreover, the citation usually substantiates the statement that has been made as for example at Rom 1,16-17. This is not the case here at 5,13b. The preceding statement v. 13a, is not substantiated by what is introduced in 13b. In addition, an introductory formula is lacking.

[221] Cf. above n. 174 and c. 3 n. 198.

[222] Cf. B. ROSNER, *Paul*, c. 3, esp. § 5.

[223] Rosner has in mind A. VON HARNACK, «Das Alte Testament», 129-141.

brought him to attach too much significance to v. 13b *vis-à-vis* claims about the OT basis of the whole argument and to overstate his case. In fact, in the conclusion to his chapter on 1Cor 5, he states, «As we navigated our course through 1 Corinthians 5 we discovered that the Deuteronomic expression in 5:13b was not a mirage but the tip of a veritable iceberg of dependence on the Jewish Scriptures»[224]. But what does Rosner mean by «mirage» and why does he use it and pose his findings as confirmation of the opposite? It seems apparent that for him, any suggestion that v. 13b is less than a flashing light which requires and justifies the excavation of 1Cor 5 for the purpose of determining the scriptural basis of Paul's argument is tantamount to treating the expression as a «mirage». The use of the term may express the author's prejudice with regard to understanding this expression in terms of its rhetorical function[225]. To signal the rhetorical function of v. 13b in the unfolding of the argument is hardly to consider the expression a mirage. Rosner falls prey to the unfortunate tendency to discount rhetorical insights as superficial. However, here we do not wish to defend the merits of synthetic approaches to the text or to question Rosner's behind-the-text approach. What we do wish to call attention to however, is that Rosner's study of 1Cor 5, even had it convincingly demonstrated Paul's dependence on OT scriptures throughout the passage, still does not prove that Paul relied exclusively on the OT as a guide to his response in this chapter. Moreover, to accent affinities between Pauline and Jewish moral teaching is not to prove that Paul's response in 1Cor 5 was based on the OT or motivated by its concerns. In 1Cor 5, community holiness and its preservation are set within the context of Christ's death through which this state of sanctification has been effected[226]. It has already been pointed out that there is only one stated reason (*gar* v. 7c) which grounds the argument and it is Christological. If one had to individuate a presupposition with which Paul apparently addresses this issue, it would seem reasonable to say, based on the text information, that his presupposition was that Christians are justified and sanctified because Christ has been slain. As the argument stands, it is the community's new sinless status that makes the sin and the sinner intolerable. Hence, the need to expunge the sinner.

---

[224] B. ROSNER, *Paul*, 91.

[225] Rosner rejects the insights of P. ZAAS with regard to the rhetorical function of v. 13b (cf. *Paul*, 62).

[226] As a number of scholars have observed, cf. e.g. J. MURPHY-O'CONNOR, *Becoming Human*, 155; R. SCHNACKENBURG, *The Church*, 83.

Of course Rosner is not alone in his conviction. In fact, to some extent he has expanded aspects of a thesis set forth in an article by T. Holtz[227] who argued that throughout 1Cor Paul approaches each discussion from the Jewish perspective. Apropos of 1Cor 5, Holtz maintains that the presupposition with which Paul approached this case of incest was «offensichtlich jüdischer Natur»[228]. The author's key argument[229] to sustain this view is that the mention of *ethnè* at 5,1 points to the fact that Paul is making a special accusation from the Jewish perspective by mentioning that this is a deed condemned even by the *ethnè*. According to Holtz – for whom the term «even» is of great moment here – this «even» implies that the condemnation was pronounced by the Jews and that this condemnation should be sufficient[230]. But this is an assumption which cannot be verified. The fact is, we simply do not know if by referring to the *ethnè* Paul intended to inject the Jewish valuative perspective as Holtz claims. It could be that Paul's purpose in this remark was to assert that the community is without excuse since, even apart from the question of whether it was bound by Jewish moral law or not, the fact is, the gentile society from which they came also prohibits such practice[231]. Moreover, if the Jewish condemnation allegedly supplied through this reference to the *ethnè* were sufficient, as Holtz claims, then one is left to wonder why Paul continued with the rest of the argument in 1Cor 5.

Holtz's claims that 1Cor 5 is permeated by a Jewish perspective appear to gain strength only *vis-à-vis* his overall thesis – if considered valid – that Paul, in his ethical instructions throughout all of 1Cor, was essentially advocating a life lived in accord with Torah. Of course a statement such as «circumcision counts for nothing» at 1Cor 7,19 does not harmonize well with this claim. Holtz, however, hastens to construe what Paul would mean by a life lived according to Torah *vis-à-vis* contemporary Judaism's understanding of Torah as a cosmic ordering principle[232]. Here Holtz

---

[227] T. HOLTZ, «Zur Frage», 385-400.

[228] T. HOLTZ, «Zur Frage», 389.

[229] Holtz also argues that Paul's use of the typical OT expression «*gynè tou patros*» clearly indicates that he was speaking from a Jewish perspective, otherwise he could have employed the term *mètryiè* (cf. 389). But against this, one could object that Paul avoids the typical OT expression «to uncover the nakedness» (cf. e.g. Lev 17,8 *apokalyptein aschèmosynè*), using instead, «to have». If Paul wanted to make the Jewish perspective transparent would he not have employed the expression «uncovering the nakedness»? Furthermore, it is curious that Paul did not cite Lev 18,8, which would amount to indisputable proof of his intention to approach this case from a Jewish perspective.

[230] T. HOLTZ, «Zur Frage», 389.

[231] Cf. above n. 47.

[232] T. HOLTZ, «Zur Frage», 394-395.

relies on Philo[233] for whom cosmic order was equal to Mosaic law. Hence, this cosmic order/Divine *nomos* is forever valid and has implications for Christian ethics which means, according to Holtz, that Christian ethics are bound to the normative content of the law[234]. This evidence reflects how Philo and his Jewish contemporaries attributed a cosmic function to the Torah[235]. But, to what extent did such a cosmic understanding of *nomos* enter specifically into Paul's reasoning here with regard to this case of incest? Furthermore, would he have drawn the consequences for Christian ethics that Holtz claims? To answer such questions affirmatively, with certainty, is not possible. Indeed Holtz himself states, «Natürlich wissen wir nicht in welcher Form Paulus diese Gedanken geteilt hat»[236].

Finally we should consider some recent comments of E. J. Schnabel who also maintains that Paul's ethical instruction is grounded in the law. Schnabel takes v. 13b as an OT citation and says, the fact that it «concludes a train of thought» shows «that Paul regards the OT as authoritative»[237]. This remark needs to be analyzed. First, Schnabel takes the last-place position of what he considers a citation from scripture to mean that Paul, by placing it at the end, has now finally arrived at *the* authoritative statement which clinches the argument and grounds the precept. Beside the fact that v. 13b has more the character of allusion than citation, as noted[238], it cannot be assumed with Schnabel and others[239] that last-place position signals or confirms importance[240]. Second, Schnabel infers from the position of this allusion to Dt that the OT is the authoritative basis for the precept here in 1Cor 5. However, Paul never deduces a rule of action from scripture[241]. Based on an examination of

---

[233] Cf. PHILO, *Op.*, 3.

[234] Cf. T. HOLTZ, «Zur Frage», 396.

[235] On the understanding of the Law as the ground plan of the universe in Hellenistic Judaism, cf. e.g. W.D. DAVIES, *The Setting*, 157ff; M. HENGEL, *Judaism and Hellenism*, I, 153-175.

[236] T. HOLTZ, «Zur Frage», 395.

[237] Cf. E.J. SCHNABEL, *Law*, 314.

[238] Cf. above n. 220.

[239] Cf. e.g. O. MERK who comments, «Das zeigt in 5,13b wo mit einem Zitat der Anlaß des Kap 5 nochmals genannt und der 'Gedankengang' abgeschlossen wird, so daß das Zitat, den Charakter einer übergeordneten oder bestätigenden Norm gewinnt» (cf. *Handeln*, 91).

[240] As already indicated, it is inadvisable to ascribe importance based on position, cf. above c. 4, ad loc.

[241] According to P. GRECH's findings there is only one case, at Rom 12,19-21, where Lev 19,18 and Prov 25,21 are given as the sole reasons for a commandment (cf. «Christological Motives», 542). See further the comments in V. FURNISH, *Theology and Ethics*, 33-34.

twenty-five scriptural allusions found in ethical contexts, Murphy-O'Connor observed that the allusions are introduced as part of the unfolding of Paul's argument, but in no case is there any indication that the scriptural allusion is accorded a particular weight[242]. A. Lindemann studied the ethical responses in 1Cor and came to the conclusion that Torah legislation is not a decisive factor in Paul's responses at all. He states, «Die konkreten Weisungen des Paulus im Ersten Korintherbrief zeigen, das Paulus sich nicht an den Inhalten der Tora orientiert, wenn er ethische Normen aufstellt oder in Konfliktfällen Entscheidungen trifft»[243]. Moreover, the fact that Paul's counsel is, in this case, in material agreement with what the OT counsels, may lead to the realization that not everything in the New Testament is new, but it does not constitute an argument for Paul's dependence on the authority of the OT as the ultimate basis and force that drives and clinches his argument in 1Cor 5[244]. On the contrary, what appears to be clear in Paul, and new, is that when issues such as the licitness of eating *eidôlothuton*, litigation among brothers, or as in this case, what to do about immorality, are treated, his responses are filtered through the Christ event with all its implications for the community and how it must act[245]. It would appear then, that neither the fact that Paul alludes to Torah legislation nor its last-place position in the argument can be appealed to as proof that the Torah was the «last word» on this subject in the sense of *the* authoritative basis on which Paul grounded his argument and the precept to expel the offender.

The positions of Rosner, Holtz and Schnabel with regard to 1Cor 5 can be viewed as a piece within the much larger controversy over whether the Law, which Paul unequivocally rejected as *Heilsweg*[246], still functioned as a *Lebensnorm*[247]. It is not our intention here to re-open that debate[248] or

---

[242] Cf. J. MURPHY-O'CONNOR, *L'existence*, 147-149; V. FURNISH notes that in 1Cor, Paul explicitly cites Sacred Scripture in relation to an ethical counsel only 5x and uses these citations in a general or indirect way (cf. «Belonging», 149). Cf. also J. COPPENS, «Les arguments», 243-253.

[243] A. LINDEMANN, «Die biblischen Toragebote», 261. For a contrasting view see G.C. KRUSE, *Paul*, esp. 115-21, 143-148. Kruse maintains that Paul uses the Mosaic Law paradigmatically. He argues, but does not make a compelling case, that in 1Cor Paul «makes repeated appeals» to the law as a paradigm for Christian behavior (cf. 274).

[244] In Paul, «even in cases of identical action the motivation is usually typically Christian» (P. GRECH, «Christological Motives», 542). Cf. also, S. WESTERHOLM, *Israel's Law*, 200.

[245] Cf. e.g. 1Cor 6,19; 6,7b; 8,11.

[246] Cf. e.g. Rm 3,21-4,25; 7,1-6; Gal 2,16-21; 3,11-29; Phil 3,7-9; Eph 2,14-17.

[247] The view that the Law had continuing validity for Christian moral living has been vigorously championed by W. SCHRAGE. The author maintains that «Der Kampf gegen den Nomismus ist kein Kampf gegen das Halten der Gebote, sondern dagegen,

analyze the arguments advanced to support the positions. Rather, what is important to the discussion at hand, is to affirm, based on the evidence in 1Cor 5 that a) the ethical decision-making turns on the consideration of the redemptive act of God in Christ and what it effects in the present[249] and b) the concrete instruction to expel the offender is constructed as a response to this redemptive event on account of which believers presently enjoy a new justified and sanctified life which cannot be compromised by evil conduct and its toleration. This bears out the general observation of W. Meeks that for Paul what must be done and the knowledge of what must be done is determined by a complex of symbols clustering always around the one central redemptive act of God's Messiah[250].

As we noted above, Paul does not enunciate the analogies or explicitly draw out the implications of this Christological reasoning but these are clear. This is a community for whom Christ has died[251]. This redemptive act of God in Christ is the source of their new identity: of who they are (5,7b) and how they must live (v. 8). Through this reasoning Paul centers on the Christ event through which the whole community has acquired a new life, a new *ethos*. To be confronted with the saving activity of God in Christ and its implications is to be confronted by the gospel and its claims. The acceptance of the Christ event and its claims on Christians must become conspicuous in ethical living.

In vv. 6-8 we have Paul's only attempt at extended reasoning in this chapter. In this reasoning process, Paul leaves aside pagan and Jewish views and concerns and relies solely on intrinsic criteria, i.e., a consideration of the holy character and sinless status obtaining in this community because of the redemptive act of God in Christ. These considerations not only illumine the minds of the Corinthians but also, in contrast to the

---

dieses Halten der Gebote zum Helisweg und zur Helisbedingung zu verdrehen» (cf. *Die konkreten Einzelgebote*, 96, cf. further 232-238).

[248] Views on the status of the law *post Christum* are set out in C.T. RHYNE, *Faith*, 1-24 and more recently in G.C. KRUSE, *Paul*, c. 1.

[249] Paul's ethical paraenesis can also be formulated in light of the coming judgement of God, cf. e.g. Rom 2,6-9; 1Cor 6,9-10; Gal 5,21. Thus, Paul can dissuade Christians from evil conduct in consideration of both the present reality of new life and future judgement (cf. J.L. HOULDEN, *Ethics*, 30-31).

[250] Cf. W. MEEKS, ed., *The Writings*, 443. See also R.F. O'TOOLE, *Who is a Christian?*, c. 2.

[251] This Christocentric focus is also displaced in R. HAYS. But Hays' claim that by introducing Dt 17,7 at 1Cor 5,13b Paul intended to address gentile Corinthians as «children of the covenant» who are herewith called «to stand with Israel and join in the covenant confession [...]» (cf. *Echoes*, 97), appears to go beyond what can be reasonably inferred from the text. Moreover, Hays fails to suggest how the rhetorical effect which he claims 5,13b was intended to produce fits in with the rest of the argumentation and aims of 1Cor 5.

arousal of negative emotions in the a and a' units, provide a positive motivation to move the community to consider changing its opinions and
behavior. These factors point up the overriding significance of this «b»
unit in the development of the argument, a significance that is enhanced
by its location in the center of the composition. However, there is much
that Paul did not enunciate or explicate in these two central verses and
much that still needs to be understood. When the analogies are carefully
considered and the figurative language replaced with the concrete we
recognize that Paul is essentially saying: a) that ethics must be commu-
nity-based ethics since ethical choices made by individuals always have
an impact on the community; b) the well-being of the community is
primary and cannot be compromised; c) when individual ethical choices
conflict with or compromise the corporate sanctified life of the community, the individual cannot be spared. In 1Cor 5, the concrete call to expel
the man, impressive in its severity, is the logical consequence of these
unenunciated affirmations. While Paul has anchored his reasoning in vv.
6-8 in a Christological affirmation, it is apparent that both the reasoning
and the call for expulsion are linked to Paul's understanding of
community and will be better understood through a consideration of
Paul's ecclesiology. This discussion will occupy us in the next chapter.

13. Conclusion to Chapter 5

In the preceding pages we have treated Paul's response to the case of
the incest under the aspect of argumentation. In the analysis of this argumentation what became apparent is that Paul is engaged in the task of
rendering the community amenable to change: change of opinions and
behavior, that will ultimately lead to the desired course of action, viz., the
expulsion of the offender. By examining the rhetorical strategy and highlighting the logical relationship of its parts we hope to have dispelled the
view that Paul's main concern here is to champion his authority and to
discipline a recalcitrant community which must now simply obey. Our
analysis has revealed, to the contrary, that Paul's concern was to impress
on the community the need to join him in what was ultimately the defense
of its own well-being through appropriate and responsible action. While
Paul used extrinsic criteria to reinforce his argument, what became clear
in the analysis is that the heart of the argument is contained in vv. 6-8
where Paul guides the community through reasoning that is ultimately
grounded in the affirmation in 7c. Flowing from this affirmation are
implications that are linked to Paul's understanding of community which
must be considered if we hope to grasp Paul's argument in this chapter
and gain some insight into the disciplinary sanction which can strike the

modern reader as not only severe and excessive but also quite removed from the approach of Jesus who forgave and even ate with sinners[252].

We now turn to chapter 6 where, in light of some of Paul's ideas about community[253], we hope to gain a more adequate understanding of his response to the case of incest and some keener insights into the moral reasoning he sets out in 1Cor 5.

---

[252] Cf. Paul's advice in 5,11.

[253] In the next chapter we will being using the terms community and church (*ekklèsia*) interchangeably. On the connotations of *ekklèsia* as found in Paul cf. below c. 6 n. 5.

CHAPTER VI

Ethics, Ecclesiology and Church Discipline

1. Introduction

At this point in our study it should be evident that Paul's concern in 1Cor 5 does not focus on a simple case of private immorality but on the threat this case of private immorality, if unchecked, posed to the community's existence. In the previous chapter we noted that in addition to what Paul states expressly in 1Cor 5, there is much that is implicit which needs closer scrutiny. We suggested that a consideration of how Paul's ecclesiological conceptions inform his moral reasoning in 1Cor 5 could illumine our understanding of what is implicit and, in consequence, the understanding of the whole chapter. The need to set the discussion of 1Cor 5 within the context of Paul's ecclesiological conceptions is further illustrated when we consider that implicit in Paul's comments in 5,6-8 is the notion that there cannot be one member of the community who is *zymè* and another *azymè*. Stated positively, this implies that the whole community, as one, is either *zymè* or *azymè* – at once, all equally, one or the other. Transposed to the moral key, this means all are either morally corrupt or morally sound. The resulting implication is that Christians form one moral entity, sharing one moral condition, for better or, as in the case at hand, for worse. In fact, this last point is vividly imaged through the proverb at 5,6b.

Considering the implications of what Paul has said, we might find ourselves spontaneously objecting – as a Corinthian might have objected – that such notions are eminently unfair. What about the Christian who is personally *azymè*, i.e., clean of sin? Why should his/her sanctified status be compromised by someone else's sin? If it could be so compromised, why should an individual strive to avoid sin?

Such questions are interesting. However, as posed, with the individual as the point of reference, they betray a perspective quite the inverse of Paul's[1] and their concerns are irrelevant to those Paul expresses in this chapter. The more we recognize that in 1Cor 5, as elsewhere, the community is the lens through which Paul views the problem and responds to it, the more evident is the inappropriateness of these questions. Moreover, in addition to the fact that such questions cannot be satisfactorily answered from the text information, they also divert attention from other questions of the type to be addressed below that are more germane to an understanding of the content of 1Cor 5.

With regard to the divergence in perspectives just signalled, the intention was not to suggest that Paul disregarded the individual but to emphasize that his primary context for reflection, and his primary concern, was the community. In fact, when we read the content of Paul's moral exhortation it is immediately apparent that it is no «how to» guide for individuals[2], replete with advice which focuses on how an individual should conduct his/her life or what paths an individual ought to follow in order to attain wisdom or happiness[3]. Even in the case at hand in 1Cor 5, there is no attempt on Paul's part to moralize, show the offender why and where he had gone wrong or lead him back on the right path. Moreover, while various motives may drive Paul's moral paraenesis[4], it is within the context of the *ekklèsia*[5] and what Paul understands about the *ekklèsia* that this moral paraenesis is shaped and the moral behavior expected of Chris-

---

[1] The contrast in perspectives has been signalled by among others, A. VERHEY, *The Great Reversal*, 103; J. MURPHY-O'CONNOR, *L'existence*, 83; ID., *Becoming Human*, 180-181.

[2] Except at Phil 4,2 where Paul addresses Euodia and Syntyche (but even here returns at v. 3 to address the whole community) and the letter to Philemon, Paul's moral exhortation is addressed to the community.

[3] As found for e.g. at Ps. 1; 111 (LXX); Sir 39,1-11; Tobit 4,5-19 or in 2Enoch J 42,6-14, or among the popular philosophers, cf. e.g. EPICTETUS, *The Discourses*, I,XXVI, 1-18; II,XIX, 29-34.

[4] Cf. e.g. O. MERK, *Handeln*; L. NIEDER, *Die Motive*; V. FURNISH, *Theology and Ethics*; P. GRECH, «Christological Motives», 541-558; K. ROMANIUK, «Les motifs», 191-207.

[5] Paul uses the term variously: a) to designate local communities (cf. e.g. 1Thess 1,1; Gal 1,2; 2Cor 8,1; Rom 16,1; b) in the phrase «*ekklèsia tou theou*» as a privileged title for the Judaean communities cf. 1Thess 2,14; c) elsewhere, e.g. 1Cor 6,4; 10,32; 12,28; Phil 3,6 a wider, supra-local conception of the church is present. For discussions of Pauline usage of *ekklèsia*, its derivation etc. cf. K.L. SCHMIDT, «*ekklèsia*», 487-536; W. MEEKS, *The First Urban Christians*, 107-108; D.E. H. WHITELEY, *Theology of Saint Paul*, 186-190; R. BANKS, *Paul's Idea*, 27-45; R. BROWN, «The New Testament Background», 114-134.

tians must be considered[6]. This will become clearer as the present chapter unfolds. Suffice it to say for the moment, that if one hopes to give a fair hearing to and make a valid evaluation of Paul's moral reasoning, as well as the disciplinary measure prescribed in 1Cor 5, a shift in perspective is in order. Practically speaking, this means that an effort has to be made to read what Paul says in this chapter through a hermeneutical lens focused on the community rather than the individual. In the majority of scholarly investigations of Paul's ethics the tendency has been to filter Paul's message through an individualistic lens[7]. An unfortunate consequence of this tendency is that these studies, with few exceptions[8], have neglected to consider the important relationship between Paul's ecclesiological conceptions and his moral reasoning. However, if the fact of the church and how Paul conceives it is fundamental to his moral reasoning and ethical expectations, as Hays emphasizes, and if, as Wendland claims, «Paulus ist [...] in der Ethik ein durch und durch 'kirchlicher' Denker»[9], then it seems reasonable to expect that his ecclesial perspective and the implications deriving from it would have significantly informed his moral reasoning in 1Cor 5. Therefore, as much as our modern predilection may be to read the moral reasoning here through individualistic lenses, in the interests of arriving at an adequate understanding of the text, we ought to view Paul's moral reasoning through *his* perspective.

In the preceding chapters of this study we have argued that our understanding of Paul's response to the incest case is skewed if the study of this text is not dissociated from the context of polemic about authority. We have now suggested that a further delimitation on our understanding may be posed by a failure to consider the ecclesiological conceptual framework and convictions which shaped the moral reasoning that Paul sets out in responding to the case of incest and the community's failure to react appropriately. This suggestion is not intended as a repudiation of the *communis opinio* that Paul's letters are occasional and that his moral paraenesis is formulated in response to the exigencies of Christian living as these manifest themselves in the various local communities. That notwithstanding, it would appear unduly short-sighted to suppose that the moral reasoning unfolded in 1Cor 5, and the disciplinary measure prescribed, though elicited by this particular occasion, are simply *ad hoc*

---

[6] See the comments in J.P. SAMPLEY, *Walking between the Times*, 37-43.

[7] As observed by R. HAYS, «Ecclesiology», 31-44.

[8] R. HAYS notes three relatively recent studies which, in varying degrees, he considers exceptions to this general tendency (cf. «Ecclesiology», 35).

[9] H.D. WENDLAND, *Ethik*, 67.

formulations[10], exclusively conditioned or qualified by the situation as if Paul had no established convictions from which his responses derived[11].

The purpose of the present chapter is not to undertake an exhaustive presentation of Paul's ecclesiology[12]. Such a presentation is not essential to our modest aim here which is to focus on a few key elements in Paul's understanding of community and convictions deriving from or associated with this understanding which, we will suggest, contributed to the shape of his moral reasoning in 1Cor 5 and had a bearing on the disciplinary measure prescribed. In particular we will focus on Paul's conception of the community as «one» and as «sinless», two notions which come clearly to the fore in 1Cor 5, which there find expression in the terms: *phyrama* at 5,6.7 and *azymè* at 5,7.

2. The Unity of Christians and Its Implications

2.1 *Collective Language and Images of Unity*

2.1.1 Collective Language

Before looking at Paul's use of *phyrama* and what it communicates about community solidarity, it would be good to consider, in broad strokes, how Paul speaks of becoming a Christian. It is apparent that Paul looked upon becoming a Christian as a pluri-dimensional phenomenon. To speak about this phenomenon he employed a multiplicity of complimentary terms such as: baptized, justified, purified, sanctified, indwelt by the Spirit, freed, bought, redeemed, adopted, etc. Each of these terms contributes in someway to our understanding of what it means for an individual to become Christian. Yet, when Paul speaks of these facets of becoming Christian he never does so from the point of view of the individual. Rather, he consistently employs the first or second person plural. For example, it is always «*we* who were buried with him by baptism» (Rom 6,4); «*our* wisdom, *our* righteousness and sanctification and

---

[10] To acknowledge that Paul provides no systematic ethic is not necessarily to affirm that his ethics were situational as A. VERHEY observes (cf. *The Great Reversal*, 107).

[11] The hermeneutical problem to which we allude here, is taken up on a grand scale in J.C. BEKER, *Paul the Apostle*; ID., *Paul's Apocalyptic Gospel*. His well known thesis that the coherent center of Paul's thought is the apocalyptic interpretation of Christ's death and resurrection from which he responds to every particular and varied situation, was tested for its applicability to 1Cor 5-7 in C. VON DEHSEN, *Sexual Relationships*.

[12] Paul's ecclesiology is treated extensively in e.g. R. BANKS, *Paul's Idea*; E. BEST, *One Body*; L. CERFAUX, *The Church*. Cf. further R. SCHNACKENBURG, *The Church*, 77-85 and passim.

redemption» (1Cor 1,30); «*we all* [...] are being changed into his likeness» (2Cor 3,18); «*you* were bought with a price» (1Cor 6,19); «*you* were washed, but *you* were sanctified» (1Cor 6,11). In other words, these key constitutive elements of Christian becoming are employed by Paul as collective categories[13]. On a purely pragmatic level Paul was obviously aware that individuals were called, baptized, sanctified, justified etc. However, as reflected in his writings, it is equally apparent that none of the preceding were conceived apart from what they signified about one's access to, or status within, a community, the *ekklèsia*. Likewise, when Paul speaks of what is attendant on this new life, viz., to keep cleansed from sin and to pursue holiness[14], these too are conceived as community affairs, for «we all» – Paul emphatically begins 2Cor 3,18 – «are being changed into his likeness from one degree of glory to another». Sampley's observation that there is «no evidence that Paul ever conceived of a solitary, isolated believer», is quite to the point[15]. Stated in other terms, in Paul's conceptualization, as reflected in his language, there existed nothing less than a justified and sanctified community. As a whole, it was to bear witness to the reality of new life. When speaking of this «whole» and especially for the purpose of emphasizing its unity and solidarity Paul relied on images. Our concern now is with the image of *phyrama* mentioned at 5,6.7.

2.1.2 An Image of Unity: *Phyrama*

The images employed by Paul to portray and to convey his insights about the unity of the *ekklèsia* are varied[16]. To express the unity of the church in its relationship to God or the Spirit, Paul uses the inanimate images of temple[17] (cf. 1Cor 3,16-17; 1Cor 6,19; 2Cor 6,16), and building (1Cor 3,9). These images are never applied to the relationship between Christ and the community[18], for which Paul prefers the dynamic organic image of body[19]. Through such a dynamic image Paul can underscore

---

[13] Cf. J. MURPHY-O'CONNOR, *L'existence*, 101.

[14] The exhortation to keep cleansed and pursue holiness is variously expressed in Paul and also directed to the community. Cf. e.g. Rom 6,19; 12,1-3; Eph 4,22-24; Col 3,1-3.

[15] Cf. J.P. SAMPLEY, *Walking Between the Times*, 37; the same point is underscored by R. SCHNACKENBURG, *The Church*, 85.

[16] Cf. L. CERFAUX, *The Church*, 232-245; P.S. MINEAR, *Images*.

[17] On Temple imagery in Paul cf. e.g. B. GÄRTNER, *The Temple*; R.J. McKELVEY, *The New Temple*, esp. 92-123.

[18] As observed by J.A.T. ROBINSON, *The Body*, 64-5.

[19] Cf. 1Cor 12,12; Rom 12,4-8; Col 1,15-19.

both the solidarity of the parts and the relationship of the parts to the whole and insist upon the communal character of Christian existence.

Another such image which Paul employs to express the unity and the solidarity of the community is *phyrama,* lump of dough. Unlike other images, there is very little remarked about Paul's use of *phyrama*[20]. For example, while there is great debate over whether the expression «body of Christ» is meant literally or metaphorically[21] and what either could signify[22], there is no debate accompanying Paul's use of the expression *phyrama*. This is probably due to the fact that the semantic incompatibility between «a community» and «a *phyrama*» is so apparent as to render unnecessary the question of how the term ought to be interpreted. *Phyrama* is taken as a metaphor, plain and simple. It is implicitly predicated of the community which is told to cleanse out the old leaven in order to be a new lump of dough, a leaven-free lump of dough (cf. 5,6b-7a.b). However, beyond the general recognition that *phyrama* is a metaphor, a more careful consideration of what it communicates is lacking.

Through this metaphor Paul intends to say something about the community. Since he uses this particular metaphor and not another, it seems reasonable to suppose that it communicates some particular Pauline perception about the community for which this metaphor was adopted as the best or most adequate expression. If so, the question that needs to be addressed is: What peculiar type of insight/s concerning the community is/are conveyed by this metaphor?

The first thing that needs to be observed is that this metaphor lies somewhere between an inanimate and dynamic type. On the one hand, a lump of dough is inanimate. On the other, it does not share the same static

---

[20] Two authors have remarked on the significance of *phyrama* as a community metaphor, cf. R.P. SHEDD, *Man,* esp. 177 and M. MITCHELL, *Paul,* 112-113. However, as we noted (cf. above c. 5 n. 28), Mitchell limits herself to a consideration of the political implications of Paul's terminology, not moral. In Minear's study (cited above n. 16), one page is devoted to the image of the church as unleavened bread at 1Cor 5,7 but there is no discussion of *phyrama* in se.

[21] An excellent discussion of these alternate ways of understanding the phrase «body of Christ» can be found in A. PERRIMAN, «"His Body"», 123-142. In this article the author points out the weaknesses of both understandings and offers helpful insights toward a better appreciation of Paul's rhetoric of metaphor.

[22] The expression is considered to refer to: a) Christ's mystical body, cf. A. WIKENHAUSER, *Pauline Mysticism;* b) Christ's real Risen Body cf. J.A.T. ROBINSON, *The Body;* c) Christ's cosmic Body, cf. R. BULTMANN, *Theology,* I, 310-311; d) an ecclesiastical body of Christ, cf. R.H. GUNDRY, *Sôma,* 228; e) the missionary body of Christ, cf. E. SCHWEIZER, «The Church», 1-11; similarly cf. J. MURPHY-O'CONNOR, «Christ», 121-136.

quality as the temple figure which communicates immovability and summons images of impervious, individual, isolated blocks of stone. Together these distinct blocks form one structure. Dough is an homogenous whole. It is porous; it rises and it falls as one mass. Thus inhering in the figure *phyrama* there is a dynamic quality – but only partially. As an image, *phyrama* lacks the individuation and articulation of parts that a transparently dynamic metaphor such as that of the body is able to communicate. Instead, what *phyrama* most patently communicates is a sense of total fusion, of indivisibility and homo-substantiality. As a metaphor for the community, it suggests that the community is one indivisible entity, a fusion of members all sharing the same substance and as such, subject in its entirety to the same influences and conditions. In the context of the argument being unfolded in 1Cor 5, these notions emerge as criteria in light of which the Corinthians are now being asked to re-consider the incest case.

This metaphor, perhaps more than others, portrays Paul's idea of the solidarity of the community. Moreover, what appears to be strikingly unique is its communication of the notion that community members are of the very same substance and are subject to the same influences. Morally speaking, this implies that the community is a moral entity which shares in one moral condition, and hence, it rises or falls – to borrow an image suggested by the metaphor – in unison. Each community member's life is herewith depicted as inextricably bound to or fused with that of every other member. Paul's vision of the community as expressed through this metaphor has implications with regard to the issue of individual ethical action as we noted at the end of the preceding chapter. These implications will be considered below.

Our concern now is to understand Paul's operative conceptual framework from which a metaphor such as *phyrama,* with its emphasis on both community solidarity and oneness of moral condition, evolved. In order to do so, we will focus attention on Paul's own teaching and ideas as presented in his letters rather than searching outside of Paul to determine the origin of the ideas he expresses in 1Cor 5. With regard to the latter pursuit, R. Shedd has already considered the question of whence came the foundational ideas that underlie Paul's conception of community solidarity as expressed in 1Cor 5. Here we can only note his findings and make a few comments. Shedd maintains that Paul's conception is traceable to the characteristic Hebrew conception of the person as more than an individual[23]. Shedd's thought was influenced by H. W. Robinson's study of the

---

[23] Cf. R. SHEDD, *Man*, esp. 93-96, 177-197.

notion of «corporate personality» in ancient Israel[24]. That we do find in Paul vestiges of the primitive idea of corporate personality is seriously questioned by J. W. Rogerson[25]. Although Rogerson's legitimate objection[26] raises doubts about probability, Shedd's suggestion that this OT concept is operative at 1Cor 5 cannot be totally discounted. On the other hand, not to be overlooked is Murphy O'Connor's warning against hastily assuming that the Pauline conception of community solidarity with its various implications is identical to the OT conception with its implications[27]. To illustrate the difference, Murphy-O'Connor notes that, unlike the OT, in Paul, ethnicity was not the basis of solidarity[28]. More reason for heeding the author's caveat is provided by 1Cor 5 itself. For example, in this chapter, while Paul represents the incest sin as corrupting leaven and therefore as having negative ramifications for the whole community, he in no way suggests that the whole community bears the guilt for this sin, is corporately responsible for it or is under Divine judgement. These elements are key corollaries of the OT concept of corporate personality[29]. In the OT where sin is discussed within the framework of this primitive concept one or more of these elements is discernible[30]. But none are present in 1Cor 5 nor can they be convincingly insinuated into the discussion[31]. On the contrary, in this chapter, the individual is judged to be guilty and is the sole object of the disciplinary action. Thus, while the sin is conceived of and presented as something which can negatively affect the whole community, it is not conceived and presented here as the sin of the whole community[32].

In sum, while Paul's accentuation of community solidarity is prominent in this chapter and community life is undeniably presented as taking precedence over the individual, we agree that Paul's idea of community

---

[24] H.W. ROBINSON, *Corporate Personality*; ID., «The Hebrew Concept», 49-62.

[25] Cf. J.W. ROGERSON, «The Hebrew Conception», 1-16.

[26] J.W. ROGERSON, «The Hebrew Conception», 6. This primitive idea of corporate personality with its corollaries was gradually superseded by the stress on the individual and the accentuation of individual moral choice and responsibility, cf. Ezek 18,1-32; Jer 31,29-30. Thus Rogerson is correct to question the claim that in Paul we have the more primitive concept.

[27] Cf. J. MURPHY-O'CONNOR, *L'existence*, 87. To the warning he adds: «Certaines modèles trouvés dans l'AT furent utiles pour Paul, mais ils furent mis au service d'une idée de solidarité qui est beaucoup plus qu'une forme supérieure de la conception vetero-testamentaire» (88).

[28] J. MURPHY-O'CONNOR, *L'existence*, 88.

[29] These corollaries are set out and discussed in R. SHEDD, *Man*, esp. 12-26. Cf. further B. ROSNER, art. cited above, c. 3 n. 198.

[30] Cf. e.g. Josh 7,1.11; Num 16,22; Ex 34,7; Dt 4,9.

[31] Cf. above, c. 3 n. 198.

[32] This distinction is overlooked by Rosner, cf. above, c. 3 n. 198.

solidarity is perhaps better viewed within his own understanding of community as it exists in Christ[33]. Therefore, we turn to Paul's own writings, in an attempt to elucidate the ideas contained in them which generated an image such as *phyrama* that communicates and accents the unity and solidarity of the community and a common moral condition. We begin first with the idea of unity.

2.2 *Unity and Solidarity in Paul*

2.2.1 God's Call to Fellowship in Christ: The Basis for Unity

At 1Cor 1,9 Paul states, «*pistos ho theos di' hou eklèthète eis koinônian tou hyiou autou lèsou Christou*». In Paul, *koinônia* is essentially an ecclesial notion[34] and with this verse[35] Paul concisely expresses key aspects of his understanding of the uniqueness of the Christian community. Both in terms of origin and purpose, the Christian community has nothing whatsoever in common with human gatherings[36]. The latter are born of human initiative and based on factors that are normally conducive to human aggregation such as ethnicity or politics. In contradistinction, the *ekklèsia* owes its existence[37] to one fact: God's call[38]. This call is part of the mystery of his divine plan[39]. Hence, for Paul, the *ekklèsia* «is a divinely created affair»[40]. Second, for the *ekklèsia*, there is but one aggregating factor: the Christ-event, by which is meant, in particular, the triad of decisive events – the passion, death and resurrection of Christ – on account of which this fellowship is possible[41]. Third, the reason for the

---

[33] Cf. D.E.H. WHITELEY, *Theology of Saint Paul*, 292.

[34] *Pace* M. FAHEY, «Church», II, 35. In Paul, *koinônia* expresses the vital union of believers. As Panikulam has shown, it is never employed with individual sharing in Christ in mind. Rather, it is always used «for someone's sharing in Christ with others» and has, in Paul, a «strict communitarian sense» (cf. G. PANIKULAM, *Koinônia*, 5).

[35] Cf. the detailed exegesis of this verse in G. PANIKULAM, *Koinônia*, 8-16.

[36] Here we underscore the distinction between the *ekklèsia* and other assemblies *vis-à-vis* origin and purpose. Other distinguishing marks as well as some resemblances are discussed in e.g. W. MEEKS, *The First Urban Christians*, 75-110; L. CERFAUX, *L'Eglise*, 11-24.

[37] On the relationship between *ekklèsia* and *kaleô* in Paul, cf. L. CERFAUX, *The Church*, 184-185. As he observes, «the idea of calling is one of the basic elements of primitive ecclesiology», 185.

[38] With few exceptions, e.g. 1Cor 10,27, Paul uses the term *kalein* to speak of the Divine act by which believers are brought to a new existence, cf. Rom 8,27; 9,11.24; 1Cor 7,17.22; Gal 1,6.15. Cf. further, K.L. SCHMIDT, «*Kaleô* [...] *ekklèsia ktl*», 487-489; G. PANIKULAM, *Koinônia*, 12-13.

[39] The Divine origin of the church is repeated by Paul a few verses later at 1,30: «*ex autou de hymeis este en Christô*». The idea is fully elaborated at Eph 1,1-10.

[40] Cf. R. BANKS, *Paul's Idea*, 31.

[41] Cf. E. SCHWEIZER, *The Church*, 63.

community's existence is also one: fellowship with Christ. In essence then, the *ekklèsia* is a network of relationships all deriving from and revolving around this common participation in the one life of Christ[42]. The basis for the unity of all believers is precisely that Christ is one[43] into whose fellowship all believers are called according to the single purpose of the Divine plan of salvation for all in Jesus Christ. This unity, willed by God in and through Christ (cf. e.g. 1Cor 1,30; 2Cor 5,19; Eph 1,10; 2,13), was perceived by Paul as fundamental to the nature of the church.

Paul's understanding of God's call to unity in Christ is linked to and must be considered in light of his teaching on baptism[44]. Paul's understanding of baptism as uniting the Christian with Christ has an obvious starting point in early tradition[45]. This union is so intimate that Paul can say the Christian «puts on Christ»[46]. However, Paul conceives baptism as more than an individualistic experience between a Christian and Christ. As he makes clear, baptism presupposes access to the community of the saved, who, baptized into the same Christ and endowed by the same spirit (cf. 1Cor 12,13 and Gal 3,27-28), constitute a special union[47]. Paul's conviction of the realism of this union is captured in his language. He writes, «*pantes gar hymeis* heis *este en Christô*» (Gal 3,29); that Christians are «hen *sôma*» (1Cor 10,17; 12,13) or «hen *sôma en Christô*» (Rom 12,5).

The unity of the *ekklèsia*, deriving from the Christian's call to fellowship with Christ, effectuated and made visible in baptismal co-participation in Christ, is the framework in which Paul views the individual and his/her actions. As persons «*en Christô*», that is, those who form the

---

[42] Cf. R. BANKS, *Paul's Idea*, 107-108; cf. further E. SCHWEIZER, *The Church*, 63-64.

[43] Cf. e.g. Rom 5,15.17; 1Cor 1,13; 10,17; 12,12; 2Cor 5,14. To say that Christ is one is not the equivalent of saying that Jesus is an individual. Beginning with the Corinthian correspondence, Christ is not «merely the title-become-proper-name of Jesus of Nazareth but also the name of the New Man» and has a collective or corporate connotation (cf. J. MURPHY-O'CONNOR, «Christ», 123-127). On Paul's conception of the «corporate Christ» cf. also E.E. ELLIS, «Biblical Interpretation», 716-718.

[44] For a complete treatment of Paul's Baptism theology, cf. R. SCHNACKENBURG, *Baptism*. A good but less extensive treatment is found in G.R. BEASLEY-MURRAY, *Baptism*, 126ff., and E. CUVILLIER, «Le baptême», 161-177.

[45] Cf. Rom 6,3; note the introductory phrase, «*hè agnoeite*», suggesting that what is about to follow is known. Paul's link with this tradition is also reflected at 1Cor 1,30; 6,11 and 2Cor 1,21-22.

[46] Cf. Gal 3,27; Eph 4,24; Col 3,10. In the middle voice, used in a figurative way, *enduô* can denote the taking on of characteristics or virtues, or entering into another's dispositions (cf. W. BAUER, BAGD, «*enduô*», 263).

[47] Cf. A. DESCAMPS, «Le baptême», 203-235.

«body of Christ»[48], Christians must look at themselves not simply in terms of their individuality[49] but also, and primarily[50], as persons now constituted in and by the community, since to be «en Christô»[51] means to be in the ekklèsia. This is such a given in Paul's thinking that he «never exhorts Christians to become the Church»[52]. While the phrase «en Christô» bespeaks the intimate relationship between the individual Christian and Christ[53], in Paul, many scholars agree that this phrase is primarily an ecclesiological formula[54] signifying that this new existence or new life in Christ is essentially ecclesial.

This exposé of some key Pauline ideas sets in relief his fundamental conviction that believers had solidarity in Christ, in and with whom they form a special union. Within such a perspective, images such as «one body» or «the body of Christ» can be seen as evolving from this basic conviction. Each in some way gives linguistic expression to this fundamental conviction. As we saw above, the metaphor phyrama also expresses the reality of the oneness and solidarity of Christians and thus it would appear reasonable to collocate this expression within this same thought complex.

---

[48] As E. KÄSEMANN points out «in Christ» and «Body of Christ» mutually interpret one another and ought to be considered together (cf. «The Theological Problem», 106).

[49] Cf. L. CERFAUX, The Church, 216; H. CONZELMANN, An Outline, 261.

[50] Cf. 1Cor 12,27. Christians are primarily the Body of Christ and in a secondary way Paul refers to them as individual members of it.

[51] The prepositional phrase en Christô is important, ubiquitous and used with various significations in Paul. At times en + Christô (or en autô as at 1Cor 1,5) has an instrumental sense, cf. e.g. Rom 3,24; 6,11; 1Cor 1,4; 2Cor 3,14; 5,19. In these instances the accent is on Christ's mediation and the phrase is similar in meaning to dia + the gen. Christou at e.g. 1Thess 5,9. More commonly, en Christô (or en + kyriô e.g. Rom 16,11.12) is used to signify the close union between Christians and Christ, cf. e.g. Rom 12,12; Gal 3,26.28; Eph 2,5.10; Phil 1,1; 2Cor 5,12.

[52] Cf. J.C. BEKER, The Triumph, 100; «Cette nouvelle existence est ecclésiale» (au.ital.) (G. THERRIEN, Discernement, 268); cf. further J. MURPHY-O'CONNOR, Becoming Human, 185.

[53] On en Christô as a formula for mystic union between the Christian and Christ cf. A. WIKENHAUSER, Pauline Mysticism, esp. 21-33; A. SCHWEITZER, The Mysticism, esp. 109-140.

[54] Cf. e.g. R. BULTMANN, Theology, I, 311; W. SCHRAGE, Die konkreten Einzelgebote, 80; J.P. SAMPLEY, Walking Between the Times, 39; A.J.M. WEDDERBURN, «The Body», 81; J. MURPHY-O'CONNOR, L'existence, 81; E. BEST, One Body, 7. By extension, the phrase can also be taken existentially, as signifying a mode of existence which is determined by Christ, cf. J. MURPHY-O'CONNOR, L'existence, 80-81.

2.3 *One Moral Entity; One Moral Condition*

Nowhere in Paul's letters is it expressly stated that Christians partake of only one moral condition. Yet, if the whole lump of dough is infected, as Paul says in 1Cor 5,6, then clearly the implication is that there is only one moral condition which Christians share in common and which can be compromised when one member of the community acts immorally. This implication is straightforward; no forcing of the text is required to make it evident. That Paul intended it to be perceived by the Corinthians seems to be a safe presumption. Is there a cluster of ideas in Paul that could accommodate such an implication? Or, does this implication take its life exclusively from this metaphor, having no further connection to Pauline ideas and no further significance beyond this context?

We have already seen that by baptism, Paul understands that all Christians participate in the one redemptive act of Christ and are gifted by the same Spirit. Most commentators agree that from this understanding it was a short step for Paul to his insight that in baptism a special union of believers is formed[55]. In fact, this insight is considered to be a logical deduction, which Paul subsequently articulated in the metaphoric language of «one body» and «body of Christ»[56]. It would seem equally reasonable to regard the implication that the Christian community forms one moral entity, sharing one moral condition, carried in the metaphor *phyrama*, as also a logical deduction from Paul's understanding of baptism. From the various discussions[57] in which he considers the significance of baptism and delineates its manifold effects we learn, *inter alia*, that in baptism Christians are washed, justified and sanctified (1Cor 6,11); obtain the forgiveness of all their trespasses (Col 2,12-13, cf. 2Cor 5,19); have «put on Christ» (Gal 3,27; Eph 4,24; Col 3,10); obtain a new moral identity and enter into a new moral existence[58] (Rom 6,4); moreover, Christians form not merely a totality but one new man[59], with one new

---

[55] Cf. e.g. C. SPICQ, *Théologie morale*, I, 80-82; L. CERFAUX, *The Church*, 236-7; A.J.M. WEDDERBURN, «The Body», 79; B. AHERN, «The Christian's Union», 203-204.

[56] Cf. J. MURPHY-O'CONNOR, *L'existence*, 165; B. AHERN, «The Christian's Union», 207.

[57] Rom 6,1-11 is considered the *locus classicus* of Paul's baptism teaching, however Paul elaborates on the significance of baptism in other texts, e.g. Gal 3,27; 1Cor 12,13; Col 2,11-12, Eph 4,5, 1Cor 6,11.

[58] The expressed purpose of baptism, cf. Rom 6,4 «*hina* [...] *houtôs kai hèmeis ev kainotèti zôès peripatèsômen*»; *peripatein* in Paul refers to moral conduct, cf. e.g. Rom 8,4; 13,13; Gal 5,16; Eph 2,10. On the relationship between Baptism and morality cf. H. HALTER, *Taufe*; S. ZEDDA, *Relativo*, esp. 33-39; J. ECKERT, «Indicativ» esp. 172-173; E. DINKLER, «Zum Problem», esp. 187-197.

[59] «The believers – people in relation to God – are therefore, in their full-grown and in no way attenuated individuality, one body, one individual in Christ. They are not a

nature (Gal 3,26-28; Col 3,11); the vital principle that animates this one new reality is the one Spirit (Rom 8,14-16; Gal 4,6) from whom all were made to drink (1Cor 12,13). Was it not an equally short step for Paul to move from an understanding that Christians become one new man with one new nature through baptism to the logical deduction that through baptism they form one moral entity possessed of one uncompartmentalized moral condition common to all members of the community? This is what is implied through the metaphor *phyrama*. The fact that the implication emerges only here at 1Cor 5,6 should not lead to the assumption that apart from this metaphor, employed for this one occasion, the implication is without further basis in Paul's thought. Here the metaphor itself may be *ad hoc*; however, it carries an implication whose content appears to be a logical deduction about the nature of the community which Paul draws from his understanding of baptism and its effects.

The moral unity that is being suggested runs counter to contemporary conceptions of moral life, moral actions, sin and salvation, which can be sharply individualistic[60]. But not for this reason can we overlook or undervalue Paul's understanding that the *ekklèsia* is a moral entity wherein the actions of each had significant ramifications, negative or positive, for the sanctified life of the whole. Nor can we consider the implication a minor or merely incidental consequence of Paul's having used this particular metaphor as if, were it not for the metaphor, we should have no hint whatsoever of Paul's thoughts about the moral unity of the community. Moral unity seems to be at the heart of other Pauline statements as well[61]. As a whole, the body «grows with a growth that is from God» (Col 2,19); the whole «grows into a holy temple in the Lord [...] the dwelling place of God in the Spirit» (Eph 2,22). It is for all, together, to attain to maturity, to the «measure of the stature of the fullness of Christ» (Eph 4,13). Christ's sacrificial death was for the *ekklèsia* which, as a whole[62], was the object of sanctification and cleansing[63] (Eph 5,25-6).

---

mass of individuals, not even a corporation, a personified society, or a "totality", but the Individual, The One, The New Man [...]» (K. BARTH, *Romans*, 443).

[60] Cf. the comments in J. MURPHY-O'CONNOR, *Becoming Human*, 175-176.

[61] The following text references are from Ephesians and Colossians. The debate over authorship does not detract from the acknowledged fact that in these letters Paul's thought is advanced. Apropos of Colossians, its authenticity has again been recently defended, cf. J. MURPHY-O'CONNOR, *Paul. A Critical Life*, 237-250.

[62] Christ's self-sacrifice, regardless of whatever thrill it awakens in every renewed heart, to paraphrase E.K. Simpson, is presented here with the whole *ekklèsia* as the focus (cf. E.K., SIMPSON, *Ephesians*, 131). The tendency to abstract and apply what is said here to the individual Christian, as Simpson does, only detracts from the ecclesial focus of Eph 5,24-27 which others have correctly underscored. Cf. e.g. M. BARTH,

Christ's intention is that the *ekklèsia* as a whole be without spot or wrinkle, holy and without blemish[64] (Eph 5,27). Hence, new life in Christ is characterized by sinlessness[65] and this trait distinguishes the church as a whole[66].

2.4 *Implications for Ethics*

Given Paul's perception that Christians form an indivisible moral entity, it follows that, for him, individual ethical action will necessarily be circumscribed by the community, with concern for its moral well-being the primary consideration of each Christian. As we have seen, since the Christian is a member of the *Heilsgemeinde*, salvation is not conceived by Paul as an individual affair, and neither is sin[67]. Since for Paul, the «esse Christianum» of the Christian is life within the body[68], it follows that a Christian, in so far as he/she is constituted by the community, apart from which he/she is not authentically Christian, always acts, and can only act, as a member of the community[69]. That being the case, while a Christian acts as an individual, his/her acts can never be, strictly speaking, autonomous. Thus Wendland is right on target when he states that «Von der ethischen Autonomie des einzelnen weiss Paulus nichts»[70]. Indeed in Paul's perspective, as it emerges in 1Cor 5, an immoral act of an individual Christian can never be considered without negative import or

---

Ephesians, 669-699; R. SCHNACKENBURG, *Ephesians*, 248-258; cf. further S.P. VAN RENSBURG, «Sanctification» esp. 80-81.

[63] The perennial majority view that «*tô loutrô tou hydatou*» is a reference to baptism is rejected by M. BARTH, *Ephesians 4-6*, 692-699. But see the criticism of Barth in H. HALTER, *Taufe*, 283. Whether the reference is to baptism or to the new life given in the Spirit (so M. BARTH, *Ephesians*, 699), nonetheless, what is emphatic is that it is common to all members of the church.

[64] «*hagia kai amômos*» are probably intended as ethical designations here as suggested by R. SCHNACKENBURG, *Ephesians*, 251; On the ethicization of the *heiligkeitsbegriff* in Paul, cf. R. ASTING, *Die Heiligkeit*, 202-15. Apropos of *amômos*, besides its occurrence here, it is used at Eph 1,4 in a statement which parallels 5,27. It occurs one other time at Phil 2,15 where again the moral/religious, not cultic, sense seems to be intended.

[65] Cf. J. MURPHY-O'CONNOR considers this passage the most formal and explicit affirmation of the Church's «impeccabilité» (sinlessness) found in Paul (cf. «Péché», 166). This new ecclesial condition of sinlessness will be discussed below, § 3.

[66] This same stress on the communitarian dimension of sanctity is also evident at Col 1,12.22.26; 3,12.

[67] This is clear from 1Cor 5,6 where Paul equates sin with infectious *zymè*. That individual sin or evil is capable of polluting others is a common Jewish notion Cf. e.g. Lev 21,1ff.; JOSEPHUS, *BJ*, 1,25,1.

[68] Cf. L. CERFAUX, *The Church*, 216.

[69] Cf. J. MURPHY-O'CONNOR, *Becoming Human*, 175-181.

[70] Cf. H. WENDLAND, *Ethik*, 65.

consequences for the whole community since a little leaven contaminates the whole mass. Here, the question of the offender's intention is not at all in view. Rather, Paul's focus is teleological; his concern centers on the negative consequences for the community. Even when these are not perceived by the community, as seems to be the case in 1Cor 5, Paul insists that the community suffers the consequences nonetheless. If they are one mass of dough and leaven is introduced, then they are all subject to contamination.

That the ethical implications arising from Paul's understanding of the community as one moral entity do not square well with an individualistic perspective is obvious. One way around this difficulty is to consider the implications as no more than the consequential offshoots of primitive collectivist thinking, now fortunately superseded by a more sophisticated ethical reflection that gives due attention to the individual, intentionality and individual responsibility. However, such a contrast is not valid since Paul was not a collectivist[71]. Rather, he begins with what he understands about the nature of the *ekklèsia* and derives his understanding of individual ethics from this. For Paul, a self who is Christian must understand his/her individuality *vis-à-vis* the *ekklèsia*, that organic unity of which he/she is necessarily a part or is not a Christian. Hence, an individual Christian must and ought to behave differently from a self that conceives of individuality as synonymous with autonomy. Since, as we have seen, it is Paul's conviction that the community is one, not just functionally speaking, but even in its core moral constitution, then it is perfectly logical and comprehensible that Paul gives primacy to the life of the community and would expect that the finality of each individual Christian's moral choices would have in view not only his/her own personal good but also the well-being of the whole community. Thus, as Paul sees it, individual ethical choice will always have to be evaluated in light of the whole[72]. In some instances a more refined discernment will be required[73]. In others, for example the case of 1Cor 5, an individually chosen course of action may so manifestly compromise the sanctified life of the whole community, that the discernment should be apparent and result in swift and appropriate remedial action. Unfortunately, as we have seen, the

---

[71] As we observed above, p. 153-154, the incest sin and responsibility for it are imputed to the individual. Likewise, it is the individual Christian who loves and does the good. But, in Paul, the individual always acts as a member of a community. Cf. further, H. WENDLAND, *Ethik*, 65-66; R. BATEY, «The *Mia Sarx* Union», esp. 279-280.

[72] This does not necessarily imply that the individual must, in every instance, defer to the whole, cf. J.A. DAVIS, «The Interaction», 1-18.

[73] Cf. e.g. 1Cor 7; 8,1-13; 12-14

community at Corinth, failed in its discernment with regard to the incestuous brother.

3. A «Sinless» Community

In 1Cor 5 the answer to why the incest sin and the perpetrator cannot be tolerated is that the community is a new, unleavened loaf. Here *azymè,* without leaven, obviously means without sin and this condition is rooted in the expiatory death of Christ (5,7c; cf. Rom 3,24-5; Eph 1,7).

The condition of sinlessness, wrought through Christ's death and linked by the early church with baptismal remission of sins (cf. e.g. Acts 2,38; 22,16; 1Cor 6,11; Eph 5,26-7), is, as commonly recognized, a traditional eschatological theme. Sinlessness was considered one of the privileges of messianic times (cf. e.g. Isa 4,4; 44,22; Ezek 36,25-29; Sir 24,22; 1Henoch 5,8-9). Along with unity (cf. e.g. Isa 11,11-14; Ezek 37, 15-28), sinlessness would characterize the elect of God on whom the Spirit would be poured out (cf. e.g. Joel 3,1-5; Isa 32,15; Zech 12,10; Ezek 39,29). The outpouring and indwelling of the Spirit was the sign that the messianic age had begun and unity and sinlessness were to be the distinguishing traits of the new *Heilsgemeinschaft.*

The tradition of the sinlessness of the eschatological community was no doubt inherited by Paul[74]. Murphy-O'Connor's conviction that this tradition figured largely into the thought of Paul and, in a particular way, in his response in 1Cor 5[75] appears to be on target. It is quite evident that basic to Paul's teaching is the conviction that Christ's death has gained for humanity that renewed existence that tradition held would characterize the promised and long-awaited new age (cf. e.g. Rom 3,21-26; 5,1-5; 16,25-26; 2Cor 5,17; 6,2; Gal 4,4-5; Eph 1,9-10). Christ's death is the eschatological salvation event. In consequence, the *ekklèsia,* whose inception is coincident with this salvation event, is, in Paul's conception, nothing other than the new eschatological community[76]. In the *ekklèsia,* the promised Spirit, the first fruit of the final consummation (Rom 8,9.11; Eph 1,13-14), has been poured out and now dwells (Rom 8,9.11; 1Cor 3,16); there is peace with God (cf. Rom 5,1), unity has been achieved and, through

---

[74] The early Christian community and the Essene community were the two communities which identified themselves as the new eschatological community of God. On similarities and differences in their respective views see the discussion in F. M. CROSS, *The Ancient Library,* esp. 197-243. The emphasis on sinlessness can be found in the writings of both communities (in the NT, besides 1Cor 5 e.g. 1Jn 3,6-9; cf. also CD XX, 2-8; 1 QS III, 3-9; 17-23; IV, 20-23; VIII, 4-9. Apropos of 1Jn 3,6-9, cf. I. DE LA POTTERIE, «L'Impeccabilità», 235-258.

[75] Cf. J. MURPHY-O'CONNOR, *L'existence,* 92-97; ID., *Becoming Human,* 158-159.

[76] Cf. R. BULTMANN, *Theology,* I, 308.

baptismal co-participation in Christ's death, the *ekklèsia* has been raised sinless (Eph 5,25; 1Cor 6,11).

Though Paul understands the *ekklèsia* as a transmundane reality, a phenomenon of the new aeon which is totally new and distinct (Gal 3,27; 2Cor 5,17), still he knows that the *ekklèsia* must live in the world (1Cor 5,10). According to Paul, in order to make this distinctiveness manifest, it was not necessary for the community to segregate itself from the world (cf. 1Cor 5,10; Phil 2,15) or even abandon social conventions or structures (cf. 1Cor 7,1.20; Rom 13,1; Col 3,18-23;). Rather, as Paul saw it, the distinctiveness of the *ekklèsia* had to manifest itself in the community's unity, in its walking by the Spirit (Rom 8,4.9; Gal 5,16), in its Spirit-guided capacity to discern and do the will of God (Rom 12,2; 1Cor 2,12-14), to live for and consecrate itself to God (Rom 6,11.13) and to show itself sinless (Phil 2,14; Eph 1,4). In sum, Paul expected that in its present world-context, the community would show itself to be the eschatological community of God, a united community whose Spirit-guided behavior would give concrete expression to its status[77].

In 1Cor, we see Paul at work to guide the community in the living out of its eschatological status. The emphasis on unity, one of the important hallmarks of the eschatological community, pervades the whole letter. Paul moves from the discussion of disunity, which he characterizes in terms of divided allegiance (cf. 1Cor 1,11-12), to the discussion of some varied, concrete issues which have divided, or have potential to divide, the community, seeking always to resolve these issues in view of the upbuilding of the community and its continued solidarity. As we noted, unity and sinlessness go hand in hand as eschatological hallmarks and thus it is reasonable to expect that this latter characteristic of the *ekklèsia* would show itself to be a key factor in Paul's response here in 1Cor 5 where it is precisely the sinless status of the community that is at stake.

To show itself sinless meant nothing less for Paul than that the whole church should live without and apart from sin. In concrete terms, this signified that it was incumbent on each community member to renounce those acts (cf. 1Cor 5,11; 6,9-10; 1Thess 4,3-7; Gal 5,19; Eph 5,3-5; Col 3,5-9) that were incongruous with God's dominion and inimical to God's will so that, as a whole, the eschatological community, the *ekklèsia*, could live according to the exigencies of its vocation to holiness[78] (1Thess 4,3; cf. Gal 5,22-25; Col 3.12-14).

---

[77] On the Spirit as «*Grundprinzip*» of genuine Christian life cf. R. ASTING, *Die Heiligkeit*, esp. 193-202.

[78] As Bonsirven points out holiness is double-sided; negatively, it means the suppression of all sin and vice which is indicated by the combined terms holy and

4. Medial Summary

We have seen that Paul's conception of the *ekklèsia* as one moral entity, a conception carried in the metaphor *phyrama*, derives from his understanding of baptism and what it effectuates. Within this conceptual framework, his insistence that one member's sinful act can have negative consequences for the whole community is fully understandable. We have also seen that Paul understands that, as a whole, the *ekklèsia* is to be *azymè*. Christ's death has effected this condition and through baptismal participation in his death and baptismal cleansing, the whole *ekklèsia* enjoys the new condition of sinlessness. This condition distinguishes the eschatological community of God, which is precisely what Paul understands the *ekklèsia* to be. The implications for ethics flowing from Paul's ecclesial conceptions are clear and we have commented on these above. But what of the implications for church discipline?

5. Implications for Church Discipline

In the case of 1Cor 5, Paul's decision was to excommunicate the offender. This discipline has a harsh ring for readers unaccustomed with this practice now reserved for cases of serious, public departure from church teaching and praxis[79]. However, if our presentation of the ecclesial conceptual framework within which Paul apparently operated is correct and if it is allowed to become the lens through which we too view the discipline announced in 1Cor 5, we can begin to appreciate that excommunication was a reasoned response to the situation. Unfortunately, by couching the interpretation of 1Cor 5 in the context of polemic over authority – a context against which we have argued – this admittedly severe disciplinary stance has come to be more associated with the politics of authority than with theology. However, when we take seriously Paul's deep convictions of the reality of the moral solidarity of the *ekklèsia* and its sinless condition as the eschatological community of God, we can see how such conviction logically demanded action aimed at repristinating and ensuring the continued sinlessness of the whole community[80]. Since, for Paul, the sinlessness of the community was not something elusive or

---

without blemish as we find in Eph 1,4; 5,27; positively, it signifies the continuing task of sanctification which supposes a dynamism always in action (cf. J. BONSIRVEN, *L'Évangile*, 286-287).

[79] Cf. *CIC*, Bk 6, «Sanctions» cans. 1331, 1354-57.

[80] How exactly excommunication would restore the community's sinless status and moral integrity, Paul does not say but his thought may reflect OT influence. There, the idea is patent that sin is a communicable phenomenon. Its negative consequences were eradicated with the eradication of the perpetrator, cf. e.g. Lev 21,9.

irreducibly metaphysical but signified concretely that the whole community was sin-free and had to live without and apart from sin, then sin had to be expunged from its midst. Hence, there emerges the need to expel the sinner whose sin and continued presence compromised the moral integrity of the community.

There is a notable tendency in treatments of 1Cor 5 to remark or speculate about the peculiar nature of this sin[81]. Whether consciously intended or not, the remarks can appear as attempts to justify Paul's decision to excommunicate. Such a severe sanction must imply a particularly abhorrent sin! Notwithstanding the reasonableness of such logic, the fact is the nature of the particular sin is less important here than the recognition of sin's nature. What matters ultimately is that incest *is* a sin and sin's nature is to infect. After the initial statement that the sin is *porneia*, qualified as incest (1Cor 5,1), Paul refers to the sin generically as leaven with all its pejorative connotations (5.6,7). By using the term *zymè*, Paul focuses attention not on *porneia* as sexual sin[82], but on the sin's penetrating and corrupting effect on the whole community. When we consider these facts alongside the ecclesiological convictions of Paul, there is no need to speculate about the peculiar nature of this sin, to explain or justify the expulsion pronouncement. Nor is it helpful to chalk his response up to an embattled situation that required a show of force to re-establish his authority, thereby turning a religious-moral issue into a politics-of-authority issue. Given his perspective, for Paul, excommunication was the logical and necessary response to the situation. Indeed the call for expulsion, an act of the *ekklèsia* on behalf of its own common life, affirms and underscores Paul's deep conviction about the moral solidarity and sinlessness of the whole community. If sinlessness were a purely individual affair and if there existed no real moral solidarity, excommunication would have no significance or efficacy in this situation. In sum, when we consider the offense and the discipline in light of Paul's ecclesial ideas, we can observe that the discipline clearly fits the offense.

---

[81] In the majority of cases where the nature of incest is the focus its peculiarly gross and abhorrent character is remarked, invariably from the Jewish perspective, and is supported by reference to the vice lists where primary place is accorded to *porneia*. For a different slant where the accent is on the «radical egoism» of sexual sins, the most blatant manifestations of turning away from God and the Spirit (cf. T. DEIDUN, *New Covenant Morality*, 93-96).

[82] Deidun treats the incest of 1Cor 5 within a broader discussion of the nature of sexual sins and Paul's view of sexual immorality as *particularly* (au. ital.) incompatible with being a Christian (cf. *New Covenant Morality*, 89-92). Deidun offers valuable insights but this does not change the fact that here in 1Cor 5, Paul's consternation over this sexual immorality has as its focus, not primarily the sexual nature of the sin but, the sin's potential to corrupt the whole community.

Compared to Jesus' response to sinners as presented in the gospels (cf. e.g. Lk 15,1ff.), Paul's disciplinary response may appear to come up on the short-side of compassion and forgiveness. However, such comparisons, though understandable, are not all together valid since differences between the contexts and motivations of Jesus and Paul exist and must be taken into consideration. When we read the gospels, we find Jesus reaching out to the lost, the marginalized and sinners, aiming to gather all men and women into God's love. The behavior of Jesus must be considered then in light of his program of in-gathering, «como una apertura conversionista»[83]. There is every reason to suppose that during his evangelizing activity, Paul was as open and welcoming as Jesus himself. Paul too apparently went to those who had been adulterers, thieves (cf. 1Cor 6,19-10) and idolaters (1Cor 12,2; 1Thess 1,9). These he invited into *koinônia* with Christ through faith, to partake of the privileges of the sons and daughters of God. But, the context of Paul's letters is not the context of the missionary campaign. In his letters, Paul addresses the communities he has already founded, those who by faith and baptism are already in Christ. What motivates Paul in this phase of written contact is no longer the conversionist concern of gathering-in but rather the concern to maintain[84] what is now established in and through Christ by ensuring that the community lives in a manner manifestly determined by Christ and therefore coherent with the reality of its new existence in Christ.

It should now be apparent that any attempt to compare the responses of Jesus and Paul to sinners which does not take into consideration the divergence in contexts and motivations to which we have just called attention is flawed from its inception and can only produce a skewed evaluation of Paul. Attentive to the context within which Paul responds and to his motivations, we must admit that far from lacking compassion or forgiveness, Paul was operating in the best interests of the community and ultimately the individual (1Cor 5,5). The consideration of Paul's profound convictions concerning the reality of the moral solidarity of the *ekklèsia* and its sinless status and the recognition that, for Paul, these convictions had pragmatic and concrete implications can help us to recognize how ultimately positive and necessary was Paul's call for expulsion.

6. Conclusion to Chapter 6

In this chapter we have argued that Paul's reasoning and response to the situation referred to in 1Cor 5 are more completely understood and

---

[83] Cf. R.T. ETCHEVARRIA, «A proposito», 138-139.
[84] Cf. R.T. ETCHEVARRIA, «A proposito», 139.

therefore more adequately evaluated when we consider certain key Pauline ecclesial convictions which appear to be fundamental to his reasoning and response. We took as our clue for individuating and investigating his convictions the terms *phyrama* and *azymè* found at 1Cor 5,6. Taken in the moral sense in which Paul clearly intended them, these metaphors communicate, *prima facie*, moral oneness and sinlessness. As we believe to have shown, though these terms are employed by Paul for this occasion, the ideas they express are linked to two of Paul's fundamental ecclesial convictions: the moral unity and sinless condition of the *ekklèsia*. These ecclesial convictions are rooted in Paul's understanding of baptism, both in terms of the moral unity it effects and the condition of sinlessness that is bestowed through it on the whole church. In addition, Paul's understanding of the *ekklèsia* as the new eschatological community of God, carries with it the conviction, inherited from Jewish tradition, that the eschatological community would be distinguished by its sinlessness. These ecclesial conceptions form a background against which Paul's choice of metaphoric language with its implications, his manner of reasoning and the form of his disciplinary response is illumined. In this light, the content of 1Cor 5 can be more fully understood and misrepresentations of Paul's aims can be avoided. If there is any sub-agenda that conditions Paul's response in 1Cor 5, it is not the need to re-assert his authority, but rather his deep ecclesial convictions. These convictions drive Paul's response, shed light on the exigency with which he attends to the problem and help us to appreciate that his reasoning is designed to draw the community into the exigency of the situation and persuade it to come to its own defense by taking the action he prescribes.

Even when we understand Paul's ecclesial convictions and see how they informed and guided his reasoning and response in 1Cor 5 we may still feel that Paul's way of reasoning and the sanction he prescribed, notwithstanding the logic of it all, were primitive and extreme. Perhaps the latter sentiment serves only to underscore how much distance there is between Paul's conceptual world and our own.

One question, concerning the placement of 1Cor 5 relative to the ordering of the other practical matters discussed by Paul, remains to be addressed. We will begin our next chapter by addressing this question. Then we will consider some of the prominent flaws and lacunae in the Corinthian understanding of Christianity especially as they come to light against the key Pauline ecclesiological conceptions highlighted in this present chapter. Chapter 7 will then conclude with a statement of general conclusions issuing from this study as a whole.

Chapter VII

Flaws and Lacunae in the Corinthian Understanding of Christianity

1. Introduction

In light of what we have set forth, especially in cc. 3, 5 and 6 of our study, we will now, by way of conclusion, take another look at the gaps in the Corinthians' understanding of Christianity, as they come to the fore in 1Cor 5. Before moving to that discussion, we will begin by considering one last question concerning the location of this discussion of incest in the ordering of the practical issues under discussion in 1Cor. A suggestion about its placement will be made in light of rhetorical-pedagogical considerations.

2. The Location of the Incest Discussion in 1 Corinthians

Even scholars who support the literary integrity of 1Cor do not conceal a certain perplexity with regard to the apparent lack of logic in the ordering of material in this letter which they concede is «loosely structured»[1]. A number of commentators observe, more or less in line with Hurd[2], that Paul responds first to information of which he had been apprised orally then, beginning at 7,1, responds to inquiries and information alleged to have come to him through a written communication. With regard to 1Cor 5, we have already noted that it is lexically linked to the preceding chapter[3]. Nonetheless, the essential theme of the whole macro-unit, cc. 1-4, is

---

[1] Cf. e.g. H. CONZELMANN, *1 Korinther*, 2; D. LÜHRMANN, «Freundschaftsbrief», 304; L. MORRIS, *1 Cor*, 28; W. DE BOOR, *1 Korinther*, 17. Reasons for what appears to be the loose organization of the letter vary cf. e.g. J. MOFFATT, *1 Corinthians*, esp. xxv-vi; J. MURPHY-O'CONNOR, *Paul. A Critical Life*, 280.

[2] For example, Conzelmann adopts Hurd's schema, however he admits that some sections of 1Cor cannot be pressed into it (cf. H. CONZELMANN, *1 Korinther*, 89).

[3] Cf. c. 4 n. 3.

not taken up in 1Cor 5. Why then did Paul begin his treatment of practical matters by discussing this case of incest? Various ways of explaining its placement are possible. For example, if one assumes that Paul's intention was to organize the letter according to responses to oral information first, then to written information, the incest discussion can be understood to be located where it is at c. 5 because it continues to discuss matter of which Paul was apprised orally and, along with c. 6, provides a transition to the responses to written queries[4]. However, beside the fact that the evidence at 11,18[5] undermines the collocation of material on this basis, this whole assumed division of material into responses-to-oral and responses-to-written information needs to be reconsidered, and perhaps jettisoned, in light of more recent considerations[6]. Hence, to explain the location of 1Cor 5 only in function of an alleged system of ordering based on a division between oral and written response material is inadequate.

Another possibility for explaining the placement of this discussion is to begin with a reflection on the nature of this sin and to speculate that Paul may have ordered his treatment of practical matters affecting the community beginning with the worst sin first. Here one would be assuming that the valuative context in which Paul operated was Judaism where *porneia*, and in particular incest, was considered a most abhorrent sin[7]. While it is possible that Paul began his ordering in light of Jewish evaluations of sin, other considerations diminish the probability of this explanation. First, if Paul ordered his discussions on a «worst-sin-first» basis, from a Jewish perspective, the discussions of idols, idolatry[8], the eating of *eidôlothutos* and the idolatrous communion resulting from such a practice (cf. c. 10,18-

---

[4] Dahl, for example, considers the epistolary function of 1Cor 5 and 6 to be a bridge between Paul's re-establishment of authority in cc. 1-4 and his authoritative response to community questions in cc. 7-16 (cf. «Paul and the Church», 57).

[5] At 11,18 Paul discusses divisions as they exist with regard to the assembly for the Lord's supper about which he had been apprised orally (*akouô schismata en hymin*). It is also possible that the topic of head-covering in the context of worship discussed in 11,1-15 was also a point of contention within the community that Paul came to know about orally.

[6] Cf. the excellent study of M. MITCHELL, «*Peri de*», 229-256. Though the «*peri de*» formula at 7,1 has been commonly taken to signal the beginning of Paul's response to written inquiries, Mitchell has argued against this assumption. The author has shown, quite convincingly, that «*peri de*» does not necessarily signal a response to a *written* query (cf. 234) nor is «*peri de*» necessarily an answering formula (cf. 244).

[7] Cf. above, c. 5 n. 190, 191, 192.

[8] From a Jewish perspective, idolatry ranked at least on par with *porneia* in terms of gravity (cf. Acts 15,20). At times, it was evaluated as the more serious offense, considered the root of all evil (cf. Ps. PHILO, 44,6). In the rabbinic texts on idolatry, it is clear that the rabbis assigned most-grievous-sin status alternately between idolatry and sexual immorality (cf. C. MONTEFIORE, *A Rabbinic Anthology*, esp. 251-253; 138).

21) should be expected to precede or immediately follow that of incest, or at any rate, at least precede discussions of matters such as the proper forum for Christian litigation (cf. 6,1-11) or advice to widows and the unmarried (cf. 7,8). Second, conceived this way, there is an implicit supposition that Paul intended to highlight Corinthian failure *vis-à-vis* Jewish ethical standards. However, from the point of view of the largely gentile audience, this does not appear highly probable. In fact, as we have already seen in chapter 5 of our study, the gravity of the situation discussed in 1Cor 5 is rooted in the fact that the man's behavior and the community's response imply a radical departure from and betrayal of the reality of new life in Christ. Therefore, even if incest were a most abhorrent sin from the point of view of Judaism, this fact does not necessarily account for Paul's ordering of material.

In a slightly different vein, one could attribute Paul's placement of the incest discussion first among practical matters to the prominent place that sexual conduct occupies in general on his moral agenda[9]. Thus, by starting the discussion of practical issues with that of incest, Paul would be going right to his main moral concern, a sexual issue. This is possible since Paul's moral discourse is concerned with sexual conduct[10]. However, as we observed in the previous chapter[11], Paul does not appear to be preeminently occupied with incest *qua* sexual sin in 1Cor 5 but rather with the sin's power to infect the community. Therefore, adducing the sexual nature of this sin or the alleged prominence of sexual sins in general in Paul's moral thought may, but does not necessarily, explain why Paul began his discussion of practical matters with incest first.

As an alternative to explanations for the placement of 1Cor 5 which rely on the oral-then-written structuring logic or are derived, in some way, from a general reflection on the sexual nature of this sin, it may be of some advantage to consider the placement of 1Cor 5 in view of its rhetorical-pedagogic function. By turning the focus to Paul's rhetorical task, both in 1Cor 5 and in the subsequent discussions of practical matters

---

[9] Some authors would maintain that, in Paul's view, sexual behavior and codes of sexual conduct bore the main weight of what it meant to be holy. Cf. e.g. P. BROWN, *The Body*, 52; M. ENSLIN, *Ethics*, 190ff.; T. DEIDUN, *New Covenant Morality*, 89-96.

[10] However, it may be somewhat of an exaggeration to insist that concern with sexual (im)morality occupies an unparalleled place of importance in Paul's moral *paraklèsis* as Schrage maintains (cf. *Die konkreten Einzelgebote*, 220). For Paul, to walk *kata pneuma*, signified that the whole person, in all things, including sexuality, would henceforth live in a manner pleasing to God (Rom 8,1-8); see also Gal 5,19 where Paul lists all the sins, not just specifically sexual ones, that Christians had to avoid in their living *kata pneuma*.

[11] Cf. above, c. 6 n. 81; 82.

affecting the community, another insight may be gained about the discussion's placement.

Based on our analysis of 1Cor 5, we have seen that Paul's task was to bring the Corinthians to acknowledge incest as evil, recognize its negative implications for the whole community and take action to correct this situation. Throughout the 1Cor 5 Paul works to persuade the community, which he has now apprised of the gravity of the situation, to execute this action, both for its own benefit and that of the brother. Paul's intervention is necessary because the community has failed to act and this is due, ultimately, to a deplorable failure in judgement. Not merely by Jewish, but by all lights[12], incest was a gross act of immorality. Hence, despite their reasons, the simple fact is that in this moral judgement the Corinthians showed themselves incompetent.

Looking at the rest of the issues in the letter, we observe that beginning at 6,1 and moving through 14,1-40, Paul's task is to assist the community in a series of moral discernments that cover a variety of issues and courses of action. By and large, these are not black and white issues[13] where there is only one correct course of action to adopt. Thus we see Paul working with the community to consider various modes of behavior which are not only possible and permissible but which are also appropriate for persons whose lives are now Christologically, and therefore ecclesially, determined. Under consideration are not only the good but also the better courses of action that Christians can adopt[14]. The recurring object of the discernment is what is beneficial (cf. 6,12b; 10,23.24; 14,4 [bis]), or edifying (cf. 14,3.5.12.26), for the community[15]. Succinctly stated then, the *ekklèsia* is the context for discernment and its well-being or edification is the object of discernment.

Community edification is one, but not the only, object of Christian moral discernment[16]. With a mind renewed[17] by the Holy Spirit (cf. Rom

---

[12] Cf. above c. 5 § 5.

[13] Exceptions are the issue of fornication with prostitutes (cf. 6,12-20) and the particular issue of *eidôlolatria* (cf. 10,14). In both cases there is only one appropriate course of action, «to flee» («*pheugete tèn porneian*», 6,18; «*pheugete apo tès eidôlolatrias*», 10,14).

[14] Cf. above c. 3 n. 121, 122, 123.

[15] This object coincides with the *telos* of deliberative rhetoric cf. above, c. 5 § 11.

[16] For a complete treatment of discernment in Paul see the excellent study of G. THERRIEN, *Le discernement*; cf. further, J.P. SAMPLEY, *Walking Between the Times*, esp. 50-69.

[17] «Commence au baptême, le renouvellement doit se poursuivre chaque jour» (G. THERRIEN, *Le discernement*, 144). Beyond the process aspect of this renewal, its collective dimension is set in relief in J. MURPHY-O'CONNOR, *L'existence*, esp. 187-191.

12,2; Eph 4,23; 1Cor 2,6-14), Christians were to discern the «will of God»[18] (Rm 12,2; cf. further 1Thess 4,2), what is «the good, acceptable and perfect»[19] (Rom 12,2), what is pleasing to the Lord (Eph 5,10, cf. Eph 5,17); what is good and what is evil (1Thess 5,21)[20].

Apropos of this case of incest, the Corinthian Christians did not show themselves capable of judging it as evil with respect to the will of God[21] (cf. 1Thess 4,3; 1Cor 6,9-10), to sin's incompatibility with Christian essence (cf. 1Cor 5,7b), and to the negative impact on the whole community (cf. 1Cor 5,6b). Perhaps nothing could have served to exacerbate Paul's consternation over the fact of the incestuous relationship more than the knowledge that the community at Corinth had bungled what should have been a rather uncomplicated judgement issuing in a unanimous denunciation of this relationship as evil.

Confronted with this fact, and having before him various other practical matters to treat which were not so patently black and white[22] and which obviously required refined and nuanced powers of discernment, could Paul, the practical pedagogue that he was, begin with more intricate issues when the community had failed to judge such a blatant transgression against the moral will of God? (cf. 1Thess 4,3). If the community could not deal with an elementary distinction between good and evil, how would it be able to work through the complexities of the other discussions? Would a group, incapable of recognizing the negative implications of this festering evil and showing no appreciation of its ecclesial constitution, to the point of indulgence toward one whose individual choice was community destroying, be able to discern authentically when community edification was the object of such discernment? Given Paul's rhetorical task in most of the remaining discussions in the letter[23] and his acknowledged

---

[18] «Le non-conformisme chrétien à l'égard de ce monde et la métamorphose de l'être profond commencé au baptême et se prolongeant dans et par le renouvellement quotidien du sens moral sont ordonnés à une fin précise: *discerner quelle est la volonté de Dieu*» [au.ital.] (G. THERRIEN, *Le discernement*, 144).

[19] On Paul's use of these three notions, cf. G. THERRIEN, *Le discernement*, 145-148.

[20] A Christian had to be «un homme de bon jugement moral qui discerne le bien et le mal et sait conduire sa vie exactement selon les principes de l'Evangile» (cf. C. SPICQ, *Théologie morale*, I, 470).

[21] Something, which according to Paul, even pagans were capable of doing, cf. Rom 1,19.32; 2,14-15. Cf. further the comments in G. THERRIEN, *Le discernement*, 128-135.

[22] Cf. e.g. 1Cor 7,25-35; 10,23-31; 14,1-24.

[23] Exceptions to Paul's task of discerning would appear to be 1Cor 13 and 15, the former generally taken as an example of encomium (epideictic rhetoric) and the latter a defense unit (forensic rhetoric). However, M. MITCHELL has recently argued that in both of these texts Paul is also involved in deliberation (cf. *Paul*, 270-279; 283-291).

pedagogical sensitivity and skill, it seems reasonable to suggest that Paul began his discussion of practical matters with the incest case, not because it was the worst sin, nor necessarily because it was a sexual sin, but rather because incest was a *sin*. Hence, by dealing with incest case at the outset of his discussion of practical matters affecting the community, Paul sought to first re-order the focus of the Corinthians within the fundamental boundaries of good and evil, an obvious pre-requisite to going forward with the remaining matters for discussion which required authentic and unimpaired Christian discernment. *In breve*, before moving on to issues that admitted of shades of grey, Paul had to get this black and white one straight in the minds of the Corinthians.

3. Key Flaws and Lacunae in the Corinthian Understanding of Christianity

The Corinthians, as the other communities Paul had founded, no doubt heard his proclamation of Jesus as *the* human freedom event, perhaps in the same programmatic formulation one hears at Gal 5,1: «For freedom Christ has set us free». By preaching Jesus as *the* human freedom event, Paul linguistically and conceptually cast the preaching of the gospel within the context of the most crucial issue with which society at large was then occupied: the (re)definition of freedom. Although Paul does not introduce the term *eleutheria* in 1Cor 5,1-13, it is probable that the issue of freedom was at the basis of the brother's *mésalliance* and the community's response to this situation. Indeed, much has been observed in the course of this study which points toward a realization that the Corinthian converts heard Paul's freedom preaching but without hearing the theological inflection which he gave to the term *eleutheria*[24] or, at least, without assimilating its theological and ethical significance. Therefore, despite whatever their own self-conceptions may have been[25], the text information at 1Cor 5 reveals that there were some serious flaws in Corinthian understanding of Christianity.

Misconceptions about freedom appear to lay at the basis of the divorce which the Corinthians apparently made between moral behavior and faith in and belonging to Christ. The divorce is manifest in the behavior discussed in 1Cor 5. For Paul, as his writings attest, belonging to Christ had no meaning apart from belonging to the God of Jesus Christ since Christ died to free us from the slavery of sin and law precisely so that we

---

[24] In Paul, *eleutheria* was «ein genuin theologisch-heilgeschtlicher Begriff [...]» (D. NESTLE, *Eleutheria*, 135).

[25] The problem of reading the language of 1Cor as a mirror of Corinthian self-perception has already been signalled, cf. above c. 3 n. 56; 57.

would be alive to God (Rom 6,11) and become slaves of God (Rom 6,22). To accept the offer of freedom which comes through Christ is to stand in a new relationship, to accept a new bondage and this carries with it ethical consequences[26]. Christians are to bear fruit for God (Rom 7,4), walk in the newness of life (Rom 6,4), yield themselves no longer to sin but to righteousness unto sanctification, the end of which is eternal life (Rom 6,15-23). Thus, the new freedom exercised by those who partake of this new life can never be absolute freedom but freedom lived within the parameters of belonging to God in Christ[27] and exercised for determined ends.

Apparently the Corinthian community failed to understand that Christ's offer of freedom from sin also carried with it bondage to God. This observation is reinforced by a consideration of the fact that, in 1Cor in general, Paul repeatedly emphasizes the relationship that exists between the community and God through Christ, employing formulations which, interestingly, appear only in this letter[28]. It is difficult to avoid the impression that the Corinthian community was greatly in need of the very basic reminder that faith in and belonging to Christ have also something to do with faith in and belonging to the God of Jesus Christ and this has ethical consequences[29]. Hence, for Paul, ethics can never be independent of God. But how could the Corinthians fail to understand that their freedom was conditioned by their belonging to God whose nature and moral will necessarily impinged on their exercise of freedom?

---

[26] Cf. the comments in F. MUßNER, *Theologie der Freiheit*, 32-36.

[27] This is illustrated at 1Cor 6,12-20 where Paul frames his discussion within these two parameters: Christians are free (6,12) but they belong to God (6,19) in and through Christ whose death constituted the price (6,20) by which they were set free from the bondage of sin.

[28] For example, at 3,21b.23 he states, «*panta gar hymôn estin* [...] *hymeis de Christou, Christos de theou*». Later in the letter, Paul refers to Christ as the head of every man, but again this bilateral relationship is re-contextualized *vis-à-vis* God, who is the «*kephalè* [...] *tou Christou*» (1Cor 11,3). These formulations at 3,21b.23 and 11,3, which emphasize the chain of relationship – Christians, Christ, God – are employed only in this letter. At 6,19, Paul, alluding to Christ's death, speaks of the price by which the Corinthians were bought (*ègorasthète*, 6,20; cf. 7,23). Thus, they are not their own (6,19), but belong to God to whom they must render glory (6,20b). Here, too, both the expression found at 6,19 «*kai ouk este heautôn*» (a similar idea is expressed at Rom 14,7 but the stress is on belonging to the Lord, where judging from v. 9, Paul is referring to Christ) and the mention of being bought – with God as the intended purchaser – are unique to this letter.

[29] Note how in 1Cor Paul emphasizes that it is God's wisdom that must be acknowledged (1,18-31); his commandments that must be kept (7,19). This God, the Father, is he for whom the Corinthians exist (8,5). It is God who is the source of the Corinthian's life in Christ (1,30) and whose glory is the object of everything that Christians do in and through Christ (1Cor 10,30).

If what we have proposed above in c. 3 is valid, viz., that the Corinthians' apprehension of Paul's preaching was Stoically conditioned, then it certainly goes a long way in explaining how the Corinthians could remove the exercise of freedom from the context of belonging to God and ultimately arrive at the divorce between ethical behavior and religion that is manifest in the behavior under discussion in 1Cor 5. Operating within Stoically conditioned ideas, the Corinthians would not have necessarily understood that belonging to the God of Jesus meant, as Paul would have intended it, belonging to a personal, yet totally other[30], Holy God whose Holiness demanded holiness (cf. Lev 19,1). By contrast, among Stoics, god was conceived as Reason with which the body was co-mingled[31], or matter, of which humans partake[32]. Hence, the Stoic notion of freedom would not be circumscribed by a relationship with a personal God. Moreover, freedom would not be expressed in behavior that accords with the moral will of the God of Jesus which Paul explicitly states is «your holiness»[33], but rather in conforming one's own reason to Reason, which is equivalent to saying, conforming one's life to the will of god, i.e., to nature[34]. Thus, a Stoic too could be heard to say that «freedom is to obey god»[35]. However, the key term, *theos,* would mean something totally different for Stoicism and Christianity and that would make all the difference with regard not only to how *eleutheria* would be understood[36] but, more importantly, how it would be expressed on the level of concrete behavior. Moreover, though in each instance good and evil would be determined in relation to the «will of god» the different conceptions of God/god would necessarily result in different evaluations of good and evil. Would the Corinthian converts who heard Paul's freedom preaching which resonated superficially with Stoic ideas that they had already heard and presumably assimilated also have perceived these fundamental

---

[30] Cf. above c. 3 n. 141.

[31] Cf. EPICTETUS, *Discourses*, I.III,1; CICERO, *De Natura,* II, 78-80; *De Finibus, III,* 64; MARCUS AURELIUS, *Meditations*, V, 27.

[32] Cf. EPICTETUS, *Discourses*, I.IX,6; I, 14,6.

[33] In 1Thess 4,3a after stating that the «will of God» is «your holiness» Paul adds four imperatives which express the concrete content of *hagiasmos*: 1) to keep away from *porneia* v. 3b; 2) to see that each one's own *skeuos* (vessel) is maintained in holiness v. 4; 3) to not transgress (*hyperbainen*) v. 6; 4) to not wrong (*pleonektein*) your brother in this matter, v. 6.

[34] Cf. the discussion in B. INWOOD, *Ethics*, 26-27.

[35] SENECA, *De Vita Beata*, 15,7; cf. further EPICTETUS, *Discourses*, IV.VII, 17-18.

[36] Commenting on the difference between Stoic and Christian notions of freedom, Y. Congar observed that, «Christian freedom consists in the perfect agreement, not of an "apathetic" will with nature, but of a love-intoxicated will with the saving will of God as it is shown forth in Jesus Christ» (cf. Y. CONGAR, «Holy Spirit», 25).

differences? As far as we have been able to see, 1Cor 5 illustrates the kind of behavior that could have resulted when the fundamental differences were not perceived[37].

Apparently absent from the Corinthian understanding of Christianity is also any appreciation of the ecclesial dimension of freedom. This can be deduced from the content of Paul's argument in 1Cor 5. Already in the first two verses of c. 5 Paul was able to communicate the fact that incest is deplorable – an evil even pagans recognize. However, the announcement of this fact does not of itself disclose the core of the problem. The core of the problem, which Paul illustrates through metaphoric language[38], is that this evil has communal consequences (vv. 6-8). Therefore, what is unequivocally an act of gross immorality[39] – a fact that Paul impresses on the community in the *a* and *a'* sections of this chapter – perpetrated by an individual member of the community, is in reality an imperilment for the whole, and thus, a community problem – a fact that Paul highlights in the *b* section of this chapter. The salient emphasis here on the community dimension of sin is perhaps to be taken as an indication of the non-community oriented thinking of the Corinthians. If so, such thinking also fits well into a Stoic schema and reinforces the possibility that the Corinthians, or at least some of them, though baptized into Christ, were still operating under the influence of Stoic thought categories.

Notwithstanding its talk of human communion, Stoic philosophy (religion) could be considered essentially a-social. Though Stoics held that all were permeated by the same *logos*, the acknowledged basis of communion, nevertheless, the focus was on the individual, one's own inner state of virtue and imperturbability, one's own striving to live in accord with nature[40]. With this stress on individualism, it should come as no surprise then that the kind of moral communion conceived by Paul where one person's sin could adversely affect all the members of the community (cf. 1Cor 5,6-8), would be inconceivable for Stoics as many of their own writings illustrate[41]. If the Corinthians were still operating within a Stoically conditioned schema, as we have argued, this would

---

[37] Cf. above c. 3 § 4.4.

[38] Discussed above c. 5 § 9; c. 6 § 2.1B.

[39] Why the Corinthians failed to consider this incestuous relationship a sin has already been discussed. Cf. above, esp. p. 82-83.

[40] Cf. above c. 5 § 4.1.

[41] «To my will the will of my neighbor is as irrelevant as is his breath or his flesh. Even though we have come into the world for each other's sake, yet our directing minds each have their own sphere of government. Else my neighbor's evil were my evil, which was not the god's intention, lest it be within another's power to bring misfortune upon me» (MARCUS AURELIUS, *Meditations*, VIII,56).

explain their apparent failure to apprehend the ecclesial inflection that Paul would necessarily have given to *eleutheria*. For Christians, freedom had to be exercised in a way that was compatible with their shared existence in Christ and with the common vocation to holiness received in Baptism. What was inimical to this shared life, sin, could never be, and could never be viewed as, an expression of Christian freedom. Moreover, in the Christian *ekklèsia* there was no room for individualists seeking to chart autonomous courses toward perfection. Christians formed One body in and through which they participated in the freedom that was the gift of Christ to the whole. Freedom, as it was exercised by each, had to promote the growth in holiness of the whole *ecclesia*, so that, as one body, it would attain to maturity, to the «measure of the stature of the fullness of Christ» (Eph 4,13).

In sum, from the text information of 1Cor 5 and what can be constructed from the contours of this argument and Paul's emphases elsewhere in 1Cor, it would seem that Paul encountered a flawed understanding of Christianity at Corinth which manifested itself in a) disregard for the life of the whole community[42] and its sinless status in Christ, b) the according of primacy to the individual and self-realization and c) disregard for the essential link between faith and belonging to Christ and moral behavior. These flaws in Corinthian thinking which probably account for the conspicuously un-Christian behavior of both the incestuous brother and the community center around a misunderstanding of what Christian freedom is, what it implies and what its *telos* is. If our perception has been correct and our argument valid, the flaws and lacunae in Corinthian thinking resulted from a situation characterized by a lack of clarity with regard to the essential differences between Stoic and Christian conceptions of freedom and its *telos*.

4. The Perils of Preaching

Some would say that by his own imprecise preaching, Paul contributed to the confusion at Corinth and the lack of clarity with which this community approached and lived Christianity[43]. However probable, and we agree that it is, we should try to avoid construing this in a totally negative way as if the situation were somehow Paul's fault – or even the Corinthians' for that matter. On the positive side, we have to consider that by preaching the gospel in categories which were familiar and of critical importance to his audience, using even identical vocabulary, Paul took a bold and

---

[42] See the remarks in E. SCHWEIZER, *The Church*, 39.
[43] Cf. e.g. J. MURPHY-O'CONNOR, *Paul. A Critical Life*, 253.

necessary step toward making the gospel accessible to the Corinthians. If we get the impression from 1Cor in general, and c. 5 in particular, that Paul took the risk but the attempt failed miserably, we may have an unrealistic expectation that a) old and familiar words, preached with radically new meanings, will immediately mean something substantially new to people who, for a long time, may have intended something else by them and b) that the new understanding, even if quickly apprehended, would immediately generate a new *ethos* that would straightaway give rise to new behavior. Whenever the gospel message is seeded in new soil certain risks are involved and misunderstanding may be inevitable. Moreover, even in ideal circumstances, the inculcating of a new *ethos* and new ethic takes time.

With regard to the situation of 1Cor 5, Paul himself wasted no time in pointing fingers but moved quickly to the important task of taking steps to correct a bad situation and to the even more important task of instructing and clarifying so that the community would understand for the future. In this chapter, correction and instruction are inseparable. To dwell only on the judgement pronouncement and disciplinary sanction risks making of 1Cor 5 no more than an *ad hoc* case of church discipline. Paul did step in to correct but he also effectively turned the treatment of this disciplinary case into a lesson for the community. Through a well crafted rhetorical argument, Paul not only provided the community with persuasive reasons for accepting his judgement and executing the sanction now but also provided the guiding criteria by which the community would be able to judge correctly for itself if ever again confronted by a similar situation. In his use of the simplest, unambiguous language of loaf and leaven and relating it to the death of Christ, Paul was able to communicate profound ideas with clarity and thereby redirect the errant thinking of the community so that it would be able to carry out the sanction, not having been coerced, but having understood and been convinced of its necessity.

5. General Conclusion

In the course of this study we have provided a conclusion to each chapter and, when appropriate, inserted medial summaries. Before the exposition of our theological reflection in the eighth and final chapter of this study we will now, for the sake of comprehensiveness and clarity, offer a summary of significant findings, conclusions and insights that have emerged from this study.

1. The claim that 1Cor 5 is a polemical text, at the heart of which is the issue of Paul's authority, cannot be sustained based on the information in

the text of 1Cor 5. This view only gains currency if one reads 1Cor 5 as illustrative of a polemic over Paul's authority which is alleged to characterize 1Cor as a whole. As we believe to have convincingly argued, this allegation is based on two false presuppositions viz., that the social situation of 1Cor is for all practical purposes the same as 2Cor and that 1Cor 1-4 and 9 are units of apologetic or forensic speech. Hence we find no compelling reason to adopt the view that the incestuous relationship and the community boasting over it were intended as an overt challenge to Paul's apostolic authority nor to read Paul's response to the incest case as a vehicle for (re)establishing or imposing his authority in a situation where it has presumably eroded.

2. By dissociating 1Cor 5 from the context of polemic over authority and recognizing it as a unit of rhetoric we were able to examine the parts of this unit in terms of their argumentative and persuasive functions. In this light, we observed that 1Cor 5 shows itself to be a well-crafted argument through which Paul attempts to persuade the community to come together, acknowledge the evil and execute the sanction which he has prescribed. Our rhetorical analysis of 1Cor 5 brings us to the conclusion that Paul's ultimate concern in the deployment of this discourse is to protect the community from the harm that this incestuous situation presents for its interior life and well-being. The harm will be avoided if the community takes action; hence, Paul's rhetorical task: to persuade the community to take the prescribed action.

3. The announcement of the judgement and disciplinary sanction need not be taken as an indication that, apropos of this case, Paul has eschewed persuasive discourse. As we believe to have convincingly argued, the judgement pronouncement has an integral role to play in the argumentative strategy. Therefore, any suggestion that the judgement pronouncement constitutes *prima facie* text evidence that Paul's intention was to champion his authority and resolve the case in a unilateral manner needs to be reconsidered. Moreover, evaluations of Paul's intention in 1Cor 5 made in light of the three-verse judgement pronouncement and not the whole chapter are necessarily skewed and may derive, as we have observed, from a desire to prove some other point, e.g. the undemocratic manner in which disciplinary decisions were arrived at in the early Church.

4. In the unfolding of the argument Paul calls on the witness of both the pagan and Jewish worlds as testimony to this immorality. While some say

that scandal to the pagans is Paul's chief concern and accounts for the severity of his response, others hold that the Jewish perspective dominates. On closer analysis we have discovered that neither dominates but both are brought to bear on the situation and, structurally speaking, provide the framework in which Paul's argument is set.

5. The key argument against the continued tolerance of the offender is provided in vv. 6-8. Here Paul apprises the community of the gravity of the situation and argues for the necessity of expelling the offender in reason of the community's essential character which results from the redemptive act of Christ. Though the reasoning is posterior to the judgement pronouncement, the execution of the sanction is ultimately contingent on the persuasive power of the reasoning and not, as we believe to have shown, on the authoritative tone or antecedent place of the pronouncement.

6. With the discussion of 1Cor 5 dissociated from the context of polemic a window opens onto the possibility of evaluating the disciplinary sanction within the context of Paul's ecclesiology. Viewed within this context, we were able to observe that the severe sanction, far from being a reactionary response to a desperate situation, emerges as a logical response to a situation which threatens the whole community.

7. It must be conceded that absolute certainty may never be had with regard to why a community member decided to live in a relationship which by all lights could be considered immoral, nor why the community tolerated and apparently touted this relationship. Our investigation into the possible backgrounds that may have contributed to the Corinthians' attitude and behavior toward this case has brought us to the conclusion that the Corinthians' apprehension of Paul's preaching, especially his proclamation of freedom, was colored by ideas from Stoicism. This admixture had the possibility of resulting in ideas and behavior that could have unfortunate effects in the Christian community and there seems to be sufficient reason to consider 1Cor 5 as a case in point.

CHAPTER VIII

Theological Reflection

1. Introduction

As we noted in the introduction, 1Cor 5 is a chapter that can be easily dismissed as irrelevant for the present day. This is especially so if Paul's response is presented primarily as part of an on-going feud between himself and a small group of converts who were contesting his authority. Unfortunately, when construed as a text in which the (re)gaining of control and power is at stake, the theological and moral content of 1Cor 5, a content that ought to occupy our attention, is eclipsed[1].

By reviewing the evidence used to substantiate the reading of 1Cor 5 within a context of polemic, by reconsidering the factors that may have induced the Corinthians to behave as they did and by looking at Paul's response through the lens of rhetoric, we hope to have dispelled the view that a polemic over authority was at the basis of Corinthian behavior or molded the dynamics that drove Paul's argument. What was at stake was the integrity of the community and we believe to have set in relief the crucial theological concerns that accounted for Paul's exigent response.

Adjusting and improving our understanding of the situation and Paul's response is important. However, the study of a biblical text is not undertaken only for the purpose of ensuring a more accurate reading of a past

---

[1] Setting the focus on the politics of authority rather than the moral and theological content of 1Cor 5 is unfortunate. However, it may go hand in hand with the increasing tendency in studies of NT ethics to abandon the «religious and theological content and concentrate on the social, economic or political underpinnings of ethical discourse» (L. KECK, «Rethinking», 8).

situation. We still must inquire about the relevance of the biblical text for us today and make every effort to continue the process of actualization[2].

An inquiry concerning the relevance of Paul's moral teaching for Christian life today is, as everyone involved in Pauline studies knows, a task surrounded by much controversy[3]. The weightiest reasons for denying the relevance of Paul's moral teaching are well known, viz., Paul's responses were occasional and his thoughts were conditioned by an eschatological perspective that no longer applies[4]. Based on these reasons some would categorically deny the relevance of Paul's moral teaching and would consider any investigation into its relevance misguided. In the case of 1Cor 5, beyond the standard reasons advanced for denying relevance to Paul's moral teaching, the fact that it is here accompanied by a call for excommunication might induce even the staunchest advocates of relevance to think twice. Excommunication is an extreme discipline in any epoch and few scholars would want to attach their names to its advocacy[5]. Moreover, given the current climate of intolerance notable in some sectors of secular and Christian society and given the increasingly urgent calls for harsher sanctions being launched by these groups[6], one must be cautious about suggesting the relevance of a text that could be politicized and marshalled to justify courses of action which are not necessarily motivated by charity.

With regard to the prevalent reasons for rejecting the relevancy of Paul's moral teaching, in the first place it can be objected that though Paul was responding to a particular situation, his moral exhortation in 1Cor 5 is nonetheless rooted in considerations that are not themselves situation-bound[7]. Hence, the moral teaching, though directed to a particular situation, is not on that account necessarily divested of value and relevancy for any other time or situation. Second, in every age, the Church is always the community who waits in faith and hope for the second and future coming of Christ. Hence, regardless of the time that has elapsed, we still do live in

---

[2] On the necessity of actualizing the biblical text and the principles on which this task is based cf. «The Interpretation of Bible» sect. IV A. in J.A. FITZMYER, *The Biblical Commission's Document*, 170-176.

[3] Cf. S. ZEDDA, *Relativo*. This monograph is entirely devoted to this issue.

[4] Some scholars marshall these reasons to reject not only the relevance of Paul's moral teaching but that of the entire NT, cf. e.g. J.T. SANDERS, *Ethics*; An interesting discussion of how both ethicists and biblicists deal with the issue of the validity of NT ethics for today is carried on in R. SCROGGS, «New Testament and Ethics», 77-93.

[5] A notable exception is V.C. PFITZNER, already signalled above, Introduction, n. 8.

[6] In the USA for example, a case in point is the call for the death penalty. To date, thirty-seven states have re-instated the death penalty (cf. *The 1997 World Almanac*, 960).

[7] Cf. above c. 5 §9;12; c. 6; cf. further S. ZEDDA, *Relativo*, esp. 73-75.

the interim period between the two comings[8]. Moreover, even if Paul's eschatological expectations for the end of history were not fulfilled as anticipated, as Christians, ever in need of renewal and purification[9], we cannot afford to relegate his message to the past. An insight of Sampley is well-worth repeating here: «When one loses sight of Paul's eschatological critique of this age and its values, then the value's of one's own age creep back into one's thought world and become formative»[10].

As for the fear of advocating excommunication, the risk of providing fuel for the fire of fundamentalists and hard-liners cannot be a deterrent to examining the relevance of Paul's insights in 1Cor 5. Nor should this risk be used as an excuse to ignore the challenge that Paul's theological insights and their many implications may pose for contemporary church life. But what of these theological insights and their challenge to us today? Let us begin with a brief review of the situation that Paul faced and then consider the present.

2. The Corinthian Situation

In the course of this study we have argued that the judgement of the Corinthians was impaired by a Stoically influenced conception of freedom skewed by individualism. The fact of the incest and the community's response to it showed a disregard for basic human morality and a deficient understanding of the key Pauline insight that the Christian is an individual who is constituted by community, draws his life from and within the context of the community and must contribute to the salvation of the community. For Paul, there was no antithesis between the individual and the community. On the contrary, they were complimentary in that, as Paul understood it, the individual Christian is constituted by community and therefore knows and becomes him/herself precisely in community, in the *ekklèsia*. However, there was necessarily a great antithesis between community and individualism, the latter understood as self-realization pursued apart from any consideration of the community context that necessarily circumscribes Christian existence.

3. The Contemporary Situation

To speak of the exercise of freedom skewed by individualism is to speak of a contemporary problem to which an increasing number of theologians, ethicists and social analysts are calling attention. Though

---

[8] Cf. R.F. O'TOOLE, *Who is a Christian?*, 136.

[9] Cf. «Lumen Gentium», 9, 39.

[10] J.P. SAMPLEY, *Walking Between the Times*, 108.

individualism is characteristic of modern western culture, Schindler has recently considered how and why American society (U.S.)[11] has been particularly suited to the development and promotion of individualism to such an extent that, as he has remarked, «individualism is the defining characteristic of this culture»[12]. For the purposes of this reflection we will keep the focus on the problem of «individualism» within the United States and consider its negative impact on the practice of Christianity within the ranks of American Catholics.

At present, radical individualism is perceived as one of the major factors contributing to the unraveling of the civic and moral life of the nation and to the destruction of freedom itself. In a work widely acclaimed[13] as a benchmark study of contemporary American society, the social analyst R. Bellah and his collaborators began with a consideration of the three cultural strands or conversations that have shaped American society since its inception: the «Biblical», the «Republican» and the «Individualist»[14]. The present crisis in the United States derives from what Bellah and his associates observed to be the dominance of «individualism» over the other two foundational cultural strands. The Biblical and Republican strands, though differing, still shared a strong ethical component and communitarian dimension[15]. Within these two traditions, the individual was not disregarded but rather placed «in a context of moral and religious obligation that in some contexts justified obedience as well as freedom»[16]. Individualism, on the other hand, whether, «utilitarian» or «expressive»[17], stresses self-interest and self-realization. Within this strand, as it has developed into our own day, center stage is occupied by the «autonomous individual» whose life choices are made not on the basis of some order of higher truths or the common good, but according to criteria that advance his/her own

---

[11] In the following we will be using the terms America/American to refer to the United States or U.S. citizens, aware, of course, that these terms have other referents.

[12] Cf. T. SCHINDLER, Ethics, 41. In c. 1, the author traces the rise of the concept of the individual as a «bounded and distinct self» to changes occurring in 12th century Europe (31), looks at the emergence of «individualism» under the influence of the classical liberal tradition (33-41) and then discusses how this concept developed and flourished within American society (41-45). A more detailed exposition of the philosophical underpinnings of modern individualism is presented in F.G. KIRKPATRICK, Community.

[13] Cf. R. BELLAH, Habits.

[14] These traditions are discussed in R. BELLAH, Habits, c. 2.

[15] R. BELLAH, Habits, esp. 29-31.

[16] R. BELLAH, Habits, 143.

[17] On utilitarian and expressive forms of individualism, cf. R. BELLAH, Habits, 32-35.

happiness and fulfillment[18]. In this perspective the individual is understood to be antecedent to society and the self is perceived as the only, or main form of reality[19]. For the self of individualism, the exercise of freedom can easily devolve into little more than the exercise of rights ordered to one's own ends apart from any concern for the common good or moral obligation[20]. The self becomes the criterion for the validation of choices. «"Values" turn out to be the incomprehensible, rationally indefensible thing that the individual chooses when he or she has thrown off the last vestige of external influence and reached pure, contentless freedom»[21].

This regnant individualism has, in various ways, infiltrated American Roman Catholicism[22]. A. Dulles S.J. has expressed his concern with regard to the inadequacy of the American categories of freedom, rugged individualism, democracy and reformability to serve as norms for the Church[23]. In discussing American reaction to Vatican Council II, Dulles has observed that the radical revision of what the Council taught in light of the implied American dogma of self-determination has served to advance claims in the interest of freedom that cannot be said to be warranted by the Council[24]. By acknowledging important American values, the Council made it easier for American Catholics to enter into the spirit of the Council and apprehend its message. However, as Dulles also observed, «the Church cannot be totally recast in the image of American liberal society»[25]. Nor, as the author contended elsewhere, can Christians grant that «freedom is to be defined simply as autonomy, still less in terms of indetermination or self-realization»[26]. On the contrary, the freedom advocated by Vatican Council II was ordered to the seeking after and adhering to the fullness of revealed truth[27]. Indeed, as the Church continues to affirm, the exercise of freedom must be rooted in and ordered

---

[18] R. BELLAH, *Habits*, 47.

[19] R. BELLAH, *Habits*, 143. On ontological individualism cf. further 244, 334.

[20] «Separated from family, religion and calling as sources of authority, duty and moral example, the self first seeks to work out its own form of action by autonomously pursuing happiness and satisfying its wants» (cf. R. BELLAH, *Habits*, 79).

[21] R. BELLAH, *Habits*, 79-80.

[22] Statistics based on some polls and studies of American Catholics which indicate in what ways and to what extent American Catholics have absorbed the individualistic attitudes of American culture are discussed in E. WCELA, «Who Do You Say?», 5-7.

[23] A. DULLES, *The Reshaping*. See esp. ch. 1, «The American Impression of the Council».

[24] A. DULLES, *The Reshaping*, 15.

[25] A. DULLES, *The Reshaping*, 16.

[26] Cf. A. DULLES, *A Church to Believe In*, 69.

[27] Cf. A. DULLES, *The Reshaping*, 15.

to truth or it risks destroying and negating itself[28]. However, even with regard to truth, radical individualism would understand truth claims as contingent upon a given set of conditions, persons and personal choices made within these conditions. Hence, from the perspective of radical individualism, truth is irreducibly relative[29].

On the grass-roots level the skewing of Christian freedom by radical individualism manifests itself in various ways among American Catholics. To begin with, one can consider the stance of some Catholics on the issue of abortion. By divorcing the practice from the religious/moral context and viewing it as a political/legal issue[30], some Catholics, like some of their Christian, non-Christian and atheist contemporaries, have also come to defend or at least tolerate[31] the practice of abortion on the grounds of individual freedom, the private nature of certain human acts[32] and the further claim that a plurality of opinions on fundamental moral issues is admissible[33]. Recourse is also had to «individual conscience» which can unfortunately be employed as a cover for egoistic self-determination[34], especially when invoked by a subject who conceives of him/herself as a self-sufficient absolute[35]. This *ethos* of individualism has also permeated attitudes and practices with regard to sexuality, sexual orientation and

---

[28] Cf. JOHN PAUL II, «Evangelium Vitae», 19, 20.

[29] On truth and relativism cf. JOHN PAUL II, «Veritatis Splendor», 84.

[30] As pointed out «Evangelium Vitae» esp. 68-72, underlying such a divorce is usually the mistaken assumption that civil law is in no way obliged by moral law as inscribed in natural law. This can lead to the further assumption that the function of civil law is not the establishment of any moral position but merely the providing of legitimate space for each individual to exercise his/her freedom in conscience. Unfortunately, when Catholics fall prey to such dichotomizing they are hardly in a position «to impress the Divine law on the affairs of the earthly city», a task proper to the laity (cf. «Gaudium et Spes», 43).

[31] The «personally opposed but [...]» position with regard to abortion as expounded by Catholics in public office is carefully critiqued in M. HIMES – K. HIMES, *Fullness*, 96-99.

[32] Privatization allows public matters to be shifted to the private arena and effectively denies the social dimension of human acts. On the «cult of privatization» and the related problem of determining what issues and human actions are to be part of the agenda of public debate, cf. M. HIMES – K. HIMES, *Fullness of Faith*, esp. 93-96.

[33] The opinion that a pluralism of opinions is admissible in the sphere of morality «questions the intrinsic and unbreakable bond between faith and morality» («Veritatis Splendor», 4).

[34] The conditioning of conscience by the drive for self-determination can darken and render it incapable of distinguishing between good and evil (cf. «Evangelium Vitae», 4).

[35] For a Christian, the recourse to conscience presupposes an acknowledgement of one's total dependence upon an Absolute, i.e. God and the requisite posture of submissiveness before God. (Cf. J. FUCHS, *Personal Responsibility*, 44-48).

marriage and divorce. It is also rearing its head with new vigor in the contemporary debate on physician-assisted suicide[36] which is gaining a sympathetic hearing on the grass-roots level even among Catholics[37], though the Church continues to affirm that no one has the right to determine whether to live or die[38]. No less egregious, but perhaps less expounded, is the negative impact of individualism on Roman Catholics with regard to social morality. Not long ago, R. McBrien remarked that the «free to choose» mentality of radical individualism has also taken hold among American Catholics, evident in the tendency to reject, or at least ignore, some of the principle tenets of Catholic social doctrine[39]. As Schindler observed, individualism, with its emphasis on separateness and the resultant loosening of bonds between the individual and society, effectively promotes the subordination of the social to the personal[40]. Concern about this state of affairs is expressed in «Evangelium Vitae». There one reads:

> If the promotion of the self is understood in terms of absolute autonomy, people inevitably reach the point of rejecting one another. Everyone else is considered an enemy from whom one has to defend oneself. Thus society becomes a mass of individuals placed side by side, but without any mutual bonds. Each one wishes to assert himself independently of the other and in fact intends to make his own interests prevail[...] In this way, any reference to common values and to a truth absolutely binding on everyone is lost, and social life ventures on to the shifting sands of complete relativism[41].

---

[36] The key argument in the justification of this practice is in the recourse to the individual's right of self-determination. As is well known, the right to choose «to exit» life, i.e., commit suicide, was defended by the Stoics in view of their whole program of self-determination, cf. e.g. EPICTETUS, *Discourses*, III.VIII, 6; III.XXIV, 96-102; I.IX,11-12 and translator's n. 2.

[37] Unfortunately, Americans of all stripes are subject to extensive manipulation with regard to physician-assisted suicide as the issue is re-cast in less-abrasive language. T. E. Quill, a very powerful and eloquent advocate of physician-assisted suicide, is a master in manipulative language as illustrated by the title of his recent book: *A Midwife Through the Dying Process. Stories of Healing & Hard Choices at the End of Life*. The softening, feminizing and associating of suicide with positive images of midwifery and healing is pure language cosmetics aimed at enticing Americans to consider suicide a humane and right thing to do.

[38] Cf. «Evangelium Vitae», 15; 47 and esp. 64-67.

[39] Cf. R. McBRIEN, «The American Experience», 10; cf. further E. WCELA, «Who Do You Say?», 6.

[40] Cf. T. SCHINDLER, *Ethics*, 9-10. While loosening the bonds between the individual and society, individualism also – one might say paradoxically – promotes individual conformity to societal expectations. On this latter point see Schindler's discussion, 163-171.

[41] Cf. «Evangelium Vitae», 20.

With regard to Roman Catholics, the subordination of the social to the personal plays itself out in an individualistic morality characterized by a lack of concern for the common good and a non-recognition of the obligations of social justice[42]. After reviewing the results of a research study on American «core» Catholics, which revealed, *inter alia*, that only 39% of those studied included a social dimension when articulating their foundational beliefs, E. Wcela had the following to say:

> The paradox for the Catholic Church in America is that it stresses communitarian values. Its members dutifully describe the church in communitarian terms such as «people of God», «body of Christ,» and «fellowship of believers». They speak of the importance of the traditional teaching which stresses assistance to the needy. At the same time they have absorbed the individualistic attitudes of American culture, economy and polity[43].

In breve, while it is clear that not all Christian living is hopelessly subverted by radical individualism still, individualism is planted deep in the American psyche. Its incursion into the practice of Christian faith is discernible at both the level of individual and social morality as we have just seen. Compounding the problem, there is a notable growing loss of the sense of sin and evil[44]. There are numerous factors contributing to this de-sensitivity not least of which are the social sciences. On the positive side, advances in these fields have provided a more adequate understanding and appreciation of the various psychological and social factors that can condition behavior. In light of this information it has become increasingly clear that culpability cannot be automatically and necessarily imputed to persons who do evil. However, a more scientifically illumined understanding of the pre-moral root causes of certain behaviors may be contemporaneously contributing to the de-construction of the whole notion of sin and to a certain indifference about the moral quality of acts themselves[45]. Recently a Catholic moral theologian, commenting on some specific sexual disorders, has expressed concern that we have «so

---

[42] In «Gaudium et Spes», 30, the Church exhorted all persons to transcend a «merely individualistic morality». Why many American Catholics still remain fixed at this level of morality is the focus of Schindler's, *Ethics*. Having acknowledged that Church opposition to individualism has been unflagging, the author went forward to examine how aspects of Church praxis could be perceived as sanctioning individualistic morality by American Catholics steeped in an individualistic culture.

[43] E. WCELA, «Who Do You Say?», 6. Wcela's comment comes after his review of some key findings of a research team from the University of Notre Dame who studied «core» Catholics, i.e., those who acknowledged a formal affiliation with a parish.

[44] The problem was put out in the open over twenty years ago (cf. K. MENNINGER, *Whatever Became of Sin?*).

[45] The object or matter of a human act can itself be considered under the moral aspect of good or evil cf. AQUINAS, *STh*, I-II Q.18 Art. 2.

thoroughly medicalized all evil-doing that there is no room left either for criminality or morality»[46].

The tendency to relativize moral wrong in the name of individual freedom grounded in the drive for self-determination, to make the self the central reality and to reject transcendental truth – not simply its content but even the possibility that there is objective truth – these tendencies challenge and to some extent have already subverted the practice of Christianity both among American Catholics and their Christian contemporaries. While it must be granted that the situations of first century Corinthian Christians and twentieth century American Christians are not perfectly analogous, this admission in no way precludes either the possibility of recognizing or the necessity of admitting that freedom skewed by individualism, whether it be rooted in and nourished by Stoic philosophy or classic liberal philosophy, is not Christian freedom. It is precisely at this point that Paul's insights in 1Cor 5 may be validly investigated in terms of what they might contribute to an understanding of where Christians today need to be and on what they should take a stand. Before looking at these insights, one more comment is in order.

Who we conceive Paul to be will obviously have a bearing on whether and how we will listen to his insights. In the course of this thesis we have had cause to challenge and revise some proposed portrayals of Paul and his intentions in 1Cor 5. This was done, not in the interest of apologetics, but simply because these interpretations appear to be wrong given the evidence. As we will see in a moment, Paul's response to the situation reflected in 1Cor 5 poses a challenge to radical individualism and to those enshrined values associated with it such as self-determination, moral pluralism and non-interference. Needless to say, those Christians who have also enshrined radical individualism and its values, adopted these as operative in their own lives and have, in consequence, slipped into moral relativism will doubtless find it difficult to appropriate what Paul had to say in 1Cor 5 in a meaningful way[47]. Lest this challenging task be unnecessarily complicated by overlaying Paul's theology with politics, it is all the more important that inaccurate interpretations of his role and intentions in 1Cor 5 be set aside.

As we just noted, the exercise of freedom skewed by individualism, emerges as a problem common to both the contemporary situation and the

---

[46] The comment is by A. Guindon, cited in N.J. RIGALI, «Church Response», 134.

[47] This conflict of interests is obviously not limited to Paul. The whole biblical *ethos* of community and commitment will always present a difficulty for an audience imbued with the *ethos* of radical individualism (cf. E. WCELA, «Who Do You Say?», 6-7).

Corinthian situation, evident in the behavior discussed in 1Cor 5. In responding to the Corinthian situation, Paul does not engage in theoretical discourse about the exercise of freedom or rights. Rather, he tackles head-on some of the symptoms that accompany the exercise of freedom skewed by individualism, in particular: moral relativism, the subordination of the communal to the personal, and the neutralizing effect the *ethos* of radical individualism can exert on how the community ought to respond to individuals whose actions are immoral. These are some of the symptoms that appear to be perennial accompaniments to the exercise of freedom skewed by individualism. The terms by which we currently refer to these symptoms are not the express terms in which Paul inscribed his discourse. However, they are terms that allow us to apprehend Paul's message, apply it to the contemporary situation and consider its value for all Christians who strive to live their Christianity within cultures characterized by radical individualism and effected by its corrosive force[48].

4. **Paul's Message**

4.1 *Paul's No to Moral Relativism*

Broadly speaking, moral relativism occurs when a person(s) making a moral choice, excludes from consideration all factors[49] other than those that justify or expedite the particular end toward which one's action is directed. In the case of the radical individualist, the end that is typically in sight is self-fulfillment and the self is usually established as the sole arbiter of truth. If we have understood the situation of 1Cor 5 correctly[50], it appears that both the offender and the community subordinated all other considerations to this one: the exercise of individual freedom in the service of self-fulfillment. Relative to this end, incest, a knowable evil, was re-conceived as an expression of freedom and concern for the community was eclipsed by concern for the self. Objectively speaking, we can consider this a case of moral relativism.

---

[48] With regard to the biblical texts which have been composed with respect to other circumstances in other times, the Church states: «To reveal their significance for men and women of today, it is necessary to apply their message to contemporary circumstances and express it in language adapted to the present time», cf. «The Interpretation of the Bible», IV.A.1.

[49] More specifically with regard to Christians, moral relativism implies a divorce between moral action and faith whereby moral action is determined apart from the data of faith and the natural law, a criterion shared by all of humanity.

[50] How Stoic influences came to bear on this whole situation have been discussed and need not be repeated here, cf. above c. 3 § 4.

Paul rejects the moral relativism into which the individual and the community has obviously slipped and begins with an unequivocal condemnation of this incest situation. The condemnation is not enunciated on the basis of OT law, nor on any qualification that can be considered specifically Christian but rather in view of human reason, adduced through the reference to the pagans at 1Cor 5,2. Implicit here is that pagans do not engage in incest because they know by reason or nature (cf. Rom 2,14) what they must and must not do[51]. Since incest is contrary to reason, it is a knowable evil apart from any prescriptive law. Paul apparently assumes that knowledge of what is right and wrong which comes through human reason is a decisive factor in all human moral behavior. Christians are in no way exempt from the dictates of reason and Paul expected the Corinthians to conform their behavior to human moral behavior. Apart from whether the community had misconstrued Paul's preaching, thereby misunderstanding certain data of faith that should have been considered in this case, still the moral relativism is manifest in the community's disregard for a dictate of human morality, knowable through the *lumen naturale*. On this basis alone the brother and community are without excuse[52]. The individual should have known that *what* he was doing was evil. Likewise, the community could and should have known that what they condoned was, in absolute, evil.

Does a Christian have a right to exercise his freedom if in doing so he acts against reason, and therefore does evil? In 1Cor 5, this question is not explicitly posed. However, Paul's unequivocal condemnation stands as an explicit negative response and is confirmed by both his explicit warning elsewhere that Christian freedom cannot be used in the service of evil (cf. Gal 5,13ff.) and by other admonitions concerning Christian posture toward evil (cf. e.g. Rom 12,9). Moreover, while it cannot be asserted with absolute certainty, the fact that Paul does not even allude to, let alone argue with the reasoning behind the incest and the community's response is probably to be taken as an implicit indication that he considered actions that were contrary to reason beyond the pale of legitimization, regardless of the criteria or the offender's possible good intention[53] to give expression to spiritual freedom. Basic to Paul's response here is the implicit

---

[51] The Church refers to the capacity to know through reason and be conscious of what is good and what is evil as the natural law, cf. AQUINAS, *STh*, I-II, Q. 91 Art. 2; Q. 94 Art. 1.

[52] Cf. Rom 1,18-21.

[53] In the text of 1Cor 5, there is no consideration of the 'intention' of the offender. As we observed above, in c. 5, for Paul the moral evil (*porneia*) determined that the brother was an evil-doer (*pornos*).

affirmation that what reason dictates cannot be ignored or relativized in light of other claims or ends.

4.2 *The Individual Within the Community*

4.2.1 The Social Dimension of a Christian's Acts

Beyond the argument adduced *vis-à-vis* the pagans and what can be known from reason, Paul recalls certain data of faith, setting the discussion in a new context, viz., the eschatological sinless community (cf. 1Cor 5,6-8). For Paul, this is the matrix that shapes Christian morality. The expiatory death of Christ (5,7) has brought about this sinless environment. This moral environment has an ecology about which each individual member must be concerned. Paul's point in vv. 6-7 is that this moral ecology can be upset and compromised by one member's sin. Here, the emphasis shifts from incest as a transgression against human moral law to how the individual's sin is an act of aggression against the whole sinless community. For Paul, the Christian who sins is not just an individual transgressing a law – natural or otherwise – but, in a very real way, a destroyer of the moral ecology of the community. By stressing the repercussions of individual action (5,6b), Paul makes it clear that an action which is personal, i.e., done by an individual, is not on that account a «private» matter. In fact, Paul emphasizes from the outset of his response that it is a problem «*en hymin*» (5,1), «*in* the midst of» and effecting the community. This is why the issue must be brought before the whole community for judgement. Moreover, the enactment of a sanction that removes the offender from the society which he has offended sets in relief the social dimension of the offense.

4.2.2 The Christian: Unique but not Autonomous

As we saw above, especially in c. 6, for Paul, all the actions of individual Christians are social as opposed to purely private in virtue of the fact that the truly Christian individual exists as one who is part of a body (1Cor 12,1ff.), as one who forms the unleavened loaf (1Cor 5,6), as one whose existence is holy *koinônia* (1Cor 1,9). The Christian individual exists not as a self who is antecedent to the community but rather, as a spiritual self brought into being precisely in so far as he/she is «in communion», i.e., ecclesially determined. Hence, within Paul's understanding of Christian existence, for a Christian individual the condition for the possibility of determining that his/her actions will be purely private having no social ramifications, does not exist. Likewise, being «in communion» necessarily excludes a solipsistically determined exercise of freedom. Since the subject of Christian freedom is one «in communion», he/she cannot be an autonomous individual (cf. 1Cor 5,6b; 12,12ff.) or the sole arbiter of truth and the ultimate criterion for the validation of choices. As a partaker in the freedom with which the whole *ekklèsia* is gifted, the exercise of freedom is, in essence, an act of participation. Hence, the Christian cannot establish the self or self-fulfillment as the exclusive end of his/her exercise of freedom. In sum, as a spiritual self whose very existence is an act of participation (cf. 1Cor 1,9), a Christian ever remains a unique person, but one whose moral life and choices must take shape within the matrix of the community. As opposed to the «I» of individualism which recognizes others but places itself before the community, the Christian «I» finds its proper place within the community.

4.2.3 Freedom and Obligation Within the Community

Finally, participation in a sinless communion makes it incumbent on each individual to use his/her freedom to avoid evil, not only as the proper object of his/her own Christian freedom but in view of the whole communion and its moral ecology. Through the expiatory death of Christ the whole *ekklèsia* has been freed and purified from sin (1Cor 5,7) and enjoys this new eschatological sinless existence as one.

Participation in this existence is dynamic; it is power: power either to contribute to the continued liberation and sanctification of all the members by one's free choice to bear fruit for God under the direction of the Spirit or, power to introduce corruption into the community by exposing it to the reign of Sin through individual sin. Those outside the communion do not have this power (1Cor 5,9-13) and those inside cannot divest themselves of it. Once in the Body, the Christian cannot withdraw into neutrality. By his/her actions each Christians shows him/herself either for or against, corrupting or sanctifying, that to which he/she has been united. In the case of the incestuous man, because he was truly *inside* the communion, in a religious and not merely sociological sense[54],he had the power to corrupt (5,6). For this reason he had to be placed *outside* the communion (5,2.7.13b).

Paul is not specific with regard to how this individual's sinful choice concretely effects the community. However, if we have correctly understood his conception of the ecclesia, then individual sin can only have been perceived by Paul as an assault on the sinless existence proper to the whole ecclesia, a pollution of its moral ecology and therefore an

---

[54] This is an important distinction which is correctly emphasized in K. RAHNER, «The Sinful Church», 274.

impediment to the fulfillment of its double vocation to mature in holiness (cf. Eph 1,4-5; 2,21; 4,13) and to be within the world an assembly distinguished by holiness, witnessing Christ to the world (cf. 1Cor 5,9; Phil 2,14).

4.3 *The Responsibility of the Community*

As the individual Christian is obligated to be responsible for the life of the community with respect to his/her own actions, so too is the assembly, in its entirety, obligated to be vigilant for its life. The *ethos* of radical individualism effects not only how individuals locate themselves *vis-à-vis* society but also how whole societies or distinct communities within a society will act *vis-à-vis* individuals. In an atmosphere saturated with talk of self-determination, free choice, the relativity of truth and the infinity of choices, whole communities, and not just individuals, may feel pressured to assume a posture of non-interference in recognition of individual freedom and moral pluralism. Such a posture is a requisite for «political correctness», a familiar and indispensable term in the lexicon of cultures where radical individualism reigns. For others, presumably more enlightened, it is not unheard of to pro-actively champion the non-criminal, albeit immoral, choices of individuals, both in view of moral pluralism and the right to self-determination. If we have correctly understood the situation of 1Cor 5, at least someone must have been uncomfortable with adopting a posture of non-interference since the matter was eventually referred to Paul, presumably so he would interfere. Others, probably the enlightened «wise» of the Corinthian community, considered the brother's action a matter of individual freedom in the service of spiritual self-fulfillment, to be accepted and championed as such for reasons already discussed that betray Stoic conditioning.

In addressing himself to the whole community, Paul makes it clear that there can be no boasting in the exercise of freedom to do evil (1Cor 5,6). Moreover, the whole community was exhorted to renounce evil (5,8), actively resist its presence and take appropriate disciplinary steps when necessary to ensure the community's integrity (1Cor 5,2.5.7.13). In sum, the Christian community cannot be a partner to moral relativism nor can it adopt a posture of non-interference. To do so would be to abdicate responsibility for the spiritual well-being of both the offender and the community. To prevent this, Paul intervened to rouse the community to assume its responsibility.

5. Paul's Challenge for Today

Paul's response in 1Cor 5 challenged the *ethos* and ethics of radical individualism within which the Corinthian community operated. The corrosive effects of this *ethos* within the life of this small Christian community were evident to Paul. His task here was to make this apparent for the community, disturb its perspective and rouse it to responsible action. The *ethos* and ethics of radical individualism are very much alive and now, as then, pose a threat to the practice of Christianity. Might we not hear – need we not hear – in Paul's message to the Corinthians in 1Cor 5 a challenge for our own day?

As we have seen, Paul presents and operates within an *ethos* of community. He insists that Christian moral life is shaped in the matrix of a community which has a common moral identity and a common moral destiny. For the radical individualist of today perhaps the most disturbing realization that emerges from 1Cor 5 is that *ethos* of community excludes the possibility of solipsistically asserting one's independence from this moral communion, exempting the self from its moral economy and slipping into moral relativism. For Paul, Christians are within a community, circumscribed and obliged by it. Within, circumscribed and obliged are terms that have no place in the language and *ethos* of radical individualism. In fact, the opposite is pronounced. There is no reality apart from the individual, no context which circumscribes. There is no obligation beyond that which one owes to one's self. The extent of commitment to others is correlated to personal gain or growth. When the latter cease, so can the commitment. Radical individualism insists that we are *bounded* selves; Christianity makes of us *bonded* selves. Christians who operate within the *ethos* of radical individualism and consider it their «first language»[55] are going to find Paul's message necessarily disturbing. A Christian, perceiving him/herself to be a self-regulating, self-contained and self-serving unit of reality, will find him/herself, *vis-à-vis* the message of Paul, confronted by the paradox and falsehood of his/her own existence.

For Paul, what the church was had to be manifested in its moral living. As reflected in 1Cor 5, it is clear that Paul's thought does not admit of two separate realities, i.e., a sinless, holy, spiritual community and then the community of the Corinthians. There was only one reality. The Corinthians were the holy, spiritual, sinless community, willed by God and brought into existence through the expiatory death of Christ. This reality

---

[55] This concept is borrowed from R. BELLAH, *Habits*, 20.

had no other manifestation than in the holy and sinless lives of the members of this community.

Some of the key implications emerging from message of 1Cor 5 with regard to Christian moral living stand as challenges to three key symptoms of the exercise of freedom skewed by radical individualism that are discernible today: moral relativism, the denial of the social significance of individual acts and the abdication of responsibility on the part of communities. 1Cor 5 stands as a scriptural witness and challenge to Christians today, co-opted by the values of radical individualism, that they cannot use their freedom to do evil nor can they relativize evil in view of self-centered ends. In 1Cor 5, the evil that could not be relativized and had to be avoided was incest. It was to be avoided not because it was part of some special moral code for Christians but because they, like the rest of humanity, are bound by the dictates of reason, i.e., by basic human morality. If, in the ethics of radical individualism, it is held that freedom is fully expressed only when the individual is exempt from every law and external constraint, Paul's response in 1Cor 5 testifies that Christian freedom has a content and boundaries.

This chapter stands further as a testimony that if Christians do evil they do, in fact, harm the body of Christ. Here, Paul allows no Christian the possibility to retreat into bounded isolation and operate within the false view that human acts are private. The sin of an individual Christian has importance for the Church and affects her being[56]. This scriptural witness to the fact that individual sin has communal ramifications for the life of the whole Christian community is reflected in the teaching of the Church[57]. Perhaps, in view of the culture of radical individualism, this point needs to be further emphasized.

Finally, as Paul does not allow the individual Christian to avoid acknowledging the serious implications of his act for the community, neither does he allow the community to ignore its failure. Indeed, as we have seen, in discussing the incest case, Paul sets responsibility for this state of affairs on the shoulders of the community and directs his rhetoric to moving it to assume its responsibility. Obviously, at present, it does not fall within the competence of local lay communities to excommunicate, nor is this discipline even invoked for individual moral transgression. However, this fact does not preclude the possibility of recognizing that

---

[56] K. RAHNER observed over thirty years ago that this was scarcely a topic which appeared in the average teaching on sin or in preaching (cf. «The Sinful Church», 278).

[57] Cf. «Lumen Gentium», 11; and further, «Indulgentiarum Doctrina», 2.

1Cor 5 challenges Christians today both to awaken from the «politically correct» passivity which can sometimes characterize their responses to immoral behavior and to cease to champion immoral choices and acts as testimonies to freedom. Freedom is a good thing which the whole Church acknowledges. However, it can be «cherished improperly» and open the way to evil[58]. This too needs to be acknowledged by Christians. Genuine ignorance and widespread confusion may lead some Christians to ignore or even champion immoral behavior. However, other Christians can be too easily co-opted by the talk of «non-interference» which goes hand in hand with the freedom ethic of radical individualism. The diverse paths which Christians travel must always be respected but they must always be directed to sanctification[59]. Hence, the church today enjoins on each the responsibility to aid one another to greater holiness of life[60]. Granted, «interference» is not a popular posture in a culture dominated by the *ethos* of radical individualism. However, Christians have an obligation to engage themselves in the process of the renewal, purification and sanctification of the Church so that, also in our own day, the Church may fulfill its vocation of witnessing to the world and contributing to its sanctification[61].

In these pages of reflection we have attempted to actualize this biblical text by listening to its message within a concrete contemporary situation and allowing its meaning and message to illumine and challenge this situation[62]. Paul's message here compels us to take a critical look at the culture of radical individualism and its values, examine the ways we are co-opted by it, assess its negative impact on how we go about living our Christian faith and, of course, to do something about it.

The process of actualizing a biblical text is advanced when what is written in dissertations and text books is transferred to and applied at the pastoral level[63]. There especially, a critical posture toward the culture of radical individualism must be adopted in order to promote the continual renewal, purification and sanctification of the whole church[64]. We will certainly feel that our efforts in producing this study will have been

---

[58] Cf. «Gaudium et Spes», 17.
[59] Cf. «Lumen Gentium», 32.
[60] «Lumen Gentium», 35.
[61] Cf. «Lumen Gentium», 31.
[62] Cf. J. FITZMYER, *The Biblical Commission's Document*, 174.
[63] J. FITZMYER, *The Biblical Commission's Document*, 183-186.
[64] Cf. «Lumen Gentium», 8; 9; 39.

rewarded should any insight from the present work contribute to that process.

If there is validity in the assertion that we discover the real authority and relevance of a biblical text when it becomes for our time «as great a disturber of our own ethos and ethics as it was originally»[65] then in 1Cor 5 we have discovered a text that has great authority and relevance for our own day. In this modest study, we have undertaken to give a coherent interpretation of 1Cor 5 and to highlight its authority and relevance for today. If in this task we have come up short, then it is our hope that others will supply for what is lacking and continue the study of a text which heretofore has not enjoyed the scholarly attention that it seems to warrant.

---

[65] Cf. L.E. KECK, «Ethos», 45.

ABBREVIATIONS

1QS	*The Community Rule* (Manual of Discipline)
4QFlor	*Eschatological Midrashim*, Qumran Cave 4
11QT	*The Temple Scroll*
AB	Anchor Bible
Ad QFr	*Epistulae Ad Quintum Fratrem*
AnBib	Analecta Biblica
ANRW	Aufstieg und Niedergang der römischen Welt
Ant.	*Antiquitates Judaicae*
au. ital.	author's italics
AustrBR	*Australian Biblical Review*
BETL	Bibliotheca Ephemeridum Theologicarum Lovaniensium
BHTh	Beiträge zur historischen Theologie
Bib	*Biblica*
BijT	*Bijdragen Tidjschrift voor Filosofie en Theologie*
BJ	Bible de Jerusalem
BJ	*De Bello Judaico*
BJRL	*Bulletin of the John Rylands Library*
Blass – Debrunner	*A Greek Grammar of the New Testament and Other Early Christian Literature*, Trans and rev. of the 9-10th German ed. by R. W. Funk. Chicago 1961.
BS	*Bibliotheca Sacra*
BTB	*Biblical Theology Bulletin*
BTrans	*The Bible Translator*
BZ	*Biblische Zeitschrift*
BZAW	Beihefte zur Zeitschrift für die alttestamentliche Wissenschaft
BZNW	Beihefte zur Zeitschrift für die neutestamentliche Wissenschaft
c./cc.	chapter/chapters
CBQ	*Catholic Biblical Quarterly*
CD	*The Damascus Document*
cf.	compare
CIC	Codex Iuris Canonici
CJT	*Canadian Journal of Theology*
ConB	Coniectanea Biblica
Contra Ap.	*Contra Apionem*

Conzelmann	*Der erste Brief an die Korinther*, Göttingen 1969[1]; english trans. *1 Corinthians*, Hermeneia, Philadelphia 1975.
CRINT	Compendium Rerum Iudaicarum ad Novum Testamentum.
De Inv	*De Inventione*
De Vita	*De Vita Contemplativa*
DoctrLife	*Doctrine and Life*
e.g.	for example
ed.	editor/s
EKK	Evangelisch Katholischer Kommentar zum neuen Testament
esp.	especially
etc.	and so on
ETL	*Ephemerides Theologicae Lovanienses*
ETR	*Etudes Theologiques et Religieuses*
EvQ	*Evangelical Quarterly*
Exp	*The Expositor*
ExpTim	*The Expository Times*
ff.	following
FRLANT	Forschungen zur Religion und Literatur des Alten und Neuen Testaments
Fs.	Festschrift
FThSt	Freiburger theologische Studien
GNS	Good News Studies
Greg	*Gregorianum*
HorBT	*Horizons in Biblical Theology*
HTR	*Harvard Theological Review*
i.e.	that is
ICC	International Critical Commentary
ID.	*Idem* (the same)
Interp	*Interpretation*
JAAR	*Journal of the American Academy of Religion*
JAC	Jahrbuch für Antike und Christentum
JB	Jerusalem Bible
JBL	*Journal of Biblical Literature*
JLT	*Journal of Literature and Theology*
JPSTC	The Jewish Publication Society Torah Commentary
JRel	*Journal of Religion*
JSNT	*Journal for the Study of the New Testament*
JSNTSS	*Journal for the Study of the New Testament Supplement Series*
JTS	*Journal of Theological Studies*
Jub	*The Book of Jubilees*
LCL	Loeb Classical Library
LeDiv	Lectio Divina
LingBib	*Linguistica Biblica*
M.Sanh	Mishnah Sanhedrin
n.	note, footnote
NCB	New Century Bible Commentary
NEB	New English Bible
Neot	*Neotestamentica*

NICNT	New International Commentary NT
NICOT	New International Commentary OT
NJB	New Jerusalem Bible
NRSV	New Revised Standard Version
NRT	*Nouvelle Revue Théologique*
NT	*Novum Testamentum*
NTM	New Testament Message
NTS	*New Testament Studies*
Op.	*De Opificio Mundi*
OTL	Old Testament Library
Ps Sol	*Psalms of Solomon*
Ps. Phoc.	*Pseudo-Phocylides*
Q. Exod	*Quaestiones et solutiones in Exodum*
Q. Gen	*Quaestiones et solutiones in Genesis*
QJS	*The Quarterly Journal of Speech*
RAC	*Reallexikon für Antike und Christentum*
RB	*Revue Biblique*
REB	Revised English Bible
RevExp	*Review and Expositor*
RevistB	*Revista Biblica*
RGG	Die Religion in Geschichte und Gegenwart
Rhet. ad Her.	*Rhetorica ad Herrenium*
RSV	Revised Standard Version
Salm	*Salmanticensis*
SBLDS	Society of Biblical Literature Dissertation Series
SBLSBS	Society of Biblical Literature Sources for Biblical Study
SBLSP	Society of Biblical Literature Seminar Papers
SBT	Studies in Biblical Theology
sect.	section
Sib Or	*Sibylline Oracles*
SJT	*Scottish Journal of Theology*
SKK	Stuttgarter Kleiner Kommentar
SNT	Supplements to Novum Testamentum
SNTSMS	Society for New Testament Studies Monograph Series
ST	Studia Theologica
STh	*Summa Theologica*
StMor	Studia Moralia
T Jud	*The Testament of Judah*
T Levi	*The Testament of Levi*
T Reub	*The Testament of Reuben*
TDNT	Theological Dictionary of the NT
ThLZ	*Theologische Literaturzeitung*
TOB	Traduction Oecumenique de Bible
tr.	Translator
trans.	Translation
TS	*Theological Studies*
TynB	*The Tyndale Bulletin*
TZTh	*Tübinger Zeitschrift für Theologie*

v./vv.	*verse/s*
VigChr	*Vigiliae Christianae*
Vita	*De vita et moribus philosophorum*
viz.	namely
VTS	Supplements to Vetus Testamentum
WMANT	Wissenschaftliche Monographien zum Alten und Neuen Testament
WUNT	Wissenschaftliche Untersuchungen zum Neuen Testament
ZNW	*Zeitschrift für die neutestamentliche Wissenschaft*
ZTK	*Zeitschrift für Theologie und Kirche*
ZWB	Züricher Werkkommentare zur Bibel

BIBLIOGRAPHY

ADINOLFI, M., «Le Metafore greco-romane della testa e del corpo», in *Studiorum Paulinorum Congressus Internationalis Catholicus 1961. Simul Secundus Congressus Internationalis Catholicus de Re Biblica completo undevicesimo saeculo post S. Paul in Urbem adventum*, AnBib 17-18, Romae 1963, 33-42.

AHERN, B., «The Christian's Union with the Body of Christ in Cor, Gal, and Rom», *CBQ* 23 (1961) 199-209.

ALETTI, J.-N., «Ethicisation de L'esprit saint. Foi et ethos dans les épîtres pauliniennes», in *Ethique, religion et foi*, ed. J. Doré, Paris 1985.

———, «L'authorité apostolique de Paul. Théorie et pratique», in *L'Apôtre Paul. Personalité, style et conception du ministère*, ed. A. Vanhoye, BETL 73, Leuven 1986, 229-246.

———, «La présence d'un modèle rhétorique en Romains: son rôle et son importance», *Bib* 71 (1990) 1-24.

———, «Problèmes de composition et de structure dans la bible. Positions et propositions», in *Naissance de la méthode critique*, Colloque du centenaire de l'École biblique et archéologique française de Jérusalem, Paris 1992, 213-30.

———, «La dispositio rhétorique dans les épîtres pauliniennes: Propositions de méthode», *NTS* 38 (1992) 385-401.

ALEXANDER, L., «Paul and the Hellenistic Schools. The Evidence of Galen», in *Paul in His Hellenistic Context*, ed. T. Engberg-Pedersen, Edinburgh 1994, 60-83.

ALLO, B., *Première épître aux Corinthiens*, Paris 1935.

ALONSO SCHÖKEL, L., «Of Methods and Models», *VTS* 36 (1985) 3-13.

ARISTOTLE, *Ars Rhetorica*, tr. J.H. Freese, LCL, Cambridge 1982.

VON ARNIM, H., *Stoicorum Veterum Fragmenta*, I-VI, Stuttgart 1905.

ASTING, R., *Die Heiligkeit im Urchristentum*, FRLANT 29, Göttingen 1930.

[AUCTOR], *Rhetorica Ad Herennium*, tr. H. Caplan, LCL, Cambridge 1981.

AUNE, D., *The New Testament in Its Literary Environment*, Philadelphia 1987.

———, *Greco-Roman Literature and the New Testament*, Atlanta 1988.

BAILEY, K., «The Structure of 1 Corinthians and Paul's Theological Method With Special Reference to 4,17», *NT* 25 (1983) 152-181.

BAIRD, W., «"One Against the Other" - Intra Church Conflicts in 1 Corinthians», in *The Conversation Continues. Studies in Paul and John*, Fs. J. Louis Martyn, Nashville 1990, 116-36.

BALCH, D., «Backgrounds of I Cor vii: Sayings of the Lord in Q; Moses as an Ascetic *ΘΕΙΟΣ ΑΝΗΡ* in II Cor iii», *NTS* 18 (1971) 351-64.

——, «1 Cor 7:32-35 and Stoic Debates About Marriage, Anxiety and Distraction», *JBL* 102 (1983) 429-39.

BANKS, R., *Paul's Idea of Community. The Early House Churches in Their Historical Setting*, Peabody 1994.

BARBAGLIO, G., *La prima lettera ai Corinzi. Introduzione, versione e commento*, Bologna 1995.

BARCLAY, J., «Mirror Reading a Polemical Letter», *JSNT* 31 (1987) 73-93.

——, «Thessalonica and Corinth: Social Contrasts in Pauline Christianity», *JSNT* 47 (1992) 49-74.

BARRETT, C.K., *A Commentary on 1 Corinthians*, London 1960.

——, «Cephas in Corinth», in *Abraham unser Vater*, Fs. O. Michel, Leiden 1963, 1-12.

——, «Christianity at Corinth», *BJRL* 46 (1964) 269-297.

BARTH, K., *Der Römerbrief*, Zürich 1940; english trans. *The Epistle to the Romans*, London 1963[6].

BARTH, M., *Ephesians. Translation and Commentary on Chapters 4-6*, AB 34A, Garden City 1974.

BARTHES, R., «L'ancienne rhétorique: aide-memoire», *Communications* 16 (1970) 172-229.

BASSLER, J., «*Skeuos* in 1 Thessalonians 4.4», in *The Social World of the First Christians*, Fs. W. Meeks, Minneapolis 1995, 53-66.

BATEY, R., «The *Mia Sarx* Union of Christ and the Church», *NTS* 13 (1967) 270-81.

BAUER, W., *A Greek-English Lexicon of the New Testament*, Trans. W. F. Arndt – F. W. Gingrich, revised and augmented by F. W. Gingrich – F. W. Danker, Chicago 1979[2].

BAUMERT, N., *Frau und Mann bei Paulus: Überwinding eines Missverständnisses*, Würzburg 1993.

BAUR, F.C., «Die Christuspartei in der korinthischen Gemeinder, der gegensatz des paulinischen und petrinischen Christentums in der ältesten Kirche, der Apostel Petrus in Rom», *TZTh* 4 (1831) 61-206.

——, *Paulus, der Apostel Jesu Christi. Sein Leben und Wirken, seine Briefe und seine Lehre*, I-II, Stuttgart 1845.

BEARDSLEE, W., *First Corinthians. A Commentary for Today*, St. Louis 1994.

BEASLEY-MURRAY, G.R., *Baptism in the New Testament*, London 1962.

BEATRICE, P.F., «Apollos of Alexandria», *ANRW* 26.2, 1232-75.

BECKER, J., *Paulus. Der Apostel den Völker*, Tübingen 1989; english trans. *Paul Apostle to the Gentiles*, Westminster 1993.

BEKER, J.C., *Paul the Apostle. The Triumph of God in Life and Thought*, Edinburgh 1980.

————, *Paul's Apocalyptic Gospel. The Coming Triumph of God*, Philadelphia 1982.

————, *Der Sieg Gottes. Untersuchung zur Struktur des paulinischen Denkens*, Stuttgart 1988; english trans. *The Triumph of God. The Essence of Paul's Thought*, Minneapolis 1990.

BELLAH, R. – AL, S., *Habits of the Heart. Individualism and Commitment in American Life*, San Francisco 1986.

BERGER, K., «Die impliziten Gegner. Zur Methode des Erschließens von "Gegnern" in neutestamentlichen Texten», in *Kirche*, Fs. G. Bornkamm, Tübingen 1980, 373-400.

BERNARD, J.H., «The Connexion Between the Fifth and Sixth Chapters of 1 Corinthians», *Exp* 7 (1907) 433-43.

BEST, E., *One Body in Christ. A Study in the Relationship of the Church to Christ in the Epistles of the Apostle Paul*, London 1965.

————, «The Power and the Wisdom of God», in *Paolo a una chiesa divisa (1 Co 1-4)*, ed. L. De Lorenzi, SMBen 5, Roma 1980, 9-39.

BETZ, H. D., *A Commentary on Paul's Letters to the Churches in Galatia*, Philadelphia 1979.

————, «The Problem of Rhetoric and Theology According to the Apostle Paul», in *L'Apôtre Paul. Personnalité, Style et Conception du Ministère*, ed. A. Vanhoye, BETL 73, Leuven 1986, 16-48.

BITZER, L., «The Rhetorical Situation», *Philosophy and Rhetoric* 1 (1968) 1-14.

BLACK, C.C. «Rhetorical Criticism and Biblical Interpretation», *ExpTim* 100 (1988-89) 252-258.

————, «Rhetorical Questions: The New Testament, Classical Rhetoric and Current Interpretation», *Dialog* 29 (1990) 62-70.

BLACK, D.A., «The Discourse Structure of Philippians: A Study in Text Linguistics», *NT* 37 (1995) 16-49.

BLACK, E., *Rhetorical Criticism: A Study in Method*, Madison 1979.

BONSIRVEN, J., *L'Évangile de Paul*, Aubier 1948.

————, *Textes Rabbinique des deux premiers siècles chrétiens*, Roma 1955.

DE BOER, M., *The Defeat of Death. Apocalyptic Eschatology in 1 Corinthians and Romans 5*, JSNTSS 22, Sheffield 1988.

————, «The Composition of 1 Corinthians», *NTS* 40 (1994) 229-45.

DE BOOR, W., *Der erste Brief des Paulus an die Korinther*, Wuppertal 1968.

BORNKAMM, G., *Paulus*, Stuttgart 1969; english trans. *Paul*, London 1975.

BRANDT, W.J., *The Rhetoric of Argumentation*, New York 1984.

BRAUDE, W.G., *Jewish Proselyting in the First Five Centuries of the Common Era. The Age of Tannaim and Amoraim*, Brown University Studies 6, Providence 1940.

BRECK, J., «Biblical Chiasmus. Exploring Structure for Meaning», *BTB* 17 (1987) 70-74.

BROWN, P., *The Body and Society. Men, Women and Sexual Renunciation in Early Christianity*, New York 1988.

BROWN, R., «The New Testament Background for the Emerging Doctrine of "Local Church"», in *Biblical Exegesis and Church Doctrine*, New York 1985, 114-34.

BRUCE, F.F., *1 and 2 Corinthians*, NCB, London 1971.

BRUNOT, A., *Le génie littéraire de St. Paul*, Paris 1955.

BULTMANN, R., «*penthos, pentheô*», *TDNT* VI, 40-3.

———, *Der Stil der paulinischen Predigt und die kynisch-stoische Diatribe*, FRLANT 13, Göttingen 1910.

———, «Das Problem der Ethik bei Paulus», *ZNW* 23 (1924) 123-40.

———, *Theologie des Neuen Testaments*, Tübingen 1948-1953; english trans. *Theology of the New Testament*, I-II, New York 1951.

BÜNKER, M., *Briefformula und Rhetorische Disposition im 1 Korintherbrief*, Göttingen 1977.

BURGESS, T.C. «Epideictic Literature», *Studies in Classical Philosophy* 3 (1902) 89-201.

BÜSCHEL, F., «*eilikrinès, eilikrineia*», *TDNT* II, 397-8.

BYRNE, B., *Paul and Christian Women*, Collegeville 1988.

CAMBIER, J., «La chair et l'esprit en 1 Cor V.5», *NTS* 15 (1968) 221-32.

CAPPELLE, W. – MARROU, H.I., «Diatribe», *RAC*, III, 990-1009.

CARRINGTON, P., *The Primitive Christian Catechism*, Cambridge 1942.

———, *The Early Christian Church*, in *The First Christian Century*, I, Cambridge 1957.

CERFAUX, L., *L'Eglise des Corinthiens*, Paris 1946.

———, *Le Christ dans la théologie de saint Paul*, Paris 1951; english trans. *Christ in the Theology of Saint Paul*, New York 1959.

———, *La Théologie de l'Église suivant saint Paul*, Paris 1948; english trans. *The Church in the Theology of Saint Paul*, New York 1959.

———, *Le chrétien dans la théologie paulinienne*, Paris 1962; english trans. *The Christian in the Theology of Saint Paul*, New York 1967.

CHARLES, R.H., *The Book of Jubilees or Little Genesis*, Jerusalem 1979.

CHARLESWORTH, J.H., *The Old Testament Pseudepigrapha*, I-II, New York 1983, 1985.

CHASE, J.R., «The Classical Conception of Epideictic», *QJS* 47 (1961) 293-300.

CHEVALLIER, M.A., 4,9 «La Construction de la communauté sur le fondement du Christ», in *Paolo e una chiesa divisa, (1 Cor 1-4)*, ed. L. De Lorenzi, SMBen 5, Roma 1980, 109-29.

CHOW, J.K., *Patronage and Power. A Study of Social Networks in Corinth*, JSNTSS 75, Sheffield 1992.

CICERO, *De Finibus Bonorum et Malorum*, tr. H. Rackham, LCL, Cambridge 1983.

——, *De Inventione*, tr. H.M. Hubbell, LCL, Cambridge 1949.

——, *De Natura Deorum*, tr. H. Rackham, LCL, Cambridge 1972.

——, *De Oratore*, tr. E. W. Sutton, LCL, Cambridge 1942.

——, *De Partitione Oratoria*, tr. H. Rackham, LCL, Cambridge 1976.

——, *Epistulae ad Quintum Fratrem*, tr. W.G. Williams, LCL, Cambridge 1989.

——, *Paradoxa Stoicorum*, tr. H. Rackham, LCL, Cambridge 1976.

——, *Pro Cluentio*, tr. H.G. Hodge, LCL, Cambridge 1927.

——, *Pro Murena*, tr. L. E. Lord, LCL, Cambridge 1937.

CLARKE, A., *Secular and Christian Leadership in Corinth. A Social-historical and Exegetical Study of 1 Corinthians 1-6*, Leiden 1993.

CLASSEN, C.J., «St. Paul's Epistles and Ancient Greek and Roman Rhetoric», in *Rhetoric and the New Testament*. Essays from the 1992 Heidelberg Conference, ed. S. E. Porter – T. H. Olbrichts, JSNTSS 90, Sheffield 1993, 265-291.

COLISH, M., The Stoic Tradition From Antiquity to the Early Middle Ages, I. Stoicism in Classical Latin Literature, Leiden 1990[2].

COLLINS, A.Y., «The Function of "Excommunication" in Paul», *HTR* 73 (1980) 251-63.

COLLINS, J.J., «Chiasmus, The "ABA" Pattern and the Text of Paul», in *Studiorum Paulinorum Congressus Internationalis Catholicus 1961. Simul Secundus Congressus Internationalis Catholicus de Re Biblica completo undevicesimo saeculo post S. Paul in Urbem adventum*, AnBib 17-18, Roma 1963, 575-84.

CONGAR, Y., «Holy Spirit and the Spirit of Freedom», in *Theologians Today: Yves Congar, O.P.*, ed. M. Redfern, London 1972, 9-46.

CONZELMANN, H., *Grundriss der Theologie des Neuen Testaments*, München 1958; english trans. *An Outline of the Theology of the New Testament*, New York 1969.

COPPENS, J., «Les arguments scriptuaires et leur portée dans les lettres pauliniennes», in *Studiorum Paulinorum Congressus Internationalis Catholicus 1961. Simul Secundus Congressus Internationalis Catholicus de Re Biblica completo undevicesimo saeculo post S. Paul in Urbem adventum*, AnBib 17-18, Roma 1963, 243-53.

CORIDEN, J. – GREEN, T. – HEINTSCHEL, D., ed., *The Code of Canon Law. A Text and Commentary*, New York 1985.

COUNTRYMAN, L.W., *Dirt, Greed and Sex. Sexual Ethics in the New Testament and Their Implications for Today*, Philadelphia 1988.

COUSAR, C. B., «The Theological Task of 1 Corinthians», in *Pauline Theology, II. 1 and 2 Corinthians*, ed. D. M. Hay, Minneapolis 1993, 90-102.

CRANFIELD, C.E.B., *A Critical and Exegetical Commentary on the Epistle to the Romans*, ICC, I, Edinburgh 1975.

CROSS, F.M., *The Ancient Library of Qumran and Modern Biblical Studies*, Grand Rapids 1980.

CRUZ, H., *Christological Motives and Motivated Actions in Pauline Paraenesis*, Frankfurt am Main 1990.

CULLMANN, O., *Die Tauflehre des Neuen Testaments*, Zürich 1948; english trans. *Baptism in the New Testament*, London 1950.

——, *Petrus. Jünger-Apostel-Märtyren*, Zürich 1960².

CUVILLIER, E., «Le baptême chrétien dans le Nouveau Testament», *ETR* 70 (1995) 161-177.

DAHL, N.A., «Paul and the Church at Corinth According to 1 Corinthians 1:10-4:21», in *Christian History and Interpretation*, ed. W.R. Farmer – C.F.D. Moule – R.R. Niebuhr, Cambridge 1967, 313-35.

——, *Studies in Paul. Theology for the Early Christian Mission*, Minneapolis 1977.

DAUBE, D., «Pauline Contributions to a Pluralistic Culture: Re-creation and Beyond», *Jesus and Man's Hope*, (Festival on the Gospels), ed., D.G. Miller – D.Y. Hadidian, Pittsburgh 1971, II, 223-45.

——, *Ancient Jewish Law*, (Three Inaugural Lectures), Leiden 1981.

DAVIES, W.D., *The Setting of the Sermon on the Mount*, Cambridge 1966.

——, *Paul and Rabbinic Judaism*, London 1970³.

DAVIS, J.A., «The Interaction Between Individual Ethical Conscience and Community Ethical Consciousness in 1 Cor», *HorBT* 10 (1988) 1-18.

VON DEHSEN, C., *Sexual Relationships and the Church at Corinth: An Exegetical Study of 1 Cor 5-7*, Ann Arbor 1987.

DEIDUN, T.J., *New Covenant Morality in Paul*, AnBib 89, Rome 1981.

DEISSMANN, A., *Light from the Ancient East*, Grand Rapids 1965.

DEMING, W., *Paul on marriage and celibacy. The Hellenistic background of 1 Corinthians 7*, SNTSMS 83, Cambridge 1995.

——, «The Unity of 1 Corinthians 5-6», *JBL* 115 (1996) 289-312.

DERRETT, J.D., «"Handing Over to Satan". An Explanation of 1 Cor 5,1-7», *Studies in the New Testament. IV. Midrash, the Composition of Gospels and Discipline*, Leiden 1986, 167-86.

——, «Judgement and 1 Corinthians 6», *NTS* 37 (1991) 22-36.

DESCAMPS, A., «Le baptême, fondement de l'unité chrétienne», in *Battesimo e Giustizia in Rom 6 e 8*, ed. L. De Lorenzi, SMBen 2, Roma 1974, 203-235.

DEWAR, L., *An Outline of New Testament Ethics*, London 1949.

DI MARCO, A., «Der Chiasmus in der Bibel», Teil 1, *LingBib* 44 (1975) 21-97.

DI MARCO, A., «Der Chiasmus in der Bibel», Teil 4, *LingBib* 36 (1979) 3-70.

DINKLER, E, «Zum Problem der Ethik bei Paulus. 1 Kor 6,1-11», *ZTK* 49 (1952) 167-200.

DIO CHRYSOSTOM, *Discourses*, tr. J. W. Cohoon, LCL, Cambridge 1932.

DIOGENES LAERTIUS, *Lives of Eminent Philosophers*, I-II, tr. R.D. Hicks, LCL, Cambridge 1979.

DODD, B.J., «Paul's Paradigmatic "I" and 1 Corinthians 6.12», *JSNT* 59 (1995) 39-58.

DODD, C.H., *Gospel and Law. The Relation of Faith and Ethics in Early Christianity*, Cambridge 1951.

DOUGHTY, D., «The Presence and Future of Salvation at Corinth», *ZNW* 66 (1975) 61-90.

DULLES, A., *A Church to Believe In. Discipleship and the Dynamics of Freedom*, New York 1982.

——, *The Reshaping of Catholicism. Current Challenges in the Theology of the Church*, New York 1988.

DUNGAN, D.L., *The Sayings of Jesus in the Churches of Paul*, Philadelphia 1971.

DUNN, J.D.G., *Unity and Diversity in the New Testament. An Inquiry into the Character of Earliest Christianity*, Philadelphia 1977.

——, *The Partings of the Ways. Between Christianity and Judaism and their Significance for the Character of Christianity*, London 1991.

ECKERT, J., «Indicativ und Imperativ bei Paulus», in *Ethik im Neuen Testament*, ed. K. Kertelge, Freiburg 1984, 168-189.

ELLIS, E.E., «Christ Crucified», in *Reconciliation and Hope*, Fs. L. Morris, Grand Rapids 1974, 69-74.

——, *Prophecy and Hermeneutic in Early Christianity*, Tübingen 1978.

——, «Traditions in 1 Corinthians», *NTS* 32 (1986) 481-502.

——, «Biblical Interpretation in the New Testament», in *Mikra. Text, Translation, Reading and Interpretation of the Hebrew Bible in Ancient Judaism and Early Christianity*, CRINT, ed. M. J. Mulder, Philadelphia 1988, 691-725.

——, «*Sôma* in First Corinthians», *Interp* 44 (1990) 132-144.

——, *Paul's Use of the Old Testament*, Grand Rapids 1991.

ENGBERG-PEDERSEN, T., «Stoicism in Philippians», in *Paul in His Hellenistic Context. Studies of the New Testament and Its World*, ed. T. Engberg-Pederson, Edinburgh 1994, 256-90.

ENGELS, D., *Roman Corinth. An Alternative Model for the Classical City*, Chicago 1990.

ENSLIN, M., *The Ethics of Paul*, Nashville 1962.

EPICTETUS, *The Discourses as Reported by Arrian. The Manual and Fragments*, tr. W.A. Oldfather, LCL, Cambridge 1979.

EPSTEIN, L.M., *Sex Laws and Customs in Judaism*, New York 1967.

ETCHEVARRIA, R. T., «A proposito del incestuoso (1 Cor 5-6)», *Salm* 38 (1991) 129-153.

FAHEY, M., «Church», in *Systematic Theology. Roman Catholic Perspectives*, II, ed. F. Schüssler Fiorenza – J. P. Galvin, Minneapolis, 3-74.

FANNING, B.M., *Verbal Aspect in New Testament Greek*, Oxford 1990.

FASCHER, E., *Der Erste Brief des Paulus an die Korinther*, Teil 1, Berlin 1975.

FEE, G., *1 Corinthians*, NICNT, Grand Rapids 1987.

———, «Toward a Theology of 1 Corinthians», ed. D. J. Lull, SBLSP 28, Atlanta 1989, 265-81.

———, «"Another Gospel Which You Did Not Embrace": 2 Corinthians 11.4 and the Theology of 1 and 2 Corinthians», in *Gospel in Paul. Studies on Corinthians, Galatians and Romans for R. Longenecker*, ed. L. A. Jervis – P. Richardson, JSNTSS 108, Sheffield 1994, 111-33.

FERGUSON, E., *Backgrounds of Early Christianity*, Grand Rapids 1987.

FIORE, B., *The Function of Personal Example in the Socratic and Pastoral Epistles*, An Bib 105, Rome 1986.

FITZMYER, J.A., *The Biblical Commission's Document «The Interpretation of the Bible in the Church». Text and Commentary*, SubBi 18, Roma 1995.

FLANNERY, A. ed., *Vatican Council II. The Conciliar and Post Conciliar Documents*, Northport 1975.

FORKMANN, G., *The Limits of the Religious Community. Expulsion from the Religious Community within the Qumran Sect, within Rabbinic Judaism and within Primitive Christianity*, ConB 5, Sweden 1972.

FUCHS, J., *Personal Responsibility. Christian Morality*, Washington, D.C. 1983.

FUNK, R., «The Apostolic Parousia: Form and Significance», in *Christian History and Interpretation*, Fs. J. Knox, Cambridge 1967, 249-68.

FURNISH, V.P., *Theology and Ethics in Paul*, Nashville 1968.

———, *II Corinthians*, AB 32A, Garden City 1984.

———, *The Moral Teaching of Paul: Selected Issues*, Nashville 1985.

———, «Belonging to Christ: A Paradigm for Ethics in First Corinthians», *Interp* 44 (1990) 145-157.

GAIUS., *Gaii Institutionum Iuris Civilis Commentarii Quatuor*, translation and commentary E. Poste, Oxford 1875.

GÄRTNER, B., *The Temple and the Community in Qumran and the New Testament*, SNTSMS 1, Cambridge 1965.

GEORGI, D., *Die Gegner des Paulus im 2 Korintherbrief. Studien zur religiösen Propaganda in des Spätantike*, Neukirchen-Vluyn 1964; english trans. *The Opponents of Paul in Second Corinthians*, Philadelphia 1968.

GERHARDSEN, B., «*Eleutheria* ("freedom") in the Bible», in *Scripture: Meaning and Method*, Fs. A.T. Hanson, Pickering 1987, 3-23

GIRARD, M., *Les Psaumes. Analyse Structurelle et Interpretation 1-50*, Recherche Nouvelle Series 2, Paris 1984.

GODET, F.L., *Commentary on First Corinthians*, Grand Rapids 1977.

GOULDER, M.D. «*Sophia* in 1 Corinthians», *NTS* 37 (1991) 516-34.

GRANT, F.C., *Roman Hellenism and the New Testament*, New York 1962.

GRANT, R.M., «Hellenistic Elements in 1 Corinthians», in *Early Christian Origins*, Fs. H.R. Willoughby, Chicago 1961, 60-65.

GRECH, P., «Christological Motives in Paul», in *Paul de Tarse*, ed. L. DeLorenzi, SMBen 8, Rome 1979, 541-58.

GROSHEIDE, F.W., *The First Epistle to the Corinthians*, NICNT, Grand Rapids 1953,

GRUNDMANN, W., «*harmartanô*», *TDNT* I, 308-313.

GUNDRY, R.H., *Sôma in Biblical Theology with Emphasis on Pauline Anthropology*, SNTSMS 29, Cambridge 1976.

GUNDRY VOLF, J., *Paul and Perseverance: Staying in and Falling Away*, Tübingen 1990.

——, «Male and Female in Creation and New Creation Interpretations of Gal 3.28c in 1 Cor 7», in *To Tell the Mystery*. Essays on NT Eschatology, Fs. R.H. Gundry, JSNTSS 100, Sheffield 1994, 95-121.

HALTER, H., *Taufe und Ethos. Paulinische Kriterien für das Proprium christlicher Moral*, FThSt 106, Freiburg 1977.

HAMMERTON-KELLY, R., *Sacred Violence. Paul's Hermeneutic of the Cross*, Minneapolis 1992.

HANSE, H., «*echô ktl*», *TDNT* II, 816-32.

VON HARNACK, A., «Das Alte Testament im den paulinischen Briefen und in den paulinischen Gemeinde», *Sitzungsberichte Preußischen Akademie Wissenschaften* Berlin (1928) 129-41 = *Kleine Schriften zur alten Kirche*, ed. W. Peek, II, Leipzig 1980, 823-41.

HARRIS, G., «The Beginnings of Church Discipline: 1 Corinthians 5», *NTS* 37 (1991) 1-21.

HAUCK, F. – SCHULZ, S., «*pornè, pornos porneia ktl*», *TDNT* IV, 579-595.

HAUERWAUS, S., *A Community of Character. Toward a Constructive Christian Social Ethic*, Notre Dame 1981.

HAVENER, I., «A Curse for Salvation – 1 Corinthians 5:1-5», in *Sin, Salvation and the Spirit*, ed. D. Durken, Collegeville 1979, 334-344.

HAYS, R., *Echoes of Scripture in the Letters of Paul*, New Haven 1989.

——, «Ecclesiology and Ethics in 1 Corinthians», *Ex Auditu* 10 (1994) 31-44.

HENGEL, M., *Judentum und Hellenismus. Studien zur ihrer Begegnung unter besonderer Berücksichtigung Palästinas bis zur Mitte des 2 Jh. vor Chr.*, Tübingen 1969; english trans. *Judaism and Hellenism. Studies in their Encounter in Palestine during the Early Hellenistic Period*, I-II, Philadelphia 1974.

HÉRING, J., *La première épitre de saint Paul aux Corinthiens*, Neuchâtel 1949; english trans. *The First Epistle of Saint Paul to the Corinthians*, London 1967[2].

HERSHBELL, J., «The Stoicism of Epictetus», *ANRW* II.36.3, 2148-2163.

HIEBERT, A., «The Foundations of Paul's Ethics», in *Essays in Morality and Ethics*, ed. J. Gaffney, New York 1980, 50-62.

HIMES, M. – HIMES, K.,*Fullness of Faith. The Public Significance of Theology*, New York 1993.

HOCK, R., *The Social Context of Paul's Ministry*, Philadelphia 1980.

HODGE, C., *An Exposition of the First Epistle to the Corinthians*, Grand Rapids 1969.

HOLLANDER, H.W. – DE JONGE, M., *The Testaments of the Twelve Patriarchs: A Commentary*, Leiden 1985.

HOLTZ, T., «Zur Frage der inhaltischen Weisungen bei Paulus», *ThLZ* 106 (1981) 385-400.

HORBURY, W., «Extirpation and Excommunication», *VT* 35 (1985) 13-37.

HORSLEY, R.A., «How Can Some of You Say that there is no Resurrection of the Dead? Spiritual Elitism in Corinth», *NT* 20 (1978) 203-231.

——, «Spiritual Marriage with *Sophia*», *VigChr* 33 (1979) 30-54.

——, «Gnosis in Corinth. 1 Cor 8,1-6», *NTS* 27 (1980) 32-51.

VAN DER HORST, P.W., *The Sentences of Pseudo-Phocylides*, Leiden 1978.

HOULDEN, J.L., *Ethics and the New Testament*, Harmondsworth 1973.

HURD, J.C., *The Origin of 1 Corinthians*, London 1965.

——, «Pauline Chronology and Pauline Theology», in *Christian History and Interpretation*, Fs. J. Knox, New York 1967, 225-248.

——, «The Sequence of Paul's Letters», *CJT* 14 (1968) 189-200.

——, «Good News and the Integrity of 1 Corinthians», in *Gospel in Paul*, Fs. R. Longenecker, ed. L. A. Jervis – P. Richardson, JSNTSS 108, Sheffield 1994, 38-62.

HYLDAHL, N., «The Corinthian "Parties" and the Corinthian Crisis», *StTh* 45 (1991) 19-32.

IGNATIUS, «Ad Magnesios», in *The Apostolic Fathers*, I, tr. K. Lake, LCL, Cambridge 1959.

INWOOD, B., *Ethics and Human Action in Early Stoicism*, Oxford 1985.

JAEGER, W., *Early Christianity and Greek Paideia*, Oxford 1961.

JAGU, A., «La morale d'Epictète et le christianisme», *ANRW* II.36.3, 2164-2199.

JEWETT, R., *Paul's Anthropological Terms. A Study of Their Use in Conflict Settings*, Leiden 1971.

——, *A Chronology of Paul's Life*, Philadelphia 1979.

JOHN CHRYSOSTOM., *In Epistulas I et II ad Corinthios Homiliae*, tr. Rev. T. Chambers, The Nicene and Post-Nicene Fathers XII, Grand Rapids 1975.

JOHN PAUL II, Encyclical Letter *Evangelium Vitae*, March 25, 1995, Città del Vaticano 1995.

——, Encyclical Letter *Veritatis Splendor*, Aug. 6, 1993. Città del Vaticano 1993.

JOHNSON, A.R., *The One and the Many in the Israelite Conception of God*, Cardiff 1942.

JONAS, H., *The Gnostic Religion. The Message of the Alien God and the Beginnings of Christianity*, Boston, 1955.

JOSEPHUS, *Works*, I-IX, tr. H. St. J. Thackeray – R. Marcus – L. H. Feldman, LCL, Cambridge 1956-65.

JOY, N.G., «Is the Body Really to Be Destroyed?», *BTrans* 39 (1988) 428-36.

JUDGE, E.A., «St. Paul and Classical Society», *JAC* 15 (1972) 19-36.

KÄSEMANN, E., *Essays in New Testament Themes*, SBT 41, London 1964.

——, «The Righteousness of God in Paul», in *New Testament Questions of Today*, Philadelphia 1969, 168-82.

——, «Sentences of the Holy Law in the New Testament», in *New Testament Questions of Today*, Philadelphia 1969, 66-81.

——, *An die Römer*, Tübingen 1974³; english trans. *Commentary on Romans*, Grand Rapids 1980.

——, «The Theological Problem Presented by the Motif of the Body of Christ», in *Perspectives on Paul*, Philadelphia 1982, 102-21.

KECK, L., «Ethos and Ethics in the New Testament», in *Essays in Morality and Ethics*, ed. J. Gaffney, New York 1980, 29-49.

——, «Rethinking "New Testament Ethics"», *JBL* 115 (1996) 1-16.

KEMPTHORNE, R., «Incest and the Body of Christ. A Study of 1 Corinthians VI,12-20», *NTS* 14 (1967) 568-74.

KENNEDY, G., *The Art of Persuasion in Greece*, Princeton 1963.

——, *Classical Rhetoric and its Christian and Secular Tradition from Ancient to Modern Times*, Chapel Hill 1980.

——, *New Testament Interpretation through Rhetorical Criticism*, Chapel Hill 1984.

KINNEAVEY, J.L., *Greek Rhetorical Origins of Christian Faith*, New York 1987.

KIRKPATRICK, F.G., *Community. A Trinity of Models*, Washington, D.C. 1986.

KLAUCK, H.J., *1 Korintherbrief*, Würzburg 1984.

KNOX, J., *Chapters in a Life of Paul*, New York 1950.

KOESTER, H., *Introduction to the New Testament*, I-II, New York 1987.

——, «Epilogue: Current Issues in New Testament Scholarship», in *The Future of Early Christianity*, ed. B. A. Pearson, Minneapolis 1991, 467-76.

KRUSE, C.G., *Paul, the Law and Justification*, Leicester 1996.

KUCK, D., *Judgment and Community Conflict. Paul's Use of Apocalyptic Judgment Language in 1 Corinthians 3:5-4:5*, SNT 66, Leiden 1992.

KUSTAS, J.L. «Diatribe in Ancient Rhetorical Theory», Protocol of the Twenty Second Colloquy. April 25, 1976. The Center for Hermeneutic Studies. Graduate Theological Union and the University of California at Berkley, 1-15.

LAMBRECHT, J., «Rhetorical Criticism and the New Testament», *BijT* 50 (1989) 239-53.

LAMPE, G.W.H., «Church Discipline and the Epistles to the Corinthians», in *Christian History and Interpretation*, Fs. J. Knox, Cambridge 1967, 337-61.

LAMPE, P., «Theological Wisdom and the "Word about the Cross": The Rhetorical Scheme in I Cor 1-4», *Interp* 44 (1990) 117-131.

LANG, F., *Die Briefe an die Korinther*, Göttingen 1986.

LAURENTI, R., «Musonio, maestro di Epitetto», *ANRW* II.36.3, 2105-46.

LAUSBERG, H., *Handbuch der Literarischen Rhetorik*, München 1960.

LE DÉAUT, R., «The Paschal Mystery and Morality», *DoctrLife* 18 (4,1968) 202-10, (5,1968) 262-69.

LENCHAK, T., *«Choose Life». A Rhetorical Critical Investigation of Deuteronomy 28,69-30,20*, AnBib 129, Roma 1993.

LEVINE, B., *Leviticus*, JPSTC, New York 1989.

LINDEMANN, A., «Die biblischen Toragebote und die paulinische Ethik», in *Studien zum Text und zur Ethik des neuen Testament*, Fs. H. Greeven, Berlin 1986, 242-65.

LITFIN, D., *Saint Paul's Theology of Proclamation. 1 Corinthians 1-4 and Greco-Roman Rhetoric*, SNTSMS 79, Cambridge 1994.

LOHSE, E., *Theologische Ethik des Neuen Testaments*, Stuttgart 1988; english trans. *Theological Ethics of the New Testament*, Minneapolis 1991.

——, «St. Peter's Apostleship in the Judgement of St. Paul», *Greg* 72 (1991) 419-35.

LONG, A.A., *Problems in Stoicism*, London 1971.

——, *Hellenistic Philosophy*, London 1974.

LUEDEMANN, G., *Paulus, der Heidenapostel*, I: *Studien zur Chronologie*, Göttingen 1980; english trans. *Paul Apostle to the Gentiles. Studies in Chronology*, Philadelphia 1984.

——, *Antipaulinismus im frühen Christentum*, Göttingen 1983; english trans. *Opposition to Paul in Jewish Christianity*, Minneapolis 1989.

LÜHRMANN, D., «Freundschaftsbrief trotz Spannungen. Zu Gattung und Aufbau des Ersten Korintherbrief», in *Studien zum Text und zur Ethik des neuen Testament*, Fs. H. Greeven, Berlin 1986, 298-314.

LUND, N.W., *Chiasmus in the New Testament: A Study in Formgeschichte*, Chapel Hill 1942.

——, «The Significance of Chiasmus for Interpretation», *The Crozer Quarterly* 20 (1943) 105-23.

LÜTGERT, W., *Freiheitspredigt und Schwarmgeister in Korinth. Ein Beitrag zur Charakteristik der Christuspartei*, Gütersloh 1908

LUTZ, C.E., *Musonius Rufus. The Roman Socrates*, Yale Classical Studies 10, New Haven 1947.

LYONNET, S., *Annotationes in Priorem Epistulam Corinthios*, Roma 1965-66.

LYONS, G., *Pauline Autobiography. Toward A New Understanding*, SBLDS 73, Atlanta 1985.

McBRIEN, R., «The American Experience», in *American Catholics*, ed. J.F. Kelly, Wilmington 1989, 3-12.

McDONALD, M., «Women Holy in Body and Spirit», *NTS* 36 (1990) 161-181.

McKELVEY, R.J., *The New Temple. The Church in the New Testament*, London 1969.

McKNIGHT, S., *A Light Among the Gentiles. Jewish Missionary Activity in the Second Temple Period*, Minneapolis 1991.

MACKY, P.W., *The Centrality of Metaphors to Biblical Thought. A Method for Interpreting the Bible*, Lewiston 1990.

MACRAE. G.W. «Nag Hammadi and the New Testament», in *Gnosis*, Fs. H. Jonas, Göttingen 1978, 144-57.

MALHERBE, A., «Self-Definition Among Epicureans and Cynics», in *Jewish and Christian Self-Definition*, III, ed. B.F. Meyer – E.P. Sanders, Philadelphia 1982, 46-59.

——, «Exhortation in First Thessalonians», *NT* 25 (1983) 238-56.

——, *Moral Exhortation. A Greco-Roman Sourcebook*, Philadelphia 1986.

——, ed., *Ancient Epistolary Theorists*, Atlanta 1988.

——, *Paul and the Popular Philosophers*, Minneapolis 1989.

——, «Hellenistic Moralists and the New Testament», *ANRW* 2.26, 267-333.

——, «Graeco-Roman Religion and Philosophy and the New Testament», in *The New Testament and its Modern Interpreters*, ed. E. J. Epp – G. W. McRae, Philadelphia 1989, 3-26.

——, «Determinism and Free Will in Paul. The Argument of 1 Corinthians 8 and 9», in *Paul in His Hellenistic Context. Studies of the New Testament and Its World*, ed. T. Engberg-Pederson, Edinburgh 1994, 231-55.

MAN, R.E. «The Value of Chiasm for New Testament Interpretation», *BS* 141 (1984) 146-57.

MANSON, T.W., «St. Paul in Ephesus: (3) The Corinthian Correspondence», *BJRL* 26 (1941) 101-02.

MARCUS AURELIUS, *Meditations*. tr. C.R. Haines, LCL, Cambridge.

MARSHALL, L.H., *The Challenge of New Testament Ethics*, London 1956.

MARSHALL, P., «Invective: Paul and His Enemies at Corinth», in *Perspectives on Language and Text*, Fs. F.I. Andersen, Winona Lake 1987, 359-73.

MARXSEN, W., «*Christliche*», *und christliche Ethik im Neuen Testaments*, Gütersloh 1989; english trans. *New Testament Foundations for Christian Ethics*, Minneapolis 1993.

MEEKS, W., ed., *The Writings of St. Paul. Annotated Text and Criticism*, New York 1972.

——, *The First Urban Christians*, New Haven 1983.

——, *The Moral World of the First Christians*, London 1987.

MEEKS, W., «The Circle of Reference in Pauline Morality», in *Greeks, Romans and Christians*, Fs. A. Malherbe, Minneapolis 1990, 305-317.

——, *The Origins of Christian Morality*, New Haven 1993.

MENNINGER, K., *Whatever Became of Sin?*, New York 1973.

MERK, O., *Handeln aus Glauben: Die Motivierung der paulinischen Ethik*, Marburg 1968.

MERKLEIN, H., «Die Einheitlichkeit des ersten Korintherbriefes», *ZNW* 75 (1984) 153-183.

MEYNET, R., *L'analyse rhétorique. Une nouvelle méthode pour comprendre la Bible*, Paris 1989.

MICHEL, O., *Das Zeugnis des Neuen Testament von der Gemeinde*, FRLANT 39, Göttingen 1941.

MILGROM, J., *Numbers*, JPSTC, New York 1990.

MINEAR, P.S., *Images of the Church in the New Testament*, Philadelphia 1960.

——, «Christ and the Congregation: 1 Corinthians 5-6», *RevExp* 80 (1983) 341-350.

MITCHELL, M.M., *«peri de* in 1 Corinthians», *NT* 30 (1989) 229-56.

——, *Paul and the Language of Reconciliation. An Exegetical investigation of the Language and Composition of 1 Corinthians*, Tübingen 1991.

MITTON, C.L., «New Wine in Old Wine Skins: IV. Leaven», *ExpTim* 84 (1972) 339-343.

MOFFATT, J., *The First Epistle to the Corinthians*, London 1947.

MONTEFIORE, C., *A Rabbinic Anthology*, London 1938.

MORRIS, L., *1 Corinthians. An Introduction and Commentary*, London 1964.

MOULE, C.F.D., «Obligation in the Ethic of Paul», in *Christian History and Interpretation*, Fs. J. Knox, Cambridge 1967, 389-406.

MUILENBERG, J., «Form Criticism and Beyond», *JBL* 88 (1969) 1-18.

MUNCK, J., «The Church Without Factions: Studies in 1 Corinthians 1-4», in *Paul and the Salvation of Mankind*, Richmond 1959, 135-167.

MURPHY-O'CONNOR, J., «Péché et communauté dans le nouveau testament», *RB* 2 (1967) 161-193.

——, *L'existence chrétienne selon saint Paul*, LeDiv 80, Paris 1974.

——, «Corinthian Slogans in 1 Cor 6:12-20», *CBQ* 40 (1978) 391-396.

——, *1 Corinthians*, NTM 10, Wilmington 1979.

——, *Becoming Human Together. The Pastoral Anthropology of St. Paul*, Wilmington 1982.

——, *St. Paul's Corinth. Texts and Archaeology*, GNS 6, Wilmington 1983.

——, «Interpolations in 1 Corinthians», *CBQ* 48 (1986) 81-94.

——, «Qumran and the New Testament», in *The New Testament and Its Modern Interpreters*, ed. E.J. Epp – G.W. MacRae, Atlanta 1989, 63-5.

——, «Christ and Ministry», *Pacifica* 4 (1991) 121-36.

MURPHY-O'CONNOR, J., *Paul et L'art épistolaire*, Paris 1994.

——, *Paul the Letter-Writer*, Collegeville 1995.

——, *Paul. A Critical Life*, Oxford 1996.

MUßNER, F., *Theologie der Freiheit nach Paulus*, Quaestiones Disputatae 75, Basel 1976.

NASH, R., *Christianity and the Hellenistic World*, Grand Rapids 1984.

NESTLE, D., *Eleutheria, Teil I: Die Griechen*, Tübingen 1967.

NESTLE, E. – ALAND, K., *Novum Testamentum Graece*, Stuttgart 1979[26].

NEUSNER, J., *The Idea of Purity in Ancient Judaism*, Leiden 1973.

NEWTON, M., *The Concept of Purity at Qumram and in the Letters of St. Paul*, SNTSMS 53, Cambridge 1985.

NEYREY, J., *Paul in Other Words. A Cultural Reading of His Letters*, Louisville 1990.

NIEDER, L., *Die Motive der religiös-sittlichen Paränese in den paulinische Gemeindebriefen. Ein Beitrag zur paulinischen Ethik*, München 1956.

NOCK, A.D., «Gnosticism», *HTR* 57 (1964) 256-79.

ORR, W. – WALTHER, J., *1 Corinthians*, AB 32, Garden City 1976.

ORTKEMPER, F.J., *1 Korintherbrief*, SKK NT 7, Stuttgart 1993.

OSTER, R.E., «Use, Misuse and Neglect of Archaeological Evidence in Some Modern Works on 1 Corinthians (1 Cor 7,1-5; 8,10; 11,2-16; 12,14-26)», *ZNW* 83 (1992) 52-73.

O'TOOLE, R.F., *Who is a Christian? A Study in Pauline Ethics*, Collegeville 1990.

PAIGE, T., «Stoicism, *Eleutheria*, and Community at Corinth», in *Worship, Theology and Ministry in the Early Church*, ed. M. Wilkins – T. Paige, JSNTSS 87, Sheffield 1992, 180-93.

PANIKULAM, G., *Koinônia in the New Testament. A Dynamic Expression of Christian Life*, AnBib 85, Rome 1979.

PEARSON, B.A., *The Pneumatikos-Psychikos Terminology in Corinthians. A Study in the Theology of the Corinthian Opponents of Paul and Its Relation to Gnosticism*, SBLDS 12, Missoula 1973.

PERELMAN, C., «Rhetoric and Philosophy», *Philosophy and Rhetoric* 1 (1968) 15-24.

——, *L'empire rhétorique: Rhétorique et argumentation*, Paris 1977; english trans. *The Realm of Rhetoric*, Notre Dame 1982.

PERELMAN, C. – OLBRECHTS-TYTECA, L., *Traité de l'argumentation: La nouvelle rhétorique*, Bruxelles 1958; english trans. *The New Rhetoric: A Treatise on Argumentation*, tr. J. Wilkinson – P. Weaver, South Bend, Ind. 1969.

PERKINS, P., *Peter. Apostle for the Whole Church*, Columbia, S. C. 1994.

PERRIMAN, A., «"His Body which is the Church...": Coming to Terms with Metaphor», *EvQ* 62 (1990) 123-42.

PESCH, R., *Paulus Ringt um die Lebensform der Kirche: Vier Briefe an die Gemeinde Gottes in Korinth*, Freiburg 1986.

PFITZNER, V.C., «Purified Community – Purified Sinner. Expulsion from the Community According to Matthew 18:15-18 and 1 Corinthians 5:1-5», *AustrBR* 30 (1982) 34-39.

PHILO, *De Opificio Mundi*, tr. F.H. Colson, LCL, Cambridge 1949.

——, *De Praemiis et Poenis*, tr. F.H. Colson, LCL, Cambridge 1939.

——, *De Specialibus Legibus*. tr. F.H. Colson, LCL, Cambridge 1954.

——, *De Virtutibus*, tr. F.H. Colson, LCL, Cambridge 1939.

——, *De Vita Contemplativa*, tr. F.H. Colson, LCL, Cambridge 1954.

——, *Hypothetica*, tr. F.H. Colson, LCL, Cambridge 1954.

——, *Legum Allegoria*, tr. F.H. Colson, LCL, Cambridge 1949.

——, *Quaestiones et Solutiones in Exodum*, tr. R. Marcus, LCL, Cambridge 1953.

——, *Quaestiones et Solutiones in Genesis*, tr. R. Marcus, LCL, Cambridge 1953.

PLUTARCH, «On Stoic Self-Contradictions», in *Moralia*, XIII, Part 2. 1033A-1086B, tr. H. Cherniss, LCL, Cambridge 1976.

——, «The Stoics Talk More Paradoxically Than the Poets», in *Moralia*, XIII, Part 2. 1057-58, tr. H. Cherniss, LCL, Cambridge 1976.

POGOLOFF, S., *Logos and Sophia. The Rhetorical Situation of 1 Corinthians*, SBLDS 134, Atlanta 1992.

PORTER, S. E., «The Theoretical Justification for Application of Rhetorical Categories to Pauline Epistolary Literature», in *Rhetoric and the New Testament*. Essays from the 1992 Heidelberg Conference, ed. S.E. Porter – T.H. Olbrichts, JSNTSS 90, Sheffield 1993, 100-22.

DE LA POTTERIE, I., «L'Impeccabilità del cristiano secondo 1 Giovanni 3,6-9», in S. LYONNET – I. DE LA POTTERIE, *La vita secondo lo spirito. Condizione del cristiano*, Roma 1967², 235-58.

PRETE, B., *Matrimonio e Continenza nel Cristianesimo delle Origini: Studio su 1 CO 7,1-40*, Brescia 1979.

PROBST, H., *Paulus und der Brief. Die Rhetorik des antiken Briefes als Form der paulinischen Korintherkorrispondenz, (1 Kor 8-10)*, WUNT 45, Tübingen 1991.

PROCKSCH, O., «*hagios, hagiazô ktl*», *TDNT* I, 88-115.

QUILL, T.E., *A Midwife Through the Dying Process. Stories of Healing & Hard Choices at the End of Life*, Baltimore 1996.

QUINTILIAN, *Institutio Oratoria*, I-IV, tr. H. E. Butler, LCL, Cambridge 1980.

RAHNER, K., «The Sinful Church in the Decrees of Vatican II», in *Theological Investigations. VI. Concerning Vatican Council II*, tr. K.H. and B. Kruger, London 1969, 270-94.

REED, J.T. «Using Rhetorical Categories to Interpret Paul's Letters: A Question of Genre», in *Rhetoric and the New Testament*. Essays from the 1992 Heidelberg Conference, ed. S.E. Porter – T.H. Olbrichts, JSNTSS 90, Sheffield 1993, 292-324.

VAN RENSBURG, S.P., «Sanctification According to the New Testament», *Neot* 1 (1967) 73-86.

RENWICK, D.A., *Paul, the Temple, and the Presence of God*, Brown Judaic Studies 224, Atlanta 1991.

RHYNE, C.T., *Faith Establishes the Law*, SBLDS 55, Chico 1981.

RICHARDSON, P., «Judgement, Immorality and Sexual Ethics in 1 Cor 6», SBLSP 19, 1980, 337-357.

———, «Judgement in Sexual Matters in 1 Corinthians 6:1-11», *NT* 25 (1983) 37-58.

RIGALI, N. J., «Church Response to Pedophilia», *TS* 55 (1994) 124-139.

RIST, J. M., *Stoic Philosophy*, Cambridge 1969.

———, *Human Value: A Study in Ancient Philosophical Ethics*, Leiden 1982.

ROBERTSON, A. – PLUMMER, A., *A Critical and Exegetical Handbook of the First Epistle of Paul to the Corinthians*, ICC, New York 1911.

ROBINSON, H.W. «The Hebrew Concept of Corporate Personality», in *Werden und Wesen des Alten Testaments*, BZAW 66, Berlin 1936, 49-62.

———, *Corporate Personality in Ancient Israel*, Philadelphia 1980.

ROBINSON, J.A.T., *The Body: A Study in Pauline Theology*, London 1957.

ROBINSON, J.M., «Kerygma and History in the New Testament», in *Trajectories Through Early Christianity*, ed. J.M. Robinson – H. Koester, Philadelphia 1971, 20-70.

———, «Gnosticism and the New Testament», in *Gnosis*, Fs. H. Jonas, Göttingen 1978, 125-43.

ROETZEL, C.J., *Judgement in the Community: A Study of the Relationship Between Eschatology and Ecclesiology in Paul*, Leiden 1972.

ROGERSON, J.W. «The Hebrew Conception of Corporate Personality: A Re-examination», *JTS* 21 (1970) 1-16.

———, *Anthropology and the Old Testament*, Oxford 1978.

ROMANIUK, K., «Les motifs parénétiques dans les ecrits pauliniens», *NT* 10 (1968) 191-207.

ROSNER, B.S., «Temple and Holiness in 1 Corinthians 5», *TynB* 42 (1991) 137-45.

———, «"*Ouchi mallon epenthèsate*": Corporate Responsibility in 1 Cor», *NTS* 38 (1992) 470-73.

———, *Paul, Scripture and Ethics. A Study of 1 Cor 5-7*, Leiden 1994.

———, *Understanding Paul's Ethics. Twentieth Century Approaches*, Grand Rapids 1995.

ROSSO UBLIGLI, L., «Alcuni aspetti della concezione della *porneia* nel Tardo-Giudaismo», *Henoch* 1 (1979) 201-245.

RUDOLPH, K., *Die Gnosis. Wesen und Geschichte einer spätantiken Religion*, Leipzig 1979; english trans. *Gnosis. The Nature and History of an Ancient Religion*, Edinburgh 1983.

SABATIER, A. *L'apôtre Paul. Esquisse d'une histoire de sa pensée*, Paris 1896³.

SAMPLEY, J.P., *Walking between the Times: Paul's Moral Reasoning*, Minneapolis 1991.

——, «The Weak and the Strong: Paul's Careful and Crafty Rhetorical Strategy in Rom 14.1-15.13», in *The Social World of the First Christians*, Fs. W. Meeks, Minneapolis 1995, 40-52.

SANDBACH, F.H., *The Stoics*, London 1975.

SANDERS, E.P., *Paul the Law and the Jewish People*, Philadelphia 1983.

——, *Paul and Palestinian Judaism. A Comparison of Patterns of Religion*, Philadelphia 1983.

——, *Judaism. Practice and Belief 63 BCE – 66 CE*, London 1992.

SANDERS, J.T., *Ethics in the New Testament*, London 1986.

SARNA, N., *Exodus*, JPSTC, New York 1991.

SCHENK, W., «Der 1 Korintherbrief als Briefsammlung», *ZNW* 60 (1969) 219-243.

SCHINDLER, T., *Ethics: The Social Dimension. Individualism and the Catholic Tradition*, Wilmington 1989.

SCHLIER, H., «*hamartanô, hamartia ktl*», *TDNT* I, 267-338.

——, «*eleutheria ktl*», *TDNT* II, 487-502.

SCHMIDT, K. L., «*kaleô, klèsis, ekklèsia ktl*», *TDNT* III, 487-536.

SCHMITHALS, W., *Die Gnosis in Korinth; eine Untersuchung zu den Korintherbriefen*, Göttingen 1956; english trans. *Gnosticism in Corinth. An Investigation of the Letters to the Corinthians*, Nashville 1971.

SCHNABEL, E.J., *Law and Wisdom from ben Sira to Paul. A Tradition Historical Enquiry into the Relation of Law, Wisdom and Ethics*, WUNT 16, Tübingen 1985.

SCHNACKENBURG, R., *Das Heilsgeschehen bei der Taufe nach dem Apostel Paulus*, Zürich 1959; english trans. *Baptism in the Thought of Saint Paul. A Study in Pauline Theology*, Oxford 1964.

——, *Die Kirche im Neuen Testament*, Freiburg 1961; english trans. *The Church in the New Testament*, New York 1965.

——, *Die sittliche Botschaft des Neuen Testamentes*, München, 1954; english trans. *The Moral Teaching of the New Testament*, New York 1965.

——, *Der Brief an die Epheser*, Zürich 1982; english trans. *The Epistle to the Ephesians. A Commentary*, Edinburgh 1991.

SCHOEPS, H., Paulus. *Die Theologie des Apostels im Lichte der jüdischen Religionsgeschichte*, Tübingen 1959; english trans. *Paul. The Theology of the Apostle in the Light of Jewish Religious History*, Philadelphia 1961.

SCHRAGE, W., *Die konkreten Einzelgebote in der paulinischen Paränese*, Gütersloh 1961.

——, *Ethik des Neuen Testament*, Göttingen 1982; english trans. *The Ethics of the New Testament*, Philadelphia 1988.

——, *Der erste Brief an die Korinther. 1 KOR 1,1-6,11*, EKK VII,1, Braunschweig 1991.

SCHÜSSLER FIORENZA, E., «Rhetorical Situation and Historical Reconstruction in 1 Corinthians», *NTS* 33 (1987) 386-403.

SCHÜTZ, J. H., *Paul and the Anatomy of Apostolic Authority*, SNTMS 26, Cambridge 1975.

SCHWEITZER, A., *Die Mystik des Apostels Paulus*, Tübingen 1930; english trans. *The Mysticism of Paul the Apostle*, New York 1968.

SCHWEIZER, E., «The Church as the Missionary Body of Christ», *NTS* 8 (1961) 1-11.

——, *Church Order in the New Testament*, SBT 32, London 1961.

——, *The Church as the Body of Christ*, Richmond 1964.

SCROGGS, R., «The New Testament and Ethics: How Do We Get From There to Here?», in *Perspectives on the New Testament*, Fs. F. Stagg, Macon 1985, 77-93.

——, «ΣΟΦΟΣ and ΠΝΕΥΜΑΤΙΚΟΣ», *NTS* 14 (1967) 33-55.

SEEBERG, A., *Der Katechismus der Urchristenheit*, München 1966.

SELLING, G., «1 Korinther 5-6 und der "Vorbrief" nach Korinth», *NTS* 37 (1991) 535-558.

——, «Hauptprobleme des ersten Korintherbriefes», *ANRW* II.25.4, 2940-3044.

SENECA, «De Vita Beata», in *Epistulae Morales*, II, tr. J. W. Basore, LCL, Cambridge 1935.

SENFT, C. *La première épître de saint Paul aux Corinthiens*, Genève 1990².

DE LA SERNA, E., «Los origines de 1 Corintios», *Bib* 72 (1991) 193-216.

SEXTUS EMPIRICUS. «Against the Ethicists», tr. R.G. Bury, LCL, Cambridge 1968.

SHEDD, R.P. *Man in Community. A Study of Paul's Application of Old Testament and Early Jewish Conceptions of Human Solidarity*, London 1958.

SIMPSON, E.K., *Commentary on the Epistle to the Ephesians*, NICNT, Grand Rapids 1970.

SNAITH, N.H. *The Distinctive Idea of the Old Testament*, London 1962.

SNYDER, G.F., *First Corinthians. A Faith Community Commentary*, Macon, GA 1992.

VON SODEN, H., «Sakrament und Ethik bei Paulus. Zur Frage der literarischen und theologischen einheitlichkeit von 1 Kor 8-10», in *Marburger Theologische Studien*, I, Fs. R. Otto, Gotha 1931, 1-40 = K.H. RENGSTORF, ed., *Das Paulusbuild in der neueren Deutschen Forschung*, Darmstadt 1964, 338-79.

SOUTH, J.T., «A Critique of the "Curse/Death" Interpretation of 1 Corinthians 5,1-8», *NTS* 39 (1993) 539-61.

——, *Disciplinary Practices in Pauline Texts*, Lewiston 1992.

SPICQ, C., *Théologie morale du Nouveau Testament*, I-II, Paris 1970⁴.

STAMPS, D.L., «Rhetorical Criticism and the Rhetoric of the New Testament», *JLT* 6 (1992) 268-79.

STAMPS, D.L., «Rethinking the Rhetorical Situation. The Entextualizing of the Situation in New Testament Epistles», in *Rhetoric and the New Testament*. Essays from the 1992 Heidelberg Conference, ed. S.E. Porter – T.H. Olbrichts, JSNTSS 90, Sheffield 1993, 193-210.

——, «Rhetorical Criticism of the New Testament: Ancient and Modern Evaluations of Argumentation», in *Approaches to New Testament Study*, ed. S. Porter – D. Tombs, JSNTSS 120, Sheffield 1995, 129-69.

STANDAERT, B., «Analyse rhétorique des chapitres 12 à 14 de 1 Co», in *Charisma und Agape (1 Kor 12-14)*, ed. L. De Lorenzi, SMBen 7, Rom 1983, 23-34.

——, «1 Corinthiens 13», in *Charisma und Agape. (1 Kor 12-14)*, ed. L. De Lorenzi, SMBen 7, Rom 1983, 127-39.

——, «La rhétorique ancienne dans Saint Paul», in *L'Apôtre Paul. Personnalité, Style et Conception du Ministère*, ed. A. Vanhoye, BETL 73, Leuven 1986, 78-92.

——, «Lecture rhétorique d'un écrit biblique», in *Naissance de la méthode critique*, Colloque du centenaire de l'École biblique et archéologique française de Jérusalem, Paris 1992, 187-94.

STEWART-SYKES, A., «Ancient Editors and Copyists and Modern Partition Theories: The Case of the Corinthian Correspondence», *JSNT* 61 (1996) 53-64.

STIREWALT, M.L. *Studies in Ancient Epistolography*, SBLSBS 27, Atlanta 1993.

STOWERS, S.K., *The Diatribe and Paul's Letter to the Romans*, SBLDS 57, Chico Press, 1981.

——, *Letter Writing in Greco-Roman Antiquity*, Philadelphia 1986.

——, «Social Typification and the Classification of Ancient Letters», in *The Social World of Formative Christianity and Judaism*, Fs. H. Clark Kee, Philadelphia 1988, 78-90.

——, «The Diatribe», in *Greco-Roman Literature and the New Testament*, ed. D.E. Aune, Atlanta 1988.

——, «Paul on the Use and Abuse of Reason», in *Greeks, Romans and Christians*, Fs. A. Malherbe, Minneapolis 1990, 253-86.

STRABO, *The Geography of Strabo*, tr. H.L. Jones, LCL, Cambridge 1961.

STRACK, H. – BILLERBECK, P., *Kommentar zum neuen Testament aus Talmud und Midrash*, III, München 1954.

TALBERT, C.H., «Artistry and Theology: An Analysis of the Architecture of Jn 1,19-5,47», *CBQ* 32 (1970) 362-66.

——, *Reading Corinthians: A Literary and Theological Commentary of 1 and 2 Corinthians*, New York 1987.

THEISSEN, G., *The Social Setting of Pauline Christianity: Essays on Corinth*, Philadelphia 1982.

THERRIEN, G., *Le discernement dans les écrits pauliniens*, Paris 1973.

THISELTON, A.C., «The Meaning of *SARX* in 1 Corinthians 5.5: A Fresh Approach in the Light of Logical and Semantic Factors», *SJT* 26 (1973) 204-228.

THISELTON, A.C., «Realized Eschatology in Corinth», *NTS* 24 (1977) 510-526.

THOMAS AQUINAS, *Summa Theologica*, I-III, tr. Fathers of the English Dominican Province, New York 1947.

THOMSON, I., *Chiasmus in the Pauline Letters*, JSNTSS 111, Sheffield 1995.

TOMSON, P.J., *Paul and the Jewish Law: Halakha in the Letters of the Apostle to the Gentiles*, CRINT, Assen/Maastricht 1990.

TOWNER, P.H., «Gnosis and Realized Eschatology in Ephesus (of the Pastoral Epistles) and Corinthian Enthusiasm», *JSNT* 31 (1987) 95-124.

TUCKETT, C., «Jewish Christian Wisdom in 1 Corinthians?», in *Crossing the Boundaries*. Fs. M. D. Goulder, Leiden 1994, 201-20.

VANNI, U., «Due città nella formazione di Paolo: Tarso e Gerusalemme», in *Atti del I Simposio di Tarso su S. Paolo Apostolo*, ed. L. Padovese, Roma 1993, 17-29.

VERBEKE, G., «Le stoïcisme, une philosophie sans frontières», in *D'Aristote a Thomas D'Aquin: Antecedents de la Pensee Moderne*. Recueil d'articles de G. Verbeke, Leuven 1990, 301-340.

VERHEY, A., *The Great Reversal. Ethics in the New Testament*, Grand Rapids 1984.

VERMES, G., *The Dead Sea Scrolls in English*, Sheffield 1987³.

VICKERS, B., *In Defence of Rhetoric*, Oxford 1988.

VOLLENWEIDER, S., *Freiheit als neue Schopfung: Eine Untersuchung zur Eleutheria bei Paulus und in seiner Umwelt*, Göttingen 1989.

WALBANK, F. W., *The Hellenistic World*, Cambridge 1980.

WATSON, D.F. – HAUSER, A.J., *Rhetorical Criticism and the Bible. A Comprehensive Bibliography With Notes on History and Method*, Leiden 1994.

WATSON, N., *The First Epistle to the Corinthians*, London 1992.

WCELA, E., «Who Do You Say That They Are? Reflections on the Biblical Audience Today», *CBQ* 53 (1991) 1-17.

WEDDERBURN, A.J.M., «The Body of Christ and Related Concepts in 1 Corinthians», *SJT* 24 (1971) 74-96.

WEIMA, J., *Neglected Endings. The Significance of the Pauline Letter Closings*, Sheffield 1994.

WEISS, J., *Der erste Korintherbrief*, Göttingen 1910.

——, *Das Urchristentum*, II, Göttingen, 1914; english trans. *The History of Primitive Christianity*, II, New York 1937.

WELBORN, L.L., «On the Discord in Corinth: 1 Cor 1-4 and Ancient Politics», *JBL* 106 (1987) 85-111.

WELCH, J.J. «Chiasm in Ancient Greek and Latin Literature», in *Chiasmus in Antiquity. Structure, Analysis, Exegesis*, ed. J.J. Welch, Hildesheim 1981, 250-68.

——, «Chiasm in the New Testament», in *Chiasmus in Antiquity. Structure, Analysis, Exegesis*, ed. J.J. Welch, Hildesheim 1981, 211-49.

WENDLAND, H.D., *Die Briefe an die Korinther,* Göttingen 1936.

——, *Ethik des neuen Testament,* Göttingen 1970.

WESTERHOLM, S., *Israel's Law and the Church's Faith. Paul and His Recent Interpreters,* Grand Rapids 1988.

WHITE, J.L., *Light from Ancient Letters,* Philadelphia 1986.

——, «Ancient Greek Letters», in *Greco-Roman Literature and the New Testament,* ed. D. Aune, SBLSBS 21, Atlanta 1988, 85-106.

——, «New Testament Epistolary Literature in the Framework of Ancient Epistolography», *ANRW* 25.2, 1730-56.

WHITELEY, D.E.H., *The Theology of Saint Paul,* Oxford 1964.

WIKENHAUSER, A., *Die Christusmystik des Apostels Paulus,* Freiburg 1956; english trans. *Pauline Mysticism. Christ in the Mystical Teaching of St. Paul,* New York 1960.

WILCKENS, U., *Weisheit und Torheit. Eine exegetisch-religionsgeschichtliche Untersuchung zu 1 Kor 1 und 2,* BHTh 26, Tübingen 1959.

WILLIS, W., «An Apostolic Apologia? The Form and Function of 1 Corinthians 9», *JSNT* 24 (1985) 33-48.

——, «Corinthusne deletus est?», *BZ* 35 (1991) 233-241.

WILSON, R. McL., «Gnosis at Corinth», in *Paul and Paulinism,* Fs. C.K. Barrett, London 1982, 102-14.

——, «How Gnostic Were the Corinthians?», *NTS* 19 (1972) 65-74.

——, «Ethics and the Gnostics», in *Studien zum Text und zur Ethik des Neuen Testament,* Fs. H. Greeven, Berlin 1986, 440-49.

WINDISCH, H., «zymè ktl», *TDNT* II, 902-06.

WIRE, A.C., *The Corinthian Women Prophets. A Reconstruction Through Paul's Rhetoric,* Minneapolis 1990.

WITHERINGTON, B., *Conflicts and Community in Corinth. A Socio-Rhetorical Commentary on 1 and 2 Corinthians,* Grand Rapids 1995.

WUELLNER, W., «Paul's Rhetoric of Argumentation in Romans. An alternative to the Donfried-Karris Debate Over Romans», *CBQ* 38 (1976) 330-351.

——, «Methodological Considerations Concerning the Genre of First Corinthians», Unpublished paper presented at the SBL Pacific Coast Regional Paul Seminar. March 1976.

——, «Greek Rhetoric and Pauline Argumentation», in *Early Christian Literature and the Classical Intellectual Tradition,* ed. W.R. Schoedel – R.L. Wilkens, Paris 1979, 177-88.

——, «Paul as Pastor. The Function of Rhetorical Questions in First Corinthians», in *L'Apôtre Paul. Personalité, style et conception du ministère,* ed. A. Vanhoye, BETL 73, Leuven 1986, 49-77.

——, «Where is Rhetorical Criticism Taking Us?», *CBQ* 49 (1987) 448-63.

YAMAUCHI, E., «Pre-Christian Gnosticism, the New Testament and Nag Hammadi in Recent Debate», in *Gnosticism in the Early Christianity,* ed. D.M. Scholer, Studies in Early Christianity 5, New York 1993, 26-33.

YARBROUGH, O.L., *Not Like the Gentiles: Marriage Rules in the Letters of Paul*, Atlanta 1985.

ZAAS, P., «Cast the Evil Man from Your Midst», *JBL* 103 (1984) 259-61.

——, «Catalogues and Context: 1 Corinthians 5 and 6», *NTS* 34 (1988) 622-29.

INDEX OF AUTHORS

TABLE OF CONTENTS

TESI GREGORIANA

Since 1995, the series «Tesi Gregoriana» has made available to the general public some of the best doctoral theses done at the Pontifical Gregorian University. The typesetting is done by the authors themselves following norms established and controlled by the University.

Published Volumes [Series: Theology]

1. NELLO FIGA, Antonio, *Teorema de la opción fundamental. Bases para su adecuada utilización en teología moral*, 1995, pp. 380.

2. BENTOGLIO, Gabriele, *Apertura e disponibilità. L'accoglienza nell'epistolario paolino*, 1995, pp. 376.

3. PISO, Alfeu, *Igreja e sacramentos. Renovação da Teologia Sacramentária na América Latina*, 1995, pp. 260.

4. PALAKEEL, Joseph, *The Use of Analogy in Theological Discourse. An Investigation in Ecumenical Perspective*, 1995, pp. 392.

5. KIZHAKKEPARAMPIL, Isaac, *The Invocation of the Holy Spirit as Constitutive of the Sacraments according to Cardinal Yves Congar*, 1995, pp. 200.

6. MROSO, Agapit J., *The Church in Africa and the New Evangelisation. A Theologico-Pastoral Study of the Orientations of John Paul II*, 1995, pp. 456.

7. NANGELIMALIL, Jacob, *The Relationship between the Eucharistic Liturgy, the Interior Life and the Social Witness of the Church according to Joseph Cardinal Parecattil*, 1996, pp. 224.

8. GIBBS, Philip, *The Word in the Third World. Divine Revelation in the Theology of Jen-Marc Éla, Aloysius Pieris and Gustavo Gutiérrez*, 1996, pp. 448.

9. DELL'ORO, Roberto, *Esperienza morale e persona. Per una reinterpretazione dell'etica fenomenologica di Dietrich von Hildebrand*, 1996, pp. 240.

10. BELLANDI, Andrea, *Fede cristiana come «stare e comprendere». La giustificazione dei fondamenti della fede in Joseph Ratzinger*, 1996, pp. 416.

11. BEDRIÑAN, Claudio, *La dimensión socio-política del mensaje teológico del Apocalipsis*, 1996, pp. 364.

12. GWYNNE, Paul, *Special Divine Action. Key Issues in the Contemporary Debate (1965-1995)*, 1996, pp. 376.

13. NIÑO, Francisco, *La Iglesia en la ciudad. El fenómeno de las grandes ciudades en América Latina, como problema teológico y como desafío pastoral*, 1996, pp. 492.

14. BRODEUR, Scott, *The Holy Spirit's Agency in the Resurrection of the Dead. An Exegetico-Theological Study of 1 Corinthians 15,44b-49 and Romans 8,9-13*, 1996, pp. 300.

15. ZAMBON, Gaudenzio, *Laicato e tipologie ecclesiali. Ricerca storica sulla «Teologia del laicato» in Italia alla luce del Concilio Vaticano II (1950-1980)*, 1996, pp. 548.

16. ALVES DE MELO, Antonio, *A Evangelização no Brasil. Dimensões teológicas e desafios pastorais. O debate teológico e eclesial (1952-1995)*, 1996, pp. 428.

17. APARICIO VALLS, María del Carmen, *La plenitud del ser humano en Cristo. La Revelación en la «Gaudium et Spes»*, 1997, pp. 308.

18. MARTIN, Seán Charles, *«Pauli Testamentum». 2 Timothy and the Last Words of Moses*, 1997, pp. 312.

19. RUSH, Ormond, *The Reception of Doctrine. An Appropriation of Hans Robert Jauss' Reception Aesthetics and Literary Hermeneutics*, 1997, pp. 424.

20. MIMEAULT, Jules, *La sotériologie de François-Xavier Durrwell. Exposé et réflexions critiques*, 1997, pp. 476.

21. CAPIZZI, Nunzio, *L'uso di Fil 2,6-11 nella cristologia contemporanea (1965-1993)*, 1997, pp. 528.

22. NANDKISORE, Robert, *Hoffnung auf Erlösung. Die Eschatologie im Werk Hans Urs von Balthasars*, 1997, pp. 304.

23. PERKOVIĆ, Marinko, *«Il cammino a Dio» e «La direzione alla vita»: L'ordine morale nelle opere di Jordan Kuničić, O.P. (1908-1974)*, 1997, pp. 336.

24. DOMERGUE, Benoît, *La réincarnation et la divinisation de l'homme dans les religions. Approche phénoménologique et théologique*, 1997, pp. 300.

25. FARKAŠ, Pavol, *La «donna» di Apocalisse 12. Storia, bilancio, nuove prospettive*, 1997, pp. 276.

26. OLIVER, Robert W., *The Vocation of the Laity to Evangelization. An Ecclesiological Inquiry into the Synod on the Laity (1987), Christifideles laici (1989) and Documents of the NCCB (1987-1996)*, 1997, pp. 364.

27. SPATAFORA, Andrea, *From the «Temple of God» to God as the Temple. A Biblical Theological Study of the Temple in the Book of Revelation*, 1997, pp. 340.

28. IACOBONE, Pasquale, *Mysterium Trinitatis. Dogma e Iconografia nell'Italia medievale*, 1997, pp. 512.

29. CASTAÑO FONSECA, Adolfo M., *Δικαιοσύνη en Mateo. Una interpretación teológica a partir de 3,15 y 21,32*, 1997, pp. 344.

30. CABRIA ORTEGA, José Luis, *Relación teología-filosofía en el pensamiento de Xavier Zubiri*, 1997, pp. 580.

31. SCHERRER, Thierry, *La gloire de Dieu dans l'oeuvre de saint Irénée*, 1997, pp. 328.

32. PASCUZZI, Maria, *Ethics, Ecclesiology and Church Discipline. A Rhetorical Analysis of 1Cor 5*, 1997, pp. 236.